American Pragmatism and Poetic Practice

Wittgenstein wrote that "philosophy ought really to be written only as a form of poetry." American poetry has long engaged questions about subject and object, self and environment, reality and imagination, real and ideal that have dominated the Western philosophical tradition since the Enlightenment. Kristen Case's book argues that American poets from Emerson to Susan Howe have responded to the central problems of Western philosophy by performing, in language, the continually shifting relation between mind and world. Pragmatism, recognizing the futility of philosophy's attempt to fix the mind/world relation, announces the insights that these poets enact.

Pursuing the flights of pragmatist thinking into poetry and poetics, Case traces an epistemology that emerges from American writing, including that of Emerson, Marianne Moore, William James, and Charles Olson. Here mind and world are understood as inseparable, and the human being is regarded as, in Thoreau's terms, "part and parcel of Nature." Case presents a new picture of twentieth-century American poetry that disrupts our sense of the schools and lineages of modern and postmodern poetics, arguing that literary history is most accurately figured as a living field rather than a line. This book will be of particular interest to scholars and students of pragmatism, transcendentalism, and twentieth-century American poetry.

Kristen Case is Assistant Professor of English as the University of Maine at Farmington.

Mind and American Literature

Edited by Linda Simon
(*Skidmore College*)

American Pragmatism and Poetic Practice

Crosscurrents from Emerson to Susan Howe

Kristen Case

CAMDEN HOUSE
Rochester, New York

Copyright © 2011 Kristen Case. All Rights Reserved.

First published 2011 by Camden House, an imprint of Boydell & Brewer, Inc., Rochester, NY, USA, and Boydell & Brewer Ltd., Woodbridge, Suffolk, UK. Reprinted in paperback 2017.

Paperback—ISBN-13: 978-1-57113-986-3; ISBN-10: 1-57113-986-9
Hardcover—ISBN-13: 978-1-57113-485-1; ISBN-10: 1-57113-485-9

Library of Congress Cataloging-in-Publication Data

Case, Kristen, 1976–
  American pragmatism and poetic practice: crosscurrents from Emerson to Susan Howe / Kristen Case.
    p. cm. — (Mind and American literature)
  Includes bibliographical references and index.
  ISBN-13: 978-1-57113-485-1 (acid-free paper)
  ISBN-10: 1-57113-485-9 (acid-free paper)
  1. American poetry—20th century—History and criticism. 2. Pragmatism in literature. 3. Poetics—History—20th century. 4. Pragmatism—History—19th century. 5. Pragmatism—History—20th century. 6. Literature—Philosophy. I. Title.
PS310.P66C37 2011
811'.509384—dc22   2011007405

Permission for use of Marianne Moore's poem "The Student" (1932 and 1941 versions) is granted by David M. Moore, Administrator of the Literary Estate of Marianne Moore. All rights reserved. Permission is also granted by Faber & Faber Limited. The 1932 version of "The Student" is also reprinted with the permission of Scribner, a Division of Simon & Shuster, Inc., from THE COLLECTED POEMS OF MARIANNE MOORE by Marianne Moore. Copyright © 1935 by Marianne Moore, renewed 1963 by Marianne Moore and T. S. Eliot. All rights reserved.

Excerpts from "The Steeple-Jack" from THE POEMS OF MARIANNE MOORE by Marianne Moore, edited by Grace Schulman, copyright © 2003 by Marianne Craig Moore, Executor of the Estate of Marianne Moore. Used by permission of Viking Penguin, a division of Penguin Group (USA).

Robert Frost's poems "After Apple-Picking," "Hyla Brook" "The Tuft of Flowers," "For Once Then, Something," "Into My Own," "The Most of It," "Design," "Mowing," and "The Need of Being Versed in Country Things," or excerpts from them, are taken from the book THE POETRY OF ROBERT FROST edited by Edward Connery Lathem. Copyright ©1923, 1930, 1934, 1939, 1969 by Henry Holt and Company, copyright © 1936, 1942, 1944, 1951, 1958, 1962 by Robert Frost, copyright ©1964, 1967, 1970 by Lesley Frost Ballantine. Reprinted by permission of Henry Holt and Company, LLC.

Excerpts from "Spring and All," "Spring and All, Section I," and "Spring and All, Section V" by William Carlos Williams, from THE COLLECTED POEMS: VOLUME 1, 1909–1939, copyright © 1938 by New Directions Publishing Corp. Reprinted by permission of New Directions Publishing Corp. and Carcanet Press Limited.

Excerpts from The Maximus Poems, by Charles Olson, copyright © 1985 and used by permission of the University of California Press. All rights reserved.

Excerpts from the following editions of Susan Howe's poetry are all reprinted by permission of New Directions Publishing Corp.: FRAME STRUCTURES, copyright © 1974 by Susan Howe; SOULS OF THE LABADIE TRACT, copyright © 2007 by Susan Howe; THE MIDNIGHT, copyright © 2003 by Susan Howe.

Printed in the United States of America. Printed on acid-free paper.

For Tom

Contents

List of Illustrations	ix
Preface	xi
Acknowledgments	xvii
1: "By Their Fruits": Words and Action in American Writing	1
2: Emerson, Moore, America	21
3: Robert Frost, Charles Sanders Peirce, and the Necessity of Form	43
4: "As Much a Part of Things as Trees and Stones": John Dewey, William Carlos Williams, and the Difference in Not Knowing	71
5: Henry Thoreau, Charles Olson, and the Poetics of Place	95
6: Howe/James	123
Works Cited	143
Index	153

Illustrations

Fig. 5.1. *Earliest Flowering of April Flowers*. From Thoreau's Kalendar.
Fig. 5.2. *General Phenomena for November*. From Thoreau's Kalendar.
Fig. 5.3. *General Phenomena for May*. From Thoreau's Kalendar.

Preface

To begin, a confession: I am a trespasser in the territory of philosophy. I come by way of poetry. It is hard to read very far in American modernist poetry, in particular, without hitting upon the question of the status of its objects — those wheelbarrows and roses and blue guitars — and the corollary question about its subjects — who is this *I*, anyway? The more poems I read the more I felt that there was something *up* with objects and subjects in American poetry, that the poems were engaging some question, or set of questions, about what it means to be a "self," and what we mean when we say we know something. My attempt to articulate these questions led me to philosophy and eventually to the writings of Charles Sanders Peirce and William James — an encounter that transformed my thinking about everything in general and about poetry in particular.

What eventually built itself out of the fragments of my old thinking and those bits of pragmatism I couldn't shake was a new picture of the field of twentieth-century poetics, one in which strains of American philosophy are picked up, dropped, and picked up again elsewhere. This book traces the way the seeds of American philosophical thought, in particular of that strain of American thinking known as pragmatism, take root in the diverse field of twentieth-century American poetry. By following the currents of pragmatist thought into the realm of poetry and poetics, I hope to trace a particular epistemology that emerges from diverse forms of American writing, one in which mind and world are understood as inseparable, and the human being is regarded as, in Thoreau's terms, "an inhabitant, or part and parcel of Nature" ("Walking," 149).

The structure of the book — an introductory chapter followed by five pairings of pragmatist thinkers and twentieth-century poets — is designed to reflect this new picture. Each chapter focuses on a particular philosophical problem, approached from the vantage points of both poetry and philosophy. The second chapter, on Ralph Waldo Emerson and Marianne Moore, centers on the relation of the real to the ideal; the third chapter describes the dialectic of form and chaos in the writings of Charles Peirce and Robert Frost; the fourth chapter, on John Dewey and William Carlos Williams, details the collapse of the subject-object dichotomy in the work of both writers; the fifth chapter investigates the relationship between subject and environment in the work of Henry Thoreau and Charles Olson; and the final chapter explores William James's concept of relation as it is embodied in the work of contemporary poet Susan Howe.

Implicit in the structure and formulation of this project is the assumption of a key relation between Emersonian transcendentalism and Jamesian pragmatism, a relation that has been forcefully established by several scholars, notably Richard Poirier, Louis Menand, and Joan Richardson. *American Pragmatism and Poetic Practice* builds on the work of these scholars, and also takes into account Stanley Cavell's linkage of Thoreau and Emerson's writings to the tradition of ordinary language philosophy.

In recent years several studies have explored the connection between American poetry and the pragmatist tradition, including Richard Poirier's *Poetry and Pragmatism*, Jonathan Levin's *The Poetics of Transition*, and Joan Richardson's *A Natural History of Pragmatism*. Each of these works highlights Emerson and James as central to the pragmatist line of thought and Stein and Stevens as their poetic inheritors. *American Pragmatism and Poetic Practice* extends the field of inquiry to include philosophers who have received less attention from literary critics (Dewey, Peirce, and Thoreau) and poets who are not generally considered among the inheritors of this tradition (Moore, Olson, and Howe). Part of my motivation to locate the seeds of pragmatist thought in a wider field of American poetry is the conviction that the discipline of literary scholarship is well served by work that disrupts traditional, linear notions of literary inheritance.

American Pragmatism and Poetic Practice also differs radically from earlier texts dealing with pragmatism and American poetry in its style and approach. Bound as it is to our persistent view of history as a linear progress, an orderly sequence of causes and effects, "the history of ideas" is most often figured as a line: a series of aesthetic and philosophical revolutions, each new "school" absorbing and then overturning the last. In spite of the critical upheavals of the past half-century, this essentially teleological view of the transmission of thought from one generation to the next remains largely unchallenged, shaping in fundamental ways our approach to American writers. The first assumption of *American Pragmatism and Poetic Practice* is that intellectual history is most accurately figured not as a line but as an organic growth. Intellectual problems and ways of approaching them are carried like seeds from one genre, one generation, one region to another, and in the field of American writing this invisible process of pollination creates connections across the artificially imposed boundary lines of critical and generic categories.

Because the pragmatist writers I investigate valued experience over the inherited problems and vocabulary of philosophy, many of their epistemological positions may be arrived at by non-philosophers in the habit of attending closely to their own experiences and relations — the kind of habit cultivated in poetic practice. In addition, by the early twentieth century the evolutionary principle that shaped the thinking of the pragmatist writers had been absorbed into the air of American thinking and writing. For these reasons, my inquiry does not focus on the question of influence, but, assuming that pragmatist principles were and are available even to those with no familiarity with pragmatism proper, rather seeks to explore the echoes of pragmatist thinking in corners where they may not be expected to sound. Though I by no means discount the role played by direct contact between the poets and pragmatist writers (James's profound influence on Frost, for example, has been admirably demonstrated by Richard Poirier, W. David Shaw, and others), the intent of this work is to widen the picture beyond such instances of direct transmission.

This project emerged from my observation that twentieth-century American poetry, with its longstanding preoccupation with the presentations of objects and the voicing of a lyric *I*, may be understood as a kind of disguised or illegible Other for post-Cartesian philosophy. As I demonstrate in the chapters that follow, American poetry has long been invested in the questions about the relation between subject and object, self and environment, reality and imagination, real and ideal that have dominated the western philosophical tradition from the seventeenth century on, but has responded to these questions from within the realm of lived experience, rather than from the imaginary exterior posited by conventional philosophical discourse. As my analyses of Moore, Frost, Williams, Olson, and Howe illustrate, American poets have responded to the epistemological questions raised by Descartes, Locke, Hume, and Kant not by positing a permanent, stable foundation for knowledge (traditionally philosophy's self-appointed task), but rather by performing, in language, continually shifting relations between mind and world. For example, as my analysis of Williams shows, the relation between subject and object can shift from poem to poem: imagination sometimes shaping the physical world, the actual — "the stiff curl of wildcarrot leaf" — sometimes imposing itself on the mind (Williams, *Collected Poems*, 2:183). Pragmatism, in its recognition of the futility of philosophy's attempt to fix the mind/world relation, announces the insight that these poets enact.

The philosophers in whom I am most interested are frequently dismissed as failed (or non-) philosophers. By extending the terrain of philosophy to include more of the texture of lived experience, Emerson, Thoreau, and James risk illegibility within the frame of philosophical discourse. This common choice — to sacrifice the mark of philosophical legitimacy to extend the range of philosophy — is a central theme of this book. For the poets whose work I consider the essential problems of our relation to the world cannot be resolved through argument; neither can they be resolved by an inherited or collective stance. For Moore, Frost, Williams, Olson, and Howe, the problems of human life — how and where we live, what we know, what our interactions with others and with our environment entail — are problems of daily living. Their writings are not solutions to these problems but lived engagements with them.

Central to my approach is a vision of scholarship as a way of coming into relation with the writers who are my subjects. William James's insistence on the primacy of relation has reinforced my belief that interpretation is always a matter of imagination, of making truth out of the fact of a text. Some of the pairings I will explore were suggested by vague resonances, remote echoes. That each has proved increasingly fruitful the further I investigate suggests not only the wide cross-pollination of ideas in the field of American thought, but also the shaping role of the reader in any meaningful reading of texts. Thus the second assumption of this work is James's insight that "in our cognitive as well as our active life we are creative," that perception is always a creative act (*Writings*, 599).

A third assumption of this project is that the meaning of any given work of literature resides not in "the work itself" nor merely in the mind of its readers, but rather in the interaction between reader and text, that this interaction, the complex relationship between a reader and a book, constitutes a legitimate object of inquiry. This extension of the notion of what constitutes the proper object of literary studies is derived from James's radical empiricism, which insists that "the relations between things, conjunctive as well as disjunctive, are just as much matters of direct particular experience, neither more so nor less, than the things themselves" (*Writings*, 826). Rather than focus exclusively on either the text as object of inquiry or the shaping role of my own or others' reading practices, my hope is to evoke the sense of a living relation between my textual subjects and myself as reader — one that involves both my pushing against the texts and the texts pushing back. One part of my approach is a situating of myself alongside my subjects, a continual re-asking of Emerson's question, "where do we find ourselves?" and an attempt to document the always-changing answer (*Essays*, 471).

The picture of mind and world that emerges in the strain of American philosophy and poetry that this work traces is at odds with conventions of writing that assume a static relation between the scholar-as-subject and the text-as-object. I know of no better articulation of the interactive model of knowledge that has determined my approach to writing this text than James's description of "Pragmatism's Conception of Truth":

> Facts come independently and determine our beliefs provisionally. But these beliefs make us act, and as fast as they do so, they bring into sight or into existence new facts which re-determine the beliefs accordingly. So the whole coil and ball of truth, as it rolls up, is the product of a double influence. Truths emerge from facts; but they dip forward into facts again and add to them; which facts again create or reveal new truth (the word is indifferent) and so on indefinitely. (*Writings*, 585)

During the period of time in which this text was conceived, several important facts pressed themselves upon my experience: U.S.-led airstrikes killed hundreds of Afghan civilians, many of them women and children. My husband's mother was diagnosed with Multiple Myeloma, a cancer now so common in her region that her doctors strongly suspect an environmental cause. I learned that my father's Parkinson's disease was likely caused by his exposure to Agent Orange during the Vietnam War. I moved to a small house surrounded by woods. I had two children. Certain of these facts, the illnesses of my father and mother-in-law, for example — remain behind the text, unannounced in my writing, but shaping in important ways my understanding of human beings' relations to the places they inhabit. Other facts — U.S. military action in Iraq and Afghanistan, my daughter's birth — have intruded so suddenly and so thoroughly into my thinking that I found rendering them invisible to be impossible. By allowing these facts to surface in my writing, I hope to enact, rather than simply describe, a pragmatist conception of knowledge.

The questions that animate the works of the writers I have been reading for this project are, for me, live questions, questions about our relationship to the world that we both constitute and inhabit, about how we come to what we call knowledge about that world. My intent is less to settle these questions, many of which may indeed be insoluble, than to bring to the critical conversation a sense of their relevance, not only to our scholarly practices but also to our practices of living. By foregrounding in the content, structure, and methodology of this work relations between poetry and philosophy, writers and readers, ourselves and our world, I hope to bring to contemporary thinking about pragmatism and American literature a living sense of the texture of these intimate but difficult-to-name relations.

Acknowledgments

I AM INDEBTED TO MANY PEOPLE for their help with this project. Linda Simon and Jim Walker at Camden House have been supportive of this project and of its author in every conceivable way. I am grateful to Heather Cass White and to Stephen Collis for their careful reading and immensely helpful editorial suggestions, and to Ian Firth for his keen eye, good humor, and indefatigable spirit in the indexing stage. Indirect but nonetheless indispensable support during the final stages of writing was provided by Gary Grieve-Carlson and Dan Gunn. I owe an incalculable debt to Daniel Peck, who responded to the email query of a complete stranger with extraordinary generosity, and whose insights about Thoreau have been foundational for my own thinking. Long having been in silent dialogue with the author of *Thoreau's Morning Work*, I took special pleasure in beginning a real conversation with Dan, whose collegiality, like his scholarship, is exemplary. For help with my research on Charles Olson and Henry Thoreau, I am very grateful to Olson's friend, now mine, Peter Anastas. My work on Thoreau also led me to the wonderful Laura Dassow Walls, to whom I am indebted for gifts both material (letters of recommendation) and spiritual (her *Seeing New Worlds*). Wayne Koestenbaum and Ammiel Alcalay have been both sources of support and, in the range and creativity of their scholarship, sources of inspiration.

For many reasons, most significantly her own seminal work, this project would have been unthinkable without Joan Richardson. The thinking reflected in the pages that follow was seeded in the fertile ground prepared by her teaching, her writing, and her friendship.

I am grateful to my husband, Tom Jessen, to whom this book is dedicated, for the continual example of his own work as an artist, for the patience with which he has endured the vicissitudes of academic life, and, most of all, for the ongoing conversation from which this writing emerged. I thank my parents for their extraordinary support and for teaching me to love my work. Finally, I thank my children, Avery and Wyatt, whose impact on the evolution of my thinking will be felt in the pages that follow.

Chapter 5, "Henry Thoreau, Charles Olson, and the Poetics of Place," first appeared in *The Concord Saunterer* NS 17 (2009), 44–72. I am grateful to the editor, Laura Dassow Walls, for permission to publish it here.

1: "By Their Fruits": Words and Action in American Writing

> *Ye shall know them by their fruits. Do men gather grapes of thorns, or figs of thistles? Even so every good tree bringeth forth good fruit; but a corrupt tree bringeth forth evil fruit. A good tree cannot bring forth evil fruit, neither can a corrupt tree bring forth good fruit. Every tree that bringeth not forth good fruit is hewn down, and cast into the fire. Wherefore by their fruits ye shall know them.*
>
> — Matthew 7:16–20

UNLIKE AN "IDEA," WHICH, once defined and categorized, may be assigned a particular history, metaphor is mercurial, harder to delimit. My intent in this opening chapter is to trace the partial history of a metaphor (which happens also to be an allusion) as it slides, serpentine, across the ground of religious, philosophical, and poetic writing in America. Following the traces of this slippery figure, I hope to provide a sense of how thinking has moved, and moves, in ways not always accounted for in influence studies, valuable though these may be in other respects. I also hope to illustrate that, in their common turn to *practice* (variously defined) as the locus of meaning, the writers who initiate the pragmatist turn in American thought destabilize the boundaries between argument and form, thought and feeling, philosophy and poetry. My justification for the unorthodox structure of this chapter — indeed, of the entire book — echoes Perry Miller's defense of his own method in his 1956 introduction to his 1940 essay "From Edwards to Emerson."

> On the crudest of levels, I am arguing that certain basic continuities persist in a culture — in this case taking New England as the test tube — which underlie the successive articulation of "ideas." Or, I might put it, the history of ideas — if it is to be anything more than a mail-order catalogue — demands of the historian not only a fluency in the concepts themselves, but an ability to get underneath them. (*Errand*, 184–85)

I will not attempt, in this chapter, to summarize the vast scholarship that already exists on the differences and similarities between, for example, Edwards and Emerson,[1] or Emerson and James. I do not intend to answer the important questions about the extent of transcendentalism's inheritance from Puritanism, or whether transcendentalism's differences from pragmatism outweigh its similarities. Rather, I wish to trace what Wittgenstein, in his *Philosophical Investigations,* called a family resemblance. In his discussion of language and language games, Wittgenstein writes:

> Instead of producing something common to all that we call language, I am saying that these phenomena have no one thing in common, which makes us use the same word for all, — but that they are related to one another in many different ways. And it is because of this relationship or these relationships, that we call them "language." (27)

In this chapter I will attempt a rough sketch for a family portrait. Necessarily, some features will be obscured as others are emphasized. Each of the figures I treat in this chapter belongs to multiple families, and other portraits have and will be drawn, highlighting other features. The language of Matthew 7:16–20 forms a dense philosophical knot, dealing simultaneously with the idea of truth and the idea of goodness. The question of *how we know what is good*, touches epistemology, ethics, and aesthetics. All of the writers to whom I refer below use the verse to articulate particular, sometimes even (as in the case of Peirce and James) opposed aspects of their thought. But amid the differences, commonalities, as Miller puts it, indeed persist.

Here is a rough map of the territory through which this chapter will travel: Jonathan Edwards and Ralph Waldo Emerson, in alluding to Matthew 7:20 within the context of Calvinist and Unitarian theology, suggest a link between knowledge and practice: the relationship between our actions in the world and what we know of our own and others' souls. In Charles Peirce and William James this link is fully articulated as (two versions of) a new, secular American epistemology: one in which knowledge is inseparable from the daily practices by which we acquire it. Frost, informed by pragmatism, brings this understanding to the particular practice of writing, which he explicitly frames as a way of making meaning. It is against the chronological unfolding presented here that the book's subsequent, largely non-chronological chapters should be read.

Sketches and maps necessarily omit features of the actual. In an attempt to restore some sense of the way the intellectual current described in this chapter moved through the daily lives of the writers who have articulated it, I have included short, biographical fragments at the end of each section. In the selection of these fragments, I was guided by poetic more than by scholarly principles. These episodes resonate with the stream of pragmatist thought in ways I cannot fully account for.

Edwards and the Affected Heart

In 1742 and 1743, in the ebb-tide of the Great Awakening, Jonathan Edwards delivered a series of sermons principally addressed to the question of how to discern authentic religious experience from the mere display of religious fervor. Later published as *A Treatise Concerning Religious Affections*, the sermons were both a defense of the much-criticized Awakening, which was characterized by widespread and highly emotional conversions, often attended by swooning and convulsions, and a warning to his parishioners against the dangers of excess imagination. "'Tis a hard thing," Edwards writes in the preface to the *Treatise*, "to be a zealous friend of what has been *good* and glorious in the late extraordinary appearance, and to rejoice much in it; and at the same time to see the evil and pernicious tendency of what has been *bad*, and earnestly to oppose that" (*Reader*, 138). The danger to which Edwards was most alert was false conversion; during the Awakening, too many citizens of Northhampton demonstrated all the outward signs of having received grace, only to return within a few weeks or months to their profligate ways. It was a phenomenon that threatened to undermine the credibility of religious revival, and Edwards's defense of emotion as essential to religious experience.

The *Treatise Concerning Religious Affections* begins by establishing the role of the affections in religious life, with particular emphasis on the union of thought and feeling in genuine religious experience.

> Never was a natural man engaged earnestly to seek his salvation: never were any such brought to cry after wisdom, and lift up their voice for understanding, and to wrestle with God in prayer for mercy; and never was one humbled, and brought to the foot of God, from anything that he ever heard or imagined of his own unworthiness and undeservings of God's displeasure; nor was ever one induced to fly for refuge unto Christ, while his heart remained unaffected. (146)

However, Edwards warns that emotional displays are not in and of themselves proof of grace, and concludes that the only reliable test of the authenticity of such emotion is to examine the believer's actions:

> I shall consider Christian practice and an holy life, as a manifestation and sign of the sincerity of a professing Christian, to the eye of his neighbors and brethren. And that this is the chief sign of grace in this respect, is very evident from the Word of God. Christ, who knew best how to give us rules to judge of others, has repeated it and inculcated it, that we should know them by their fruits. (166)

As William James would observe in 1902 in *The Varieties of Religious Experience*, Matthew 7:20 is the focal point of Edwards's text. James summarizes the *Treatise* as follows:

> In the end it had to come to our empiricist criterion: By their fruits ye shall know them, not by their roots. Jonathan Edwards's Treatise on Religious Affections is an elaborate working out of this thesis. The roots of a man's virtue are inaccessible to us. No appearances whatever are infallible proofs of grace. Our practice is the only sure evidence, even to ourselves, that we are genuinely Christians. (*Writings*, 26)

Edwards's use of Matthew 7:20 to illustrate the idea of truth as located in practice has (at least) a double resonance. With respect to his parishioners, the meaning is clear: only in examining our practice can we know the truth of our own lives. Here is the first pragmatist principle in Edwards's formulation: truth is not something hidden, some invisible essence that we must endeavor to uncover. Truth lives in the open air, and is manifest in our actions. The verse — or more precisely, the new idea of truth that Edwards uses it to announce — also has a special meaning for Edwards's practice as a preacher. Truth is never, in Edwards's view, simply communicated through words. Rather, the words must trigger an experience for the listener, and truth is located here, in this act, in this *practice*.

Though recent scholars have questioned Perry Miller's famous, almost mythological account of "the boy of fourteen" who "grasped in a flash . . . that Locke was the master-spirit of the age," there can be little doubt that John Locke's *An Essay Concerning Human Understanding* was indeed central to the epistemology Edwards announces in *A Divine and Supernatural Light* (Miller, *Jonathan Edwards*, 52).[2] As Miller illustrates, Edwards took from Locke an understanding of the way language operates:

> In the hypothetical state of nature, words might stand for the signs of basic realities, but as society grew more complex, the words would become separated from their objects and lead a life of their own. This was psychologically explicable: the tongue can say the word when no idea is in the mind; the mind itself can take the idea for granted and retain the word after the perception is utterly forgotten. Instead of being annexed to an object, the word itself becomes an object, a pallid object as compared with the thing it stands for, but the only object the mind any longer knows. (156–57)

Edwards saw his task as that of bringing language back to experience. His sermons were not descriptions of reality but rather ways of *making something happen* in the minds of his listeners.[3]

This *something*, as Miller further illustrates, is the perception of grace, a perception that involves feeling, as well as understanding. Edwards acknowledges that "there must be light in the understanding," for "where there is heat without light, there can be nothing divine or heavenly in that heart." Yet he insists that, "on the other hand, where there is a kind of light without heat, a head stored with notions and speculations, with a cold and unaffected heart, there can be nothing divine in that light" (148). Here, then, is a second pragmatist principle at play in Edwards's reference to Matthew 7:20: the fruit of Christian practice grows from a perception of truth that involves both thought and feeling. Man is, and should be, acutely *interested* in his own salvation, and this interest is intimately connected to his perception of grace. As Miller notes, Edwards "asserted the radical conception of a man as an active, interested, passionate being whose relation to objective reality is factual to the extent that he is concerned about it" (184). Here, Miller echoes John Dewey's formulation of the pragmatist epistemology in *Democracy and Education:* "If the living, experiencing being is an intimate participant in the activities of the world to which it belongs, then knowledge is a mode of participation, valuable in the degree in which it is effective" (Dewey, *Middle*, 9:347).

Underlying Edwards's sense of language as a way of making something happen — or, in a more orthodox formulation, as participating in the unbreakable chain of causation initiated by God — is his understanding, derived from Newton, of the workings of the physical universe. George Marsden notes that

> following a suggestion of Newton, Edwards argued in a very early set of entries concerning atoms, that the essence of these smaller particles must be their indivisibility, that is, they cannot be made any smaller. So solidity did not have to do most basically with taking up a certain amount of space ("extension" the Cartesians called it) but was essentially a power, the power of resistance. This power must, of course, arise ultimately from God, the Creator. (*Jonathan Edwards*, 71)

For Edwards, power is the essence of creation, which was not a single event but rather *is* an ongoing process: "The universe is created out of nothing every moment, and if it were not for our imaginations, which hinder us, we might see that wonderful work performed continually" ("Of Atoms," *Works*, 6:12). Language, like every other element of the universe, participates in the power of this continual creation.

Words/Actions

June 1, 1735

Edwards's uncle, Joseph Hawley II, respected Northampton merchant, effectively ends the Awakening by slitting his own throat.

After this, multitudes in this and other towns seemed to have it strongly suggested to 'em, and pressed upon 'em, to do as this person had done. And many that seemed to be under no melancholy, some pious persons that had no special darkness, or doubts about the goodness of their state, nor were under any special trouble or concern of mind about anything spiritual or temporal, yet had it urged upon 'em, as if somebody had spoke to 'em, "Cut your own throat, now is a good opportunity: now, NOW!" So that they were obliged to fight with all their might to resist it, and yet no reason suggested to 'em why they should do it. (*Reader*, 84–85)

March 13, 1737

A Sabbath day, two years after the height of revival. It is still winter in Northampton. With dismay, Edwards has lately noted "how we decline," and observed that "what decays that lively spirit of religion suffers among us." Frost heaves shift the wall of the meetinghouse, dislodging the joints that support the back gallery. As Edwards begins to speak, the crowded gallery cracks and splits, the timbers fracture, bodies crash upon bodies (Marsden, 184).

Emerson and the Visible Truth

Emerson gave two sermons on Matthew 7:20, one written in 1829, and one in 1830, the year before his wife Ellen's death and two years before his resignation from the Church. The first of the sermons deals with the question of the role of faith versus the role of good works in securing salvation. This little-discussed sermon is remarkable for its anticipation of Jamesian pragmatism, and deserves to be considered as a key text in the debate — which it is beyond the scope of this chapter to fully engage — about the extent to which Emerson belongs to the pragmatist lineage.[4] After declaring that, in reality, the principles of faith and works "cannot be divorced," Emerson concludes that, nevertheless, "if one [of these principles] is to be commended . . . it is safer to commend works to men, rather than faith" (*Sermons*, 47). It is in this context that Emerson makes his most Jamesian statements: "Precisely so great a sacrifice as you can make, precisely so fervent is your faith"; "Works of this day are the mercury of the day's merit"; and "Let me see your conquest of your passions today. Let me see your imitation of your Master. It is better than any confession of faith" (49). Compare these to James's articulation of the "Meaning of Pragmatism," as derived from Peirce's "pragmatic maxim":

> Mr. Peirce, after pointing out that our beliefs are really rules for actions, said that, to develop a thought's meaning, we need only

determine what conduct it is fitted to produce: that conduct is for us its sole significance. And the tangible fact at the root of all our thought-distinctions, however subtle, is that there is no one of them so fine as to consist in anything but a possible difference in practice. (*Writings*, 506)

Emerson's privileging of works over faith is consistent with Unitarian theology, which marked its difference from Calvinism in part on this question. Consistent with Unitarianism's Arminian roots, too, is the insistence on the ability of each individual to discern for himself, without the aid of dogma, goodness in action: "The upright and healthy mind will give for a little virtue at the bottom of the heart, a little pure and humble love of what is right, all the strictness of faith, all the surrounding pretensions of the Churches." In a statement that foreshadows the individualism that marks such later texts as "Self Reliance" and "The Divinity School Address," Emerson adds, parenthetically, that "it is not a church but an individual that goes to heaven or hell" (48).

In addition to articulating something remarkably like the pragmatist definition of meaning, Emerson's 1929 sermon on Matthew 7:20 evokes two other significant strains of what would become pragmatist thought. First, Emerson, like Edwards, stresses the role of the active, interested individual mind in arriving at truth. The "upright and healthy mind" is not only capable of discerning goodness for itself, it is compelled to do so. Mere knowledge of church teachings is no guarantee of salvation, since "it is not a church but an individual that goes to heaven or hell" (48). Indeed, technical or academic knowledge, even of the gospel, may obscure the living good that is manifest in action:

> A proficient in Ethics does not always know that the height of virtue may be often studied at the low bedside of almshouses. . . . [There] you shall find the rags of poverty speaking to your heart with an eloquence of duty which the careful arguments of the pulpit can never attain. The gospel itself with its pages illuminated with light from heaven shall not speak so persuasively as this *practice* of the gospel, this unsuspected testimony to the glory of religion, where life calls unto life, one that has been sorely tried and has prevailed, to you that are sorely tried. (50)

Central to Emerson's depiction of the discernment of virtue is the experience of empathy, a sense of common experience and fellow feeling, "where life calls unto life." It is *feeling* in Emerson's view that allows virtue "to speak to your heart" in a way that "the careful arguments of the podium never can." Echoing Edwards's emphasis on "the sense of the heart," Emerson links knowledge to feeling, insisting that the knower is involved in what he knows.

The second feature of pragmatism that emerges from Emerson's meditation on Matthew 7:16 is a view of truth as accessible and manifest. "As we understand the language of the human face," he writes, "so we apprehend the meaning of *works*. There is no mistake about them. There is no hypocrisy about them. A man that uniformly does good works is good, and a man that uniformly does bad works is bad, let him say what he will, let him believe what he will" (48). This characterization of the truth, like many of Emerson's positions, exists in tension with ideas expressed elsewhere, particularly later in his life. In 1851 he writes in his Journal, "Mediator, mediation. There is nothing else; there is no immediate known to us. Cloud on cloud, degree on degree, remove one coat, one lamina, and another coat or lamina just like it is the result, — to be also removed" (*Journals*, 16:424). The double-sidedness of Emerson's view of truth as at once radically accessible and perpetually beyond our grasp corresponds to a similar doubleness both in Edwards's reading of Matthew 7:20, and in James's later formulations of truth. James's summary of Edwards's *Treatise* highlights not only what we can know — "Our practice is the only sure evidence, even to ourselves, that we are genuinely Christians" — but also what we cannot — "The roots of a man's virtue are inaccessible to us. No appearances whatever are infallible proofs of grace" (26). Indeed, Edwards's interest in the question of discerning true from false conversion was driven in part by his doubts as a young man about the state of his own soul.

In "Experience," his fullest and most difficult statement of this double-sided view, Emerson begins by lamenting the knowledge we can't have — "we may have a sphere for our cricket ball, but not a berry for our philosophy" (*Essays*, 473) — and ends by celebrating, even finding transcendence in, that which we can — "the old world, wife, babes, and mother, Concord and Boston, the dear old spiritual world, and even the dear old devil not far off" (480). In ceding our claims to know any permanent absolute, Emerson suggests, we awaken to that knowledge we already had — our intimacy with the world of everyday objects and people and actions, with ordinary good and evil. It is in this realm that truth — the truth we read in faces, and in actions — is plainly manifest. James articulates his version of this doubleness in his 1907 lecture "Pragmatism's Conception of Truth":

> The "absolutely" true, meaning what no further experience will ever alter, is that ideal vanishing point toward which we imagine that all our temporary truths will someday converge. It runs on all fours with the perfectly wise man, and with the absolutely complete experience; and if these ideals are ever realized, they will all be realized together. Meanwhile, we have to live to-day by what truth we can get to-day, and be ready tomorrow to call it falsehood. (*Writings*, 584)

Consistent with Emerson's belief in the accessibility of "the meaning of works," or, in James's terms, "the truth we can get to-day" — is his aesthetic preference for the everyday. In his identification of the "low bedside of the almshouse" as a site of a more readily discernable, clearly communicable goodness than even "the gospel itself with its pages illuminated with the light of heaven," Emerson articulates what would become a consistent aesthetic scheme — the privileging of "the near, the low, the common" that emerges in "The American Scholar" (*Essays*, 68).

These two features of pragmatist thought — the role of *interest* in human knowledge and the radical accessibility of the truths of everyday experience — point to a significant corollary: that there can be no bright line drawn between how things seem to us and what they are. In his 1830 sermon on the verse, Emerson emphasizes the second feature, the idea that the truth will out — or, more precisely, that the truth is always already out to begin with:

> As every tree bears its fruit a mark by which its class and species may be indisputably known and distinguished from all other plants, so every mind has its mark and character which cannot be concealed, by which he may be known for that which he is, whatever pains are taken to disguise it. (*Sermons*, 216)

In his most radical statement of this position, Emerson notes that, though it is certainly possible for people to deceive others, there is no absolute line between seeming and being, or, in Aristotelian terms "essence" and "accident." A sufficiently thorough imitation of goodness would become actual goodness: "There are certain affects proper to virtue that nothing but virtue can produce, — a certain height and regularity of good action: To counterfeit that, would need a simulation of virtue so assiduous that it would become virtue itself" (217).

The centrality of *action* to Emerson's concept of truth had implications for his writing (particularly in later years), as it had had for Edwards's. As Robert Richardson writes, "Much of Emerson's Journal is not intended as finished work or public utterance, nor even as the record of private conviction. He is concerned to explore — and then to save — impulses, essays, hints, trials, spurts, exaggerations, the most fleeting and evanescent flowers of the mind" (*Emerson*, 201). The energy and the circuitousness, even the contradictions, of Emerson's writing, are in part attributable to his belief, remarkably similar to Edwards's notion of continual divine creation, that there is "nothing, at last, in success or failure, than more or less vital force supplied from the Eternal" (*Reader*, 483).

Visible Invisible

In early 1825 Emerson was struck by the eye disease uveitis, probably caused by his tuberculosis, the disease that would later kill his brothers Charles and Edward, as well as his first wife, Ellen. Richardson records that "over the next nine months Emerson underwent two operations in which his cornea was punctured with a cataract knife" (R. Richardson, *Emerson*, 63). In a notebook entry from the period, Emerson's small and regular script gives way to a large, uneven scrawl. Edward's note in pencil, on the side of the manuscript, reads, "this page of writing shows that RWE's eyes were weak" (*Journals*, 2: plate IV). The text reads: "But our author should remember that there are some things so absolutely impossible as not to be found by the most curious & microscopic eye 'For what never was will not easily be found not even by the most curious'" (2:386).

From *Nature* (1836):

> In the woods, we return to reason and faith. There I feel that nothing can befall me in life, — no disgrace, no calamity, (leaving me my eyes,) which nature cannot repair. Standing on the bare ground, — my head bathed by the blithe air, and uplifted into infinite space, — all mean egotism vanishes. I become a transparent eyeball; I am nothing; I see all. (*Essays*, 10)

Peircian Fruit, Jamesian Fruit

Both of the original articulators of pragmatism, Charles Peirce and William James, referred multiple times to Matthew 7:20, agreeing on its meaning (that concepts should be judged by their practical effects), but disagreeing about what kinds of effects were to be considered "fruits." As we will see, James's answer to this question, his expansion of Peirce's original formulation of pragmatism, advances the view of truth suggested by Emerson's two sermons on the verse — that truth (at least, the only truth with which we need concern ourselves) is radically accessible, already part of our daily experience.

In his 1878 "How to Make Our Ideas Clear," Peirce first articulated what became known as "the pragmatic maxim": "Consider what effects, that might conceivably have practical bearings, we conceive the object of our conception to have. Then, our conception of these effects is the whole of our conception of the object" (*Essential*, 1:132). By the time James delivered his lectures on pragmatism in 1906–7, he had absorbed and expanded "the principle of Peirce, the principle of pragmatism" (*Writings*, 507) into a broad philosophical approach, according to which

> there can *be* no difference that does not *make* a difference elsewhere — no difference in abstract truth that doesn't express itself in

concrete fact and in conduct consequent upon that fact, imposed on somebody, somehow, somewhere, and somewhen. The whole function of philosophy ought to be to find out what definite difference it will make to you and me, at definite instants of our life, if this world-formula or that world-formula be the true one. (508)

James's expansion of Peirce's principle implies the philosophical significance of the actual consequences attending individual choices; in other words, it implies the philosophical significance of real, everyday life. The pragmatist, James notes, "turns away from abstraction and insufficiency, from verbal solutions, from bad *a priori* reasons, from fixed principles, closed systems, and pretended absolutes and origins. He turns toward concreteness and adequacy, towards facts, towards action, and towards power" (508–9). James had already put the pragmatic method to work in his 1901–2 lectures on *The Varieties of Religious Experience,* in which he writes that the only way to accurately evaluate religious life is to observe its effects on believers and in the world. It is in this context that James refers to Jonathan Edwards, noting that the *Treatise* represents "an elaborate working out" of the thesis "by their fruits ye shall know them, not by their roots" (*Writings*, 26). (The phrase, "not by their roots," it should be noted, is James's addition.)

By the time it was fully developed, James's pragmatism had departed in significant ways from Peirce's more circumscribed method. James told an audience in California in 1898 that Peirce's maxim "should be expressed more broadly than Peirce expresses it." As Sami Pihlström notes, "Attempting to do this [James] appears to slide from acknowledging Peirce's notions of *possible* differences and *conceivable* effects to the stronger requirement that those differences or effects should be actualized in our concrete practices" (37). Peirce appeared already to be aware of this possible alteration of his intent in 1893, when he added the following footnote to the text of "How to Make Our Ideas Clear."

> Before we undertake to apply this rule, let us reflect a little upon what it implies. It has been said to be a skeptical and materialistic principle. But it is only an application of the sole principle of logic which was recommended by Jesus; "Ye may know them by their fruits," and it is very intimately allied with the ideas of the gospel. We must certainly guard against understanding this rule in too individualistic a sense. . . . [The] fruit is, therefore, collective. It is the achievement of a whole people. (*Collected*, 5:402n2)

The idea that the *collective* fruit is that by which truth is known is consistent with Peirce's scholastic realism, "the principle that generality is operative in nature," and reflects his belief in a "foreordained goal" toward which inquiry inexorably tends (Pihlström, 37).

> Different minds may set out with the most antagonistic views, but the process of investigation carries them by a force outside of themselves to one and the same conclusion. This activity of thought by which we are carried, not where we wish, but to a foreordained goal, is like the operation of destiny. (*Essential*, 1:138)

Peirce's warning against "too individualistic" an interpretation of the pragmatic rule seems almost certainly to have been directed at James, who, in Peirce's view, infected Peirce's original formulation with "seeds of death in such notions as that of the unreality of all ideas of infinity and that of the mutability of truth" (*Essential*, 2:450). By defining the fruit by which truth is to be judged as "collective" — that is, as "the opinion which is fated to be ultimately agreed to by all who investigate" — Peirce sought to preserve the possibility of an objective Absolute (*Essential*, 1:139). In this context, it is worth noting that Peirce reinforces the connection to the Gospel, asserting the essential compatibility of his philosophy with Christianity.

In his own 1904 lecture, "What Pragmatism Means," James defined the "attitude" of pragmatism as one "of looking away from first things, principles, 'categories,' supposed necessities; and of looking towards last things, fruits, consequences, facts" (*Writings*, 510). James's own interpretation of what is meant by the "consequences," or "fruits" of the pragmatic maxim was both more individualistic and more immediate than Peirce's. As Israel Scheffler observes, in James's view, truth is

> to be seen as relating sensibly satisfactory consequences with the actions undertaken in banking on given beliefs. It is not, in particular, a matter of relating experience to a reality outside experience, but rather a matter of the relation which *certain* experiences bear to *others*. It is thus always accessible to us as acting and perceiving beings. (103)

In his emphasis on individual action and belief, and in his insistence that truth is a matter of relating experiences to other experiences, and not to a "foreordained goal" or extra-experiential reality, James expanded the meaning of Peirce's allusion to Matthew 7:20, bringing the fruit by which we discern the truth into the realm of daily life.[5]

By 1897, Peirce was aware of his differences from James, noting in a March 13 letter:

> That everything is to be tested by its practical results was the great text of my early papers; so, as far as I get your general aim . . . I am quite with you in the main. In my later papers, I have seen more thoroughly than I used to do that it is not mere action as brute exercise of strength that is the purpose of all, but say generalization, such action as tends toward regularization, and the actualization of

the thought which without action remains unthought. (*Collected*, 8:250)

In his emphasis on the general over that particular, and thought over action, Peirce parts company from James, who cited with approval Faust's replacement of the biblical "in the beginning was the word" with "In the beginning was the act" (R. Richardson, *William James*, 92). Peirce's concern was primarily to devise a method for settling questions that arose within the practice of science; he did not advocate, as James did, the application of his pragmatic method to matters of everyday life. As Pihlström observes,

> Peirce's scholastic realism, emphasis on community, antipsychologistic view of logic, and emphasis on pragmatism as a logical principle conflicted with James's nominalism, psychological orientation, and psychologistic interpretation of pragmatism. These conflicts are not unrelated to how they viewed the notion of practical consequences. (38)

In announcing this shift toward the recognition of a radically accessible truth, locatable in the particulars of daily experience, James struck a note that had been resounding in America since Edwards located "Images or Shadows of Divine Things" in such ordinary things as corn and mother's milk (*Images*, 93). It is the note of the everyday, the assertion of the philosophical significance of ordinary life, which would find its early twentieth-century echo in the words of poets such as Robert Frost, Marianne Moore, and Williams Carlos Williams. "No ideas but in things," Williams declared, while Moore, lover of the prickly particular, whispered to the rose "your thorns are the best part of you" (Williams, *Collected*, 2:55; Moore, *Poems*, 120).

Last Things

In January of 1910, the last year of his life, James's family hosted a dinner to celebrate the presentation of a large portrait of James by the painter Bay Emmet to Harvard University. Josiah Royce thought it failed to capture James's power: "I see in you more Titanic features, *beside* those that the portrait gets." James, already worried about what he saw as the inevitable diminution of his reputation after his death, agreed (Simon, 374–75).

He was, by this time, a national celebrity. He spoke to packed lecture halls, and had been chosen in 1898 to speak at the Decoration Day unveiling of a statue of Robert Gould Shaw at the Boston State House — an honor indicative of his stature as a public figure.

As Linda Simon observes, "James had been chosen not because he was a professor of psychology at Harvard; not because he had written an acclaimed textbook and many philosophical articles. . . . He was chosen because he had the rare talent to inspire, even to mesmerize his audiences" (xiv).

Still, the responses to his later works was not what he hoped. He was dismissed by some of his contemporaries, even some friends, as unserious, anti-intellectual, undisciplined. His instructions regarding his final manuscript betray lingering doubts: "Say it is fragmentary and unrevised. Call it: 'A beginning of an introduction to Philosophy.' Say that by it I hoped to round my system, which is now too much like an arch built up only on one side" (in Simon, 383).

*

When he died of cancer in 1914, Peirce was, despite the best efforts of James and other friends, unknown to all but a small circle of intellectuals. Despite his evident and wide-ranging genius, he was never able to secure a permanent academic post. Peirce left behind a handful of published works, a sprawling, unfinished mansion (called Arisbe, about which more will be said in chapter 3), a pile of debts, a destitute wife, a library of some three thousand volumes, and a mountain of unpublished manuscript pages.

In the months that followed his death, the philosopher Josiah Royce, Peirce's friend and admirer, sought the transfer of the manuscripts to Harvard, a transaction that was eventually realized, though its circumstances remain a subject of some debate. According to Kenneth Laine Ketner, it is unclear whether Peirce's widow, Juliette, agreed to gift the manuscripts (and the rights to publish them) to Harvard, as the university claimed, or whether she simply sought to have them housed there (45–46). Whatever the case, Harvard paid the desperate Juliette five hundred dollars, and removed the mountain of papers and books to Cambridge. (Juliette had hoped the library would remain intact, but Harvard dispersed the books — with the concession of memorial book plates — into its regular collection. Ketner notes that they can still be found in the stacks of Widener Library [50]).

Frost: Work and Value

Robert Frost's debt to William James has been forcefully established elsewhere, by Richard Poirier, John Sears, and others. As Sears notes in his essay "William James, Henri Bergson, and the Poetics of Robert Frost," James became important to Frost when he read James's essay, "Is Life Worth Living?," at a time when his morale was very low. At Harvard, Frost studied the *Psychology* and later used it as a textbook when he taught at the Plymouth Normal School in New Hampshire. He was influenced by *Pragmatism* too, but it is with the *Psychology* that the richest and most interesting connections exist. Frost later said in reference to James: "My greatest inspiration, when I was a student, was a man whose classes I never attended." (Sears, 342)

Jamesian (and, as I will argue in chapter 3, Peircian) notes can be heard in may of Frost's poems and essays, perhaps nowhere more clearly than in his descriptions of the practice of writing. As Sears notes, Frost's description of poetic making in the following passage echoes James in attributing meaning to the act of making a choice:

> Every single poem written regular is a symbol small or great of the way the will has to pitch into commitments deeper and deeper to a rounded conclusion and then be judged for whether any original intention it had has been strongly spent or weakly lost; be it in art, politics, school, church, business, love, or marriage, in a piece of work or in a career. Strongly spent is synonymous with kept. (*Poetry and Prose*, 401)

In Frost's Jamesian view, meaning is not something exterior to the self that a passive mind receives, rather, it emerges from the act of "pitch[ing] into commitments deeper and deeper." That is, it is defined principally by human decision and action.

Frost's poem, "After Apple Picking," included in his 1914 volume, *North of Boston*, takes up the basic epistemological question Matthew 7:20 purports to answer: how do we know what we know? By what yardstick do we measure truth and value? Though Frost does not quote the verse — with which he was familiar[6] — the poem's thematic content, as well is its central image, seem to point to it. The poem moves between waking and sleeping life, work and the dream of work:

> I cannot rub the strangeness from my sight
> I got from looking through a pane of glass
> I skimmed this morning from the drinking trough
> And held against the world of hoary grass.
> It melted, and I let it fall and break.
> But I was well
> Upon my way to sleep before it fell,
> And I could tell
> What form my dreaming was about to take.
> Magnified apples appear and disappear,
> Stem end and blossom end,

And every fleck of russet showing clear. (70)

In its movement between dream-like labor and a dream of labor, Frost's poem suggests a radical uncertainty about the real nature of experience. The sheet of ice through which the speaker looks at the world distorts it, as does his exhaustion, and then his dreams — "Dream delivers us to dream, and there is no end to illusion" (Emerson, *Essays*, 473). Finally, however, Frost offers, if not a solution for how we may identify the real, a kind of Jamesian dissolution of the question:

> There were ten thousand thousand fruit to touch,
> Cherish in hand, lift down and not let fall.
> For all
> That struck the earth,
> No matter if not bruised or spiked with stubble,
> Went surely to the cider-apple heap,
> As of no worth.

In Frost's formulation, it is human labor (or, as he expresses it in "The Constant Symbol," human commitment) alone — not any intrinsic property of an object — that determines its value. The burden this places on the farmer is evident: "There were ten thousand thousand fruit to touch, / Cherish in hand, lift down and not let fall." Each apple — each object in the world — requires our attention and tenderness. That to which we do not attend, the fruit that strike the earth, are not valued by us, and thus have no worth. It is easy to misread the final line of the selection so that the poem says that the apples are sent to the cider heap "As *if* of no worth" — but Frost excludes that "if." They are sent to the cider heap "*As* of no worth" — because they have been determined, by the inattention of the farmer, *not* to have worth. It is the farmer's actions alone, not the condition of the apple, that determine its value.

Frost's poem announces a final strand in the pragmatist web — one that has a direct bearing on the meaning of twentieth-century American poetic practice: in the pragmatist epistemology, meaning is generated through the interaction of mind and world — it is *made*. Knowing is not a passive activity, the mere beholding of an object by a perceiving subject, it is a kind of work, a by-product of active engagement with the world. Frost writes in his notebook,

> Facts come to us as stars come out in the . . . sky, scattered broadcast, thin at first and then thick enough to suggest constellation. The lines X between them that bring out the figures are ours . . . the final and only conscious part of our world building. A world you didn't make? Yes you did too. (310)

This sense of the epistemological value of work, of knowledge as world building, underlies much of twentieth-century poetry in America, and is particularly significant for the poets whose work I discuss in the chapters that follow. In very different ways, poets including Frost, William Carlos Williams, Charles Olson, Susan Howe and others shifted their attention from the made to the making, from the finished poem to the process of writing and its mirror, the process of reading. Here is Frost in 1939:

> It is but a trick poem and no poem at all if the best of it was thought of first and saved for the last. It finds its own name as is goes and discovers the best waiting for it in some final phrase at once wise and sad. (*Poetry*, 394)

And Olson in 1951:

> What makes most acts — of living and of writing — unsatisfactory, is that the person and/or the writer satisfy themselves that they can only make a form (what they say or do, or a story, a poem, whatever) by selecting from the full content some face of it, or plane, some part. And at just this point, by just this act, they fall back on the dodges of discourse, and immediately they lose me, I am no longer engaged, *this is not what I know is the going-on*. (*Human*, 157, my emphasis)

This sense of reality as "the going-on" is more often recognized in poets like Olson and Williams than it is in Frost, who, despite the critical interventions of scholars like Richard Poirier, Frank Lentricchia, and others, is still widely perceived as a sort of naïve reactionary — a misperception with which he often played along. This vision of Frost is based principally on his devotion to form, and comments such as his famous comparison of writing free verse to playing tennis with the net down. But Frost's commitment to meter must always be considered in the context of a universe in which, as John Cunningham writes, "humanity is on its own, the only locus of value, intention, self-consciousness, presence" (Cunningham, 261). Unlike his contemporary Ezra Pound, who understood form as inherent, organic, and essential, Frost always assumed that meaning in general, and poetic meaning in particular, was made. Meter, in his poems, reflects the way the human mind imposes order and meaning on a world from which it is otherwise absent.

Two Letters

To M. L. Burton, July 7, 1921:

> The point is that neither knowledge nor thought is an end and neither is nearer an end than the other. The end they both serve, perhaps equally, is deeds in such accepted and nameable forms as the sonnet, the story, the vase, the portrait, the landscape, the hat, the scythe, the gun, the food, the breed, the house, the home, the factory, the election, the government. (*Selected Letters*, 270)

To Louis Untermeyer, October 26, 1940, two weeks after the suicide of Frost's son, Carol:

> I took the wrong way with him. I tried many ways and every single one of them was wrong. Some thing in me is still asking for the chance to try one more. There's where the greatest pain is located. I am cut off too abruptly in my plans and efforts for his peace of mind. . . . Two weeks ago I was up at South Shaftsbury telling Carol how to live. Yesterday I was telling seven hundred Harvard freshman how to live with books in college. Apparently nothing can stop us once we get going. I talk less and less however as if I knew what I was talking about. . . . He failed in farming and he failed in poetry (you may not have known). He was splendid with animals and little children. If only the emphasis could have been put on those. He should have lived with horses. (492)

Conclusion

Implicit in the structure and approach of this book is an argument for the centrality of philosophical questions to American poetry, as well as an argument for looking at poetic making as a philosophically meaningful activity — indeed, as an activity central to the pragmatist sense of what meaning is. In an important sense, the writing of a poem is, as Frost suggests, an activity like building a house, or the construction of a life. The difference lies in the fact that poetic making — the acts of thinking that culminate in the written poem — discloses itself (in words) in a way that other kinds of making don't. The poems I will examine in the chapters ahead bear traces of the practices that generated them, and it is on these practices, rather than on the poems as artifacts, that I will focus. As Charles Morris notes, "what is historically distinctive of the pragmatist orientation — and as unique as anything in philosophy is unique — is the view that there is an intrinsic connection between meaning and action, such that the nature of meaning can be clarified only by reference to action" (28). Writing is a particular kind of action — one that speaks its own history. Writing poems is a particular kind of writing — one in which choice (which word, where to break the line — in Frost's words, where the emphasis is put) is always at issue.[7]

The title of this book puts the emphasis on poetic practice, not poetry, for several reasons. First, and most obviously, because of the centrality of practice — that is, activity — to pragmatic thought. But "practice" resonates in several other ways as well. In contrast to performance, practice suggests repetition, dailiness, and fallibility. It suggests on-going activity, not completed action. I have chosen the poems and other writings I will discuss in the chapters that follow not because they are extraordinary as literary artifacts (though in fact most of them are), but because I believe they demonstrate something about the writers' habits of mind.

"Practice" is a good term for what I'm doing in these pages, as well. I do not expect to have the last word on the vast subject of American poetry and the pragmatist tradition, nor do I expect my readings of any of the poems to be seen as definitive. Rather, I see my own writing as an attempt to push the boundaries of a conversation by introducing a few new voices, and perhaps a new tone. My approach reflects my acceptance of Cleanth Brooks's concept of the heresy of paraphrase (*Urn*, 192): poems defy paraphrase because they speak to us in ways we can't entirely explain, from outside the bounds of domesticated thought, from what James calls the fringe of consciousness (*Principles*, 192–214). They serve the end of advancing thought by pushing at its edges. I hope the fragments of my own text that are not immediately recognizable as scholarly writing will serve the same function. I am interested in edges, and have tried to keep the horizon of my own thought visible in the pages that follow.

Notes

[1] This complex relationship has been a source of much fruitful discussion, beginning with Perry Miller's "From Edwards to Emerson" (*Errand*), and continuing in, among other texts, Terrence Erdt's *Jonathan Edwards*, Sacvan Bercovitch's *Puritan Origins*, Mason A. Lowance's *Language of Caanan*, and Robert Milder's "From Emerson to Edwards."

[2] See, for example, Marsden's treatment of Edwards, Locke, and Miller (60–64).

[3] It is important to note that, in Edwards's view, his parishioners' conversions were "caused" by his sermons only in the very limited sense of being linked in a longer, ultimately inviolable chain of cause and effect. As Ryan Tweney notes, Edwards's theology hinged upon a

> systemic determinism in which a variety of causal factors operate continuously to produce the proximal, moment-by-moment, phenomena of human action. . . . In elaborating upon his notion of cause, Edwards made a distinction between cause as "that which has a positive efficiency or influence to produce a thing," versus causes which "have truly the

nature of a ground or reason why some things are, rather than otherwise.... Thus the absence of the sun in the night, is not the cause of the falling of the dew at that time, in the same manner as its beams are the cause of the ascending of the vapors in the daytime." (372)

Edwards could thus view his sermons as "causing" changes in the hearts of his parishioners in the former, limited sense, without contradicting his essential determinism.

4 See Richard Poirier's *Poetry and Pragmatism* and Stanley Cavell's "What's the Use of Calling Emerson a Pragmatist?" in his book *Emerson's Transcendental Etudes.*

5 In 1920, Dewey used Matthew 7:20 in much the same way that James had, noting its centrality to the pragmatist conception of truth in his *Reconstruction In Philosophy:*

> If ideas, meanings, conceptions, notions, theories, systems are instrumental to an active reorganization of the given environment, to a removal of some specific trouble and perplexity, then the test of their validity and value lies in accomplishing this work.... Handsome is that handsome does. By their fruits shall ye know them. That which guides us truly is true — demonstrated capacity for such guidance is precisely what is meant by truth. The adverb "truly" is more fundamental than either the adjective, true, or the noun, truth. An adverb expresses a way, a mode of acting. Its active, dynamic function is the all-important thing about it, and in the quality of activity induced by it lies all its truth and falsity. The hypothesis that works is the true one; and truth is an abstract noun applied to the collection of cases, actual, foreseen and desired, that receive confirmation in their works and consequences. (*Middle*, 12:169)

6 Frost alludes to Matthew 17:20 in a notebook he kept between 1930 and 1940 (*Notebooks*, 303, 749n41).

7 This characterization applies to chance or constraint-generated poetries such as Kenneth Goldsmith's *The Weather,* as well as more conventional lyric poetries. The difference is in the timing of the choices made: Goldsmith selects the conditions of his transcriptions and then simply transcribes, while Frost, for example, selects and excludes within the process of composition. Both practices foreground the act of making choices in the construction of a verbal artifact.

2: Emerson, Moore, America

IT WAS PERHAPS SIMPLY the coincidence of my having recently worked on an essay about Marianne Moore that caused me to note in the margins of a passage of Emerson's *Nature,* "like Marianne Moore." It seemed, at the time, a wholly spurious connection; aside from the coincidence of Emerson and Moore having edited, respectively, the first and last issues of the *Dial* magazine, there seemed no reason to press this odd echo for meaning. As I read further into Emerson, however, the echo lingered, and I felt increasingly that the *atmosphere* of Moore's poems was related to that of Emerson's prose. I came to feel that both writers sought to respond to what we typically think of as problems of philosophy — questions about the basis of our knowledge and the limits of our perception — in the language of lived experience. A further hypothesis suggested itself: that this response itself marks the tradition of one strain of American thought from Emerson to Dewey, and that Moore's work might fruitfully be reconsidered as part of this tradition.

It seems important, at the outset, to acknowledge that I come to philosophy by way of an abiding interest in twentieth-century American poetry, and that I am therefore a kind of tourist in the territory of philosophy per se. Such amateurism, while a constant source of frustration to *me,* is perhaps not wholly inappropriate to a discussion of an American philosophical orientation. Emerson established passionate amateurism as one kind of American thinking, and it has the advantage of enabling unlikely correspondences between distant regions of thought — a hallmark of both Emerson and Moore's best writing. I will endeavor, therefore, to model my own thinking after theirs, and to use what must be owned as a limitation as, simultaneously, a kind of tool.

As Dalia Judovitz has demonstrated, Plato's exclusion of poetry from the Republic may be seen as philosophy's founding gesture.

> The effort to distinguish philosophical knowledge from all other ways of knowing — poetry, painting and music — becomes the first systematic effort to define philosophy in an absolute sense: as the "mark of differentness" (to use Plato's term) from all other domains . . . this conflict (*diaspora* or difference) can be shown to function as the constitutive operation in the founding of philosophy as a metaphysical discourse. (27)

The definition of philosophy as the foundational discourse to which other discourses must ultimately appeal for their justification has been challenged in recent decades. Richard Rorty and others have argued that we might reconfigure the task of philosophy as "the project of finding new, better, more fruitful ways of speaking," a project Rorty identifies with an understanding of philosophy as merely one voice in a conversation, rather than the arbiter of absolute truth (*Philosophy*, 360). It is in the spirit of this rethinking of the relation between philosophy and other modes of discourse, particularly literature, that I have sought to make Emerson and Moore speak (philosophically) to each other.

Emerson's Evolution

In his biography of Emerson, Robert Richardson retells the familiar story of Emerson's absorption and translation of German idealism via Coleridge and James Marsh, an engagement that reaches its zenith in the 1836 volume *Nature*, which Richardson calls "a modern version of Plato, an American version of Kant":

> It is a brief for the priority of law over fact, aim over action, intent over outcome, pattern over print. The plan, idea or concept of anything, whether a simple tool or the most complex piece of legislation, precedes the actual hammer or the actual voting rights act and determines it. In this sense, the plan is more real — more important — than the physical product. This is the mainmast of idealism and Emerson lashed himself to it for life. (234)

Certainly, the Emerson of *Nature* seems to be clear about the supremacy of mind over mere phenomena. In the chapter entitled "Idealism," Emerson delivers what can be read as the book's central thesis: "It is the uniform effect of culture on the human mind, not to shake our faith in the stability of particular phenomena, as of heat, water, azote; but to lead us to regard nature as a phenomenon, not a substance; to attribute necessary existence to spirit; to esteem nature as an accident and an effect" (*Essays*, 33). As I will argue below, however, Emerson did *not* lash himself to the mainmast of idealism for life, but rather used its insights to counterbalance his attraction to and absorption in the material world. The resulting tension, I contend, drove the change in style evident when one compares the 1836 *Nature* and the 1844 "Experience." Ultimately, Emerson's relation to idealism resembles his relation to Unitarianism, Swedenborgianism, and all other systems of thought. "These books," he writes in his essay on Swedenborg, "should be used with caution. It is dangerous to sculpture these evanescing images of thought. True in transition, they become false if fixed" (682).

Even in *Nature*, his most straightforward statement of philosophical idealism, one senses Emerson's ambivalence. In "Beauty," the third chapter of *Nature*, he writes:

> But beside this general grace diffused over nature, almost all individual forms are agreeable to the eye, as is proved by our endless imitations of some of them, as the acorn, the grape, the pine-cone, the wheat-ear, the egg, the wings and forms of most birds, the lion's claw, the serpent, the butterfly, sea-shells, flames, clouds, buds, leaves and the forms of many trees, as the palm. (14)

The passage is remarkable in its attention to, and evident fascination with, the stuff of the empirical world. The list of natural forms, which is presented as a mere illustration of the idea which precedes it, becomes a catalogue of objects which capture Emerson's and our interest in their own right. The list exceeds the purpose it is designed to fill (that of illustrating the ideal), and its particularity and self-generating lyrical energy point us back to the world, back to nature itself. This kind of verbal excess — elsewhere exemplified by hyper-detailed descriptions, analogies, metaphors, puns, and wordplay[1] — is typical of Emerson, and reflects the dialectical movement between "Nature" and "Spirit" continually working itself out in the material ground of his writing.

Here, as elsewhere, Emerson's language seems to undercut itself, to insist on possibilities that exceed rational commitment.[2] While "Idealism" enumerates the arguments for the subordination of matter to spirit, the next chapter, "Spirit," begins with a deeply ambivalent summation of these arguments:

> Idealism is a hypothesis to account for nature by other principles than those of carpentry and chemistry. Yet, if it only deny the existence of matter, it does not satisfy the demands of the spirit. It leaves God out of me. It leaves me in the splendid labyrinth of my perceptions, to wander without end. Then the heart resists it, because it balks the affections in denying substantive being to men and women. Nature is so pervaded with human life, that there is something of humanity in all, and in every particular. But this theory makes nature foreign to me, and does not account for that consanguinity which we acknowledge to it.
>
> Let it stand, then, in the present state of our knowledge, merely as a useful introductory hypothesis, serving to apprize us of the eternal distinction between the soul and the world. (41)

Committed to the reality of the spirit, Emerson was nevertheless dissatisfied with a theory that he acknowledged alienated human beings from the natural world, failing to account for "that consanguinity which we acknowledge to it" (41).³

Emerson's intellectual restlessness, his habitual distrust of *systems* of thought, leads him away from the expository, and more-or-less philosophically legible mode of *Nature*, toward a method of writing that discloses its epistemology in the twin acts of writing and reading, a philosophy that, in Robert Frost's phrase "finds its own name as it goes" (*Poetry and Prose*, 394). This shift, from understanding writing as a way of telling something about the world to seeing it as a way of making something happen, is a move that renders Emerson virtually incomprehensible in philosophical terms until the advent of pragmatism.

As Michael Jonik observes in his analysis of Emerson's engagement with post-Kantian German thought, Emerson altered the text of *Nature* for its 1849 reissue, removing the epigraph from the Neoplatonic philosopher Plotinus, and replacing it with his own poem:

> A subtle chain of countless rings
> The next unto the farthest brings;
> The eye reads omens where it goes,
> And speaks all languages the rose;
> And, striving to be man, the worm,
> Mounts through all the spires of form.

"Far from any mere caprice," Jonik writes, "these new lines indicate a continuing shift in emphasis in Emerson's thought from a Neoplatonic, 'emanationsit' understanding of nature to one that implies an immanent 'evolutionary' idea of form" (7). The distinction is a crucial one; while Emerson's writing, early and late, always seeks the point of intersection or equilibrium between mind and world, the balance in his later work has decidedly shifted. Forms, in Emerson's later thought, are not perfect, unchanging ideals from which the physical world "emanates," but rather exist *within* the physical, and continually evolve. This shift, Jonik notes, aligns Emerson with post-Kantian German thought. Specifically, it "marks a continued, if gradual, departure from Emerson's early idealism (marked by natural theological understanding of the universe) to one closer to the half-way point of Goethe and Schiller, the point at which the speculative mind always keeps empirical experience within its sight" (7).

While in *Nature* Emerson seeks to articulate a mediated philosophical position in philosophical terms — he is an idealist, but with significant reservations — in his later work he eschews this philosophical vocabulary in favor of a poetic language that allows him to build (and enact) his own complex, often self-canceling epistemology. Just as Emerson found himself having expanded beyond the bounds of his religious home in Unitarianism, "Experience" shows him to be pushing past the philosophical and linguistic limits imposed by the idealism he entertains in *Nature*

(Goodman, 43). Emerson's solution to this philosophical homelessness is to build himself a home in writing, an active model of the reciprocity between mind and world. As Leonard Neufeldt observes, "The source of knowing for Emerson is, in a sense, the world of one's horizons, but more precisely it is the transaction between the individual and his world, in 'a harmony of both.' The focus is neither on nature, nor on the self, but on the self in nature: that is, the engaging of one's world" (27). As I will argue in the analysis of "Experience" below, Emerson's alienation from, on the one hand, the "carpentry and chemistry" worldview of materialism, and, on the other, the untethered abstractions of idealism, prompts the creation of a style that "replicate[s] in language the motions of the mind as it thinks through how much, and how, it can know anything" (Buell, *Emerson*, 215). In other words, a model, rather than a description, of the mind-world relation.

In "Experience," published in 1844, just a few years before the reissue of *Nature,* Emerson seeks not merely to explain but rather to enact the mind's engagement with the world. This enactment encompasses both our profound sense of distance from nature — "this evanescence and lubricity of all objects, which lets them slip through our grasp when we clutch hardest" — and our intimacy with it. In the first half of the essay, Emerson reminds us of the "innavigable sea that washes between us and the things we aim at and converse with" (*Essays,* 473). The essay's opening evokes just this feeling of being adrift:

> Where do we find ourselves? In a series of which we do not know the extremes, and believe that it has none. We wake and find ourselves on a stair; there are stairs below us, which we seem to have ascended; there are stairs above us, many a one, which go upward and out of sight. But the Genius which, according to the old belief, stands beside the door by which we enter, and gives us the lethe to drink, that we may tell no tales, mixed the cup too strongly, and we cannot shake off the lethargy now at noonday. (471)

The language simultaneously demands interpretation and denies the possibility of a simple symbolic equivalence. Where *do* we find ourselves in Emerson's series of complex and shifting figures? On a staircase? Waking from a dream? On the far side of a door? If the stairs above and below us represent the future and the past, what is the meaning of the door, and where is it located vis-à-vis the stairs? What do we make of the "Genius" and his dream-inducing lethe? Such disorientation does not obscure Emerson's meaning from us, it *is* his meaning. Life is comprised of distortion, and surface; we cannot know our real life. "Dream delivers us to dream, and there is no end to illusion" (473).

In his most devastating illustration of the way the world evades our attempts to know it absolutely, Emerson describes his response to the death of his son:

> In the death of my son, now more than two years ago, I seem to have lost a beautiful estate, — no more. I cannot get it nearer to me. If tomorrow I should be informed of the bankruptcy of my principal debtors, the loss of my property would be a great inconvenience to me, perhaps, for many years; but it would leave me as it found me, — neither better nor worse. So is it with this calamity: it does not touch me: some thing which I fancied was a part of me, which could not be torn away without tearing me, nor enlarged without enriching me, falls off from me, and leaves no scar. It was caducous. I grieve that grief can teach me nothing, nor carry me one step into real nature. (473)

The passage seems calculated not only to illustrate his own alienation in the starkest possible terms, but also to alienate his audience: to enact the distance he describes by forcing his hearers to recoil from his words. In "Experience," feeling — the source of Emerson's parenthetical ambivalence about idealism in *Nature* — becomes constitutive of his epistemology: "Grief too," he writes, "will make us idealists" (473).

But this feeling of distance between mind and world, this idealism, is only half of the picture that Emerson gives us in "Experience." Just as we have adjusted to the slipperiness of Emerson's language, adopting as instructions for reading his declaration that "we live among surfaces, and the true art of life is to skate well upon them," Emerson changes course, and we find ourselves once again in the presence of "the old world, wife, babes, and mother, Concord and Boston, the dear old spiritual world, and even the dear old devil not far off" (480). No less changeful, the world is nonetheless now felt to be intimately our own, and the dizzying, shapeshifting figuration of the essay's opening gives way to familiar images of farm, bar-room and home. The shift from the lament of the first half of the essay to the acceptance, even celebration of impermanence in the latter half confirms Emerson's assertion that "life is a train of moods like a string of beads" (473). That "most unhandsome part of our condition," our inability to "anchor" ourselves in stability or certainty, is now expressed as "the miracle of life which will not be expounded, but will remain a miracle" (484). "Experience" is a dizzying piece of writing to read: by turns bewildering, exhilarating, strange, and familiar. It is, finally, an experience, not an argument.

Central to the epistemology that Emerson enacts in "Experience" is the idea of ordinariness, the hinge that connects him to the pragmatist tradition. In "The American Scholar," Emerson defines "the topics of the time" as "the literature of the poor, the feelings of the child, the philosophy of the street, the meaning of household life." The appropriate subject for the American writer and thinker are not "the sublime and beautiful" but rather "the near, the low, the common" (*Essays*, 68). It is the particular duty of the *American* scholar to demonstrate the workings of the ideal within and among the commonplace, the everyday. Listing the worldly manifestations of spiritual essence, Emerson demonstrates again his abiding fascination with the local and particular, "the meal in the firkin; the milk in the pan; the ballad in the street; the news of the boat; the glance of the eye; the form and gait of the body." This ordinary world, available to housewives and farmers and poets alike, is, for Emerson, our point of access to "divine presence" (69). Emerson sets out to speak simultaneously of ordinary life and of philosophy, of nature and of spirit, of the particular and the universal, and the result is a language that is as elusive as it seems accessible, simultaneously pointing to the natural world in the most concrete terms, and gesturing to the cosmos.

As Russell Goodman has demonstrated, Emerson "counters . . . the solipsistic implications of his flirtation with Berkelian idealism in *Nature*, by speaking of a relationship between mind and world that, like those depicted in Wordsworth and Coleridge's poetry, resembles a marriage" (43). This sense of intimate connection between the self and nature, of "an occult relation between man and vegetable," reflects Emerson's simultaneous commitments to the shaping power of mind and the real presence of nature (11). It is significant that Emerson inherits the framework of his response to the "problem" of the relation between mind and world not from philosophy, but from poetry. In "Experience," Emerson finds the spiritual to be present in exactly the same way that those with whom he is most intimate are present: "In the morning I awake, and find the old world, wife, babes, and mother, Concord and Boston, the dear old spiritual world, and even the dear old devil not far off" (480). In his description of waking to "the old world" as he wakes to his wife and children, Emerson picks up the romantic trope of the marriage of self and world, "the 'love and holy passion' with which Wordsworth sees us wedded to the universe" (Goodman, 20). The intimacy of this relation is Emerson's answer to what I have called his philosophical homelessness. Cavell traces the implications of this approach:

> I believe Emerson may encourage the idea of himself as a solipsist or subjectivist, for example, in such a remark late in the same essay [*Nature*], as "Thus inevitably does the universe wear our color." But whether you take this to be subjective or objective depends on whether you take the colors or moods to be subjective or objective. My claim is that Emerson is out to destroy the grounds on which such a problem takes itself seriously, I mean interprets itself as a metaphysical fixture. The universe is as separate from me, but as intimately a part of me, as one on whose behalf I contest, and who

therefore wears the colors I bear. We are in a state of "romance" with the universe (to use a word from the last sentence of the essay); we do not possess it, but our life is to return to it. (*Emerson*, 13)

The complexity of Emerson's position vis-à-vis the recognizable schools of philosophic thought has resulted in the widespread assumption of his philosophical naiveté, what Cavell calls the "unrelenting insistence upon Emerson's inability to think and write rigorously" (2). In a 1953 review of *Emerson's Angle of Vision,* Sherman Paul's synthesis of Emerson's philosophy, Joseph Blau expels Emerson from the field of legitimate philosophy with a remarkable sense of authority: "The very expertness of Paul's work," Blau writes, "lends emphasis to the realization that Emerson, however profoundly expounded, has little philosophical value today. This, I am sure, is not the conclusion Paul hoped his readers would reach; but it is the conclusion to which one is irresistibly led" (195). If, as Dalia Judovitz contends, the exile of poetry (and more broadly, of the aesthetic experience) from philosophy in Plato can be understood as philosophy's founding gesture, that gesture finds its echo in the rejection of Emerson as philosopher. Ultimately, professional philosophy's dismissal of Emerson has led to, in Cavell's view, the repression of an important strain — perhaps *the* important strain — of American philosophical thinking.

In the Emersonian tradition, language becomes the living body of thought. The faculty that Plato considered "a species of mental poison," the poet's ability to use the sound of words to elicit feeling, becomes, in Emerson's later essays and lectures, the driving force of thought: a way out of the dualism that had come to paralyze nineteenth-century philosophy (Havelock, 4). "The heart resists it," Emerson says of idealism, noting the failure of existing philosophical systems to account for the way knowing is informed by feeling — the fact that our intimacy with the world, "that consanguinity which we acknowledge to it," is part of what we call knowledge. In "Experience," Emerson makes explicit the relation between knowledge and feeling, demonstrating both our alienation from and our connection to the world in the most intimate terms.

Exiled from philosophy as such, the Emersonian vision of thought as wedded to feeling, and wedded to the world, finds refuge in the work of American poets.

The Call of the Quotidian

Many philosophers have written about the distance between philosophy and daily life. Stanley Cavell, for example, notes that, "philosophical thinking is not something that a normal human being can submit to all the time, or anytime he or she may choose."

> Philosophical questions — say as to whether we can know that God or the world or others exist, or why it is that something exists rather than nothing, or whether we can know that we are not now asleep and dreaming that we are awake, or whether ethical and aesthetic values have an objective basis, or whether mind and body are one thing or two things, or whether men and women are the same or different — are not questions that are alive for one at just any time. (*Emerson*, 26)

Hume expressed it this way:

> Most fortunately it happens, that since reason is incapable of dispelling these clouds, nature herself suffices to that purpose, and cures me of this philosophical melancholy and delirium, either by relaxing this bent of mind, or by some avocation, and lively impression of my senses which obliterate all these chimeras. I dine, I play a game of back-gammon, I converse, I am merry with my friends; and when, after three or four hours amusement, I wou'd return to these speculations, they appear so cold, and strain'd, and ridiculous, that I cannot find it in my heart to enter into them any farther. (Hume, 175; qtd. in Michael, 33)

I read these passages with an enormous sense of relief. It was some years of trying and failing to reconstruct Cartesian thought experiments before I asked myself whether these failures were not philosophy's as much as my own.

William James writes of one of his students that "he had always taken for granted that when you entered into a philosophic classroom you had to open relations with a universe entirely different from the one you left behind in the street. The two were supposed, he said, to have so little to do with each other that you could not possibly occupy your mind with them at the same time" (*Writings*, 495). It is, of course, just this separateness of philosophy from daily life that James set out to correct. In his lectures on pragmatism, James admits into the philosophical conversation the stubborn world of personal experience that I had never been able to lay down, voicing *as* philosophy my own embarrassed, internal objection *to* philosophy: that we can't live as though objects were just shadows of ideal forms, or phenomena echoing some remote and unknowable noumena, or disembodied sensations animated by God's ideas.

What does it mean to wish to answer the questions posed by philosophy with the particulars of daily life? To respond to speculation about the ultimate ground of being or the knowableness of things in themselves with Emerson's "the meal in the firkin, the milk in the pan; the ballad in the street; the news of the boat; the glance of the eye, the form and gait of the body," or Moore's "cat-tails, flags, blueberries and spiderwort"

(Emerson, *Essays*, 69; Moore, *Poems*, 416)? What is at stake in the attempt to make this way of speaking mean something philosophically? What does it mean to want to bring these two registers, these two kinds of talk, into the same conversation?

Marianne Moore: Imagining the Actual

In a 1922 review of an exhibit by the sculptor Alfeo Faggi, Marianne Moore writes that "the preoccupation today is with the actual" (*Prose*, 73). Indeed, "the actual" was one of Moore's own most intense preoccupations, stemming in part from her extensive course work in biology and zoology, which included exposure to Darwinian theory, at Bryn Mawr (D. R. Anderson, 32). Like Emerson's, however, Moore's interest was more particularly the point of intersection between "the actual," that is, physical reality, and the spiritual. As Jennifer Leader observes, "although Moore has less overtly religious and biblical symbolism in her poetry than many of her more skeptical contemporaries, she repeatedly engages questions of spirituality and ethics from a position firmly grounded in Judeo-Christian suppositions" (30). Moore's epistemology, derived from her simultaneous commitments to science and to religious faith, is perhaps most concisely articulated in her description of Faggi's sculpture of Dante: "the realm of the spirit is the only realm in which experience is able to corroborate the fact that the real can also be the actual. Such work as Mr. Faggi's is a refutation of the petulant patronage which for instance assigns Plato to adolescents — which remarks: 'How Plato hated a fact!'" (*Prose*, 74). Moore's view — that "the actual" is coincident with the metaphysically "real," that the spiritual realm is accessible to empirical "experience," and that Plato's idealism is perfectly compatible with a reverence for scientific fact — is, like Emerson's, difficult to square with recognizable realist or idealist philosophical positions. Indeed, as I will argue below, Moore didn't write *from* any epistemological position at all, but rather wrote *toward* one, allowing what Lisa Steinman calls her "dual commitment to mind and matter" to shape and modify her poems over time (223).

Moore published "The Steeple-Jack" in *Poetry* magazine in 1932 alongside "The Student" and "The Hero" in the sequence "Part of a Novel, Part of a Poem, Part of a Play." This title was maintained when the poem appeared in Moore's *Selected Poems*, edited by T. S. Eliot in 1935, but "The Student" was dropped from the sequence. Moore later eliminated the collective title altogether but continued to present "The Steeple-Jack" and "The Hero" consecutively, though all three poems were revised multiple times, and different versions of each appeared in later collections. "The Steeple-Jack" was the first poem in every collection in which it appeared from 1935 on.

Like Emerson's *Nature*, "The Steeple-Jack" demonstrates, on the one hand, a commitment to ideals and abstractions, and, on the other, a radical investment in the particular. The long textual history of the sequence[4] — in particular Moore's excision and replacement of key lines and stanzas in both "The Steeple-Jack" and "The Student" — reveals the delicate balancing act she sought to perform, like Emerson, building and modifying an epistemological home in language. For Moore, as for Emerson, "form — whether natural form, object-form, political or moral form, forms of the self or of the mind — to remain vital can only be understood in terms of metamorphosis" (Jonik, 4). The construction of these poems, and Moore's continual revision of them, reflect that for her, writing was a way of engaging, making, and enacting the always-changing relation between mind and world.

In the 1932 version of "The Steeple-Jack" as in many of her poems of the 1930s, Moore announces her interest in seeing, and enacts, in Emersonian fashion, a complex, difficult, persistently-shifting vision.

> Dürer would have seen a reason for living
>   in a town like this, with eight stranded whales
> to look at; with the sweet sea air coming into your house
> on a fine day, from water etched
>   with waves as formal as the scales
> on a fish. (*Poems*, 415–16)

Moore establishes in the first two lines of the poem the primacy of sight: the "eight stranded whales" provide enough visual interest as to constitute a "reason for living." What is seen — the whales, the town, the "college student / named Ambrose," the crooked steeple and the steeple-jack C J Poole — is less important here than the act of seeing, which in Moore's writing, as in Emerson's, is always representative of the mind's power to impose order on the flux of experience. In the poem's first three stanzas order prevails: the water is "etched / with waves as formal as the scales / of a fish," the seagulls fly over the town clock "one by one, in two's, in threes," and even the storm that enters in stanza four is introduced in aesthetic terms, as a "whirlwind fifeanddrum." The poem's rigorous syllabic structure (the thirteen stanzas are six lines each, following, with minor variations, a pattern of 11, 10, 14, 8, 8, and 3 syllables per line), reminds us that the scene being described is a constructed one.

In stanza four, however, the storm and its attendant "confusion" disrupts both the landscape ("disturbs stars in the sky and the / star on the steeple") and the grammatical clarity of the poem.

>   . . . . it is a privilege to see so
> much confusion. Disguised by what

> might seem austerity, the sea-
> side flowers and
>
> trees are favored by the fog so that you have
> the tropics at first hand

Most difficult here is the phrase "disguised by what / might seem austerity," since it is not at all clear how austerity acts to disguise "the sea- / side flowers and / trees." Adding to the difficulty of this formulation is the qualifier "might seem," suggesting a hidden relation between a seemingly "austere" eye and its lush, tropical vision. Unpacking the syntax of these lines, I understand them to say something like "Disguised by the seeming austerity of the ordering eye, the seaside flowers and trees take on the appearance of tropical vegetation." The power of Moore's lines, however, comes from the way they enact, rather than describe, the intricate relations between order and confusion, perception and imagination. Here, as elsewhere in the poem, grammatical ambiguity is balanced by the poem's strict visual and syllabic patterns. As Margaret Holley has demonstrated, "The Steeple-Jack" opens with a "model stanza," in which line breaks correspond to natural breaks in the rhythm of the grammatical sentence. The stanzas that follow retain the syllabic pattern established by the first stanza "through grammatical sequences that are independent of the design, often startlingly so" ("Model Stanza," 183). Syntax and stanzaic pattern are resolved in the final stanza, in which the line breaks once again correspond to natural phrasing.

Related to the dialectics of form and chaos, observer and observed that operate in the poem is the movement between the general ("a town like this") and the minutely particular ("daisies — /the yellow and the crab-claw blue ones with the green bracts —"). Indeed, Moore's revisions of the poem over the years suggest the centrality of this relation: most of the changes have to do with the poem's level of detail. In *Becoming Marianne Moore,* her impressive textual history of Moore's early poems, Robin Shulze describes how traditional editorial practice, dependant on the concept of authorial intention, is challenged by "poets like Moore, who, over the course of her career seemed to want her public to have numerous different published versions of her texts." Shulze advocates replacing the term "authorial intention" with "authorial selection," which suggests that "the author's goal in each new version of his or her text is, in fact, the local fitness of that text in relation to its social, cultural or textual environment, rather than the achievement of some always present abstract ideal of perfection" (11). Shulze's Darwinian metaphor is apt: in each of her revisions of "The Steeple-Jack" and "The Student," Moore sought to achieve a momentary balance between the givenness of objects and the creative power of mind.

Like Emerson, Moore refused ready-made structures of language and thought and instead used writing, her chosen mode of acting upon the world, to construct a habitat of her own, one in which mind and matter determine each other reflexively, in a balance established not through stasis but rather through continual fine adjustments, first in one direction, then in the other.

Stanza six of "The Steeple-Jack," a stanza Moore cut for the 1935 version of the poem and later replaced, is a list of local vegetation.

> . . . cat-tails, flags, blueberries and spiderwort,
>   striped grass, lichens, sunflowers, asters, daisies —
> yellow and crab-claw blue ones with green bracts — toad-plant,
> petunias, ferns; pink lilies, blue
>   ones, tigers; poppies; black sweet-peas. (*Poems*, 416)

The list resembles Emerson's in *Nature:* "the acorn, the grape, the pine-cone, the wheat-ear, the egg, the wings and forms of most birds, the lion's claw, the serpent, the butterfly, sea-shells, flames, clouds, buds, leaves and the forms of many trees, as the palm" (*Essays*, 14). Like Emerson's catalogue, Moore's detailed and lyrical list of names seems excessive, and its excess is the point. The poem is organized around abstractions — "hope," "truth," "a town like this," — and the list tips the scale back in the direction of local particularity, modifying our bird's-eye view of the landscape by insisting on a renewed attention to the real.

Moore's revision of the poem from its original publication in 1932 until the end of her life confirms this reading of the poem as balancing act. Moore subtracted key lines and stanzas, most notably the catalogue of local plants noted above, only to restore them in subsequent versions. Many of the textual variants of "The Steeple-Jack" have the effect of tipping the balance of the poem in the direction of the abstract or the particular. A reference to "Maine stone," for example, is dropped in an early draft, shifting the setting of the poem from New England to an imaginary anytown referred to simply as "a town like this" ("The Steeple-Jack"). In adjusting these elements, Moore sought to establish what Joan Richardson, in her description of Wallace Stevens's work, refers to as the "homeostatic balance" that, in evolutionary terms, enables an organism "to go on, to continue" (22). Like Emerson, Moore embraced the flexibility of language, the possibilities it offered for minute revisions and re-calibrations, using words to compose a continually evolving epistemological home that was more nuanced, more alive, than any theological or philosophical system, or even any completed poem.

The idiosyncrasy of Moore's epistemology, her simultaneous commitment to Calvinist ideals and to the particulars of the natural world, makes her, like Emerson, a figure difficult for literary scholarship to place. Kenneth Burke begins his 1942 essay "Motives and Motifs in the Poetry of

Marianne Moore" by quoting from the poem "He 'Digesteth Harde Y'ron'" the lines "the power of the visible / is the invisible." Burke concludes that it is "a relation between external and internal, or visible and invisible, or background and personality, that [Moore's] poems characteristically establish" (87). Burke draws distinctions between symbolism, imagism, and objectivism, noting that while all three foreground the image, the relation between object and subject (or image and meaning/interpretation of image) is distinct in each. "In objectivism, though an object may be chosen for treatment because of its symbolic or subjective reference, once it has been chosen it is to be studied in its own right" (88). Burke classifies Moore as an objectivist, suggesting that the local particularities of poems such as "The Steeple-Jack" should be read as mimetically depicted *real* objects, rather than (simply or primarily) as symbols of the ideal.

Interestingly, Morton Zabel, a contemporary of both Moore and Burke, makes the opposite argument. In his reading of Moore, Zabel emphasizes the role of the ideal over that of the real.

> In her poem *Poetry* Miss Moore improves Yeats' characterization of Blake by insisting that poets must be "literalists of the imagination"; they must see the visible at that focus of intelligence where sight and concept collide, and where it becomes transformed into the pure and total idealism of ideas. (329–30)

Zabel's argument is similar to that of Ralph Rees, who asserts the centrality of Moore's conception of imagination to her poetics, noting that "she finds imagination as much a part of reality as fact. . . . The imagined, because it is more individual and more personal than the other phenomena, seems to her the very essence of reality" (231). Imagination, according to Rees, is for Moore "poetry's mechanism for ideation" (232). Rees contends that lines such as "What is more precise than precision? Illusion" (from "Armour's Undermining Modesty") reflect Moore's belief that facts are only important insofar as they provide stimuli to the imagination, the true locus of "reality."

The critical debate about the relative importance of the imagined/ ideal and the real in Moore's poetry suggests the degree to which the two are intertwined. By insisting on the primacy of one half of this dialectic over the other, these critics miss the balance that Moore's work seeks to establish. Lisa Steinman, in her wide-ranging discussion of "The Student," acknowledges Moore's "dual commitment to mind and world, process and fact," but calls such a position "problematic" (223).

Like Emerson's writing, Moore's becomes "problematic" when translated into familiar philosophical language: she is neither an idealist nor a materialist, but a "literalist of the imagination." Her work, particularly of this period, emphatically demonstrates the way mind shapes experience, and is in turn shaped by facts that resist easy assimilation. As Margaret

Holley points out, throughout the poems of the 1930s, Moore "raise[s] the issue of nature and art not to drive a wedge but to discover the compatibility between them." Holley notes, in particular, "the yoking [of] the literal with the figurative, the actual with the imagined" (*Poetry*, 90). Similarly, Rachel Buxton, in her important essay tracing Moore's relationship to pragmatist thought, describes the way Moore, like Emerson, dissolves the "problem" of the relation of mind and world. Buxton notes "the apparent conflict we see in Moore's poetry between her responsibility to the 'physical world' and her responsibilities to the assertions of the imagination." But, Buxton insists,

> This is a conflict only if one accepts a neat, rationalist division between "world" and "mind," between "subjective" and "objective," between "reality" and "imagination" — and such an opposition is rejected by pragmatists, who argue that the mind cannot be separated from the environment in which it functions, and that the relations between things are as real as the things themselves. (536)

Just as Emerson's insistence on both nature and spirit forced him into philosophical homelessness, Moore's insistence on both the startling materiality of the world and the shaping power of mind means that she does not fit easily within the aesthetic camps carved out by her modernist peers. Stevens, Eliot, and Williams each describe her work in terms of their own poetic projects. As Roy Harvey Pearce points out, however, Moore's poetry resists such easy placement. "*Contra* Williams she insists on having ideas about the thing; *contra* Eliot her meditations are tied to and mediated by the thing, not released by it" (154).

The Emersonian impulse in "Part of a Novel" is made explicit by "The Student," the poem that was later excised from the series and published separately. The poem refers, in both its early and later versions, to Emerson's "The American Scholar" and announces that the epistemological position Moore establishes in "The Steeple-Jack" is explicitly an American position, necessary to a young democracy struggling to balance its ideals and its material success,[5] its emphasis on individualism with a national identity. As Lisa Steinman notes, Moore's intent in "The Student" "seems to be to emphasize how all human encounters with the world, be they scientific, industrial, or literary — are similar in that they involve reclassifying, revaluing, and thereby in some sense changing the world" (215–16).[6] Steinman's description of Moore's project in "The Student" serves equally well as a gloss on pragmatist epistemology, which William James describes as follows:

> In the realm of truth-processes, facts come independently and determine our beliefs provisionally. But these beliefs make us act, and as fast as they do so, they bring into sight or into existence new

facts which re-determine the beliefs accordingly. So the whole coil and ball of truth, as it rolls up, is the product of a double influence. Truths emerge from facts; but they dip forward into facts again and add to them; which facts create or reveal new truth (the word is indifferent) and so on indefinitely. (*Writings*, 585)

In "The Student," Moore, a reader of both James and Dewey, dramatizes this process on a national scale. Because the American "experiment" is, as Einstein says of science in the seventh stanza of the 1932 version, "never finished," Americans must remain open to new facts, which will generate new pictures of reality; in James's terms, new truths.

As with "The Steeple-Jack," Moore's first published version of "The Student" balances generalizations about education ("Education augments our natural forces") and America ("we're not / hypocrites, we're rustics") with catalogues of particular facts drawn from biology, zoology, and physics, as well as military life and "the world of sport." While "The Steeple-Jack" enacts the mind-world relation by illustrating the dialectic between the givenness of the material world and the shaping power of imagination, "The Student" engages the same epistemological question by demonstrating the relation between "facts" and creative power in American education. Thus, in the original version of the poem, Moore both includes facts ("horned owls have one ear that opens up and one / that opens down") and insists that such facts are not the end of education but the beginning: "Education augments our natural forces and / prompts us to extend the machinery of advancement to those who are without it." Still, though the heroic mental activity of the student is what Moore views as the proper end of education, facts are important, too: "one does not care to hold opinions / that fright / could dislocate" (*Poems*, 418). As Lisa Steinman notes, Moore's view in "The Student" is that "science is not inert fact; poetry, science and education in America are all concerned with creative energy and ongoing process; but facts are still facts and not to be ignored" (222).

The immediate source of the dialectic Moore establishes between facts and imagination in "The Student" was most likely John Dewey. As Steinman notes in her discussion of Moore's Reading Diary, Moore read and took notes on Dewey's *Democracy and Education,* and was particularly attentive to "Dewey's attempt to reconcile his emphasis upon developing character with his respect for facts" (229). Observing the dual commitment to mind and world throughout her work, Rachel Buxton argues that Moore's work is best understood alongside the American pragmatists: "Moore's poetry negotiates between situatedness on the one hand and the prescriptions of the imagination on the other. It is a negotiation which lies at the heart of the American pragmatist project" (532). In "The Student," however, Moore tips her hat not to Dewey or James, but to Emerson's "American Scholar," to which she refers in stanza 14 of the original version ("One fitted / to be a scholar must have a heroic mind, Emerson said"), and stanza 5 of the 1941 version ("But someone in New / England has known enough to say/ that the student is patience personified, / a variety / of hero") (*Poems*, 418 and 185–86). Moore translates Emerson's dual emphasis on the power of mind and the significance of the material details of everyday life — "the meal in the firkin; the milk in the pan; the ballad in the street; the news of the boat; the glance of the eye; the form and gait of the body" (*Essays*, 69) — into her own dialectic of given and made, fact and imagination in "The Steeple-Jack" and "The Student," poems that each underwent significant revision during Moore's lifetime.

Much like her dramatic 1951 revision of "The Steeple-Jack," Moore's revision of "The Student" for the 1941 volume *What Are Years* dramatically reduces the complexity of the poem by eliminating much of its detail. Gone are many of the poem's catalogues of fact, its references to football, racing, and zoology. In the later version Moore offers a single fact: "Wolf's wool is the best of wool, / but it cannot be sheared, because the wolf will not comply." And unlike the litany of facts presented in the original version, this one is immediately related to the poem's central theme: "With knowledge as / with wolf's surliness, / the student studies voluntarily, refusing to be less / than individual" (*Poems*, 185–86). Unlike "The Steeple-Jack," however, "The Student" never regained its catalogues of details. Moore restored much of the material excised in her 1935 and 1951 revisions of "The Steeple-Jack" in 1961, while "The Student," presented separately from "The Steeple-Jack" and "The Hero," which would appear together (though without the collective title) in subsequent volumes, remained in the form Moore settled on in 1941. While the form of "The Steeple-Jack," Moore's most direct expression of her complex epistemological position, continued to evolve, performing the always-changing relation between mind and world, Moore seems to have been content to allow "The Student" to become a poem *about* American education rather than a model of the interaction between fact and imagination.

In thinking through the relationship between epistemology and aesthetics at the heart of both Emerson and Moore's writing, it is helpful to return to Michael Jonik's distinction between a conception of form as "emanation" from an ideal, and one that perceives form as "immanent," emerging from the actual. Jonik's observation that Emerson's thought evolves from "a Neoplatonic, 'emanationsit' understanding of nature to one that implies an immanent 'evolutionary' idea of form" is supported by what we know of Emerson's changing practice as a writer (7). While his early notebooks, entitled "Wide World," were pre-ordered by topic, in the 1830s he began writing first and indexing afterwards, a reflection of his shifting understanding of the relationship between form and process (R. Richardson, 200–201). Robert Richardson notes that Emerson

> spent a good deal of time methodically copying and recopying Journal material, indexing, alphabetizing indexes, and eventually making an index of indexes. When he came to write a lecture, he would work through his indexes, making a list of possible passages. He then assembled, ordered and reordered these into the talk or lecture. (201)

The particular balance between attention to the physical world and recognition of the ordering impulse of the mind that Emerson and Moore each sought to achieve in the act of writing manifests itself most clearly in an aesthetic of emergent form. Like Emerson's essays, pulled together from Journal passages indexed by topic, Moore's poems, revised repeatedly even after publication, demonstrate an understanding of form as the product of ongoing evolution. Bonnie Costello observes that

> Revision and composition were one to Moore's restless imagination. With every new publication (and even in printed copies she sent to friends) she would set to work adding, deleting, reworking lines to the dismay of critics like myself who have tried to trace the record. Many fine early poems never saw their way into collections, others underwent such drastic stylistic or thematic changes as to become new works. (4)

The practices of both writers suggest that for them, truth was not perceived and then declared, but rather emerged through the act of writing and, crucially, re-writing. Both writers' works represent, in this regard, important instances of an American epistemological tradition that understands writing as a record of thought in the act of disclosing itself to the thinker.

In an interview with Donald Hall in 1963, Moore states, "I think the most difficult thing for me is to be satisfactorily lucid, yet have enough implication in it to suit myself" (Hall, 31). Emerson and Moore shared this double use of language as both a means for lucidity — clear, direct reference to a world of real things — and as a means of implication — a gesturing toward what language cannot contain. This particular, complex orientation toward language characteristically works itself out in forms that do not look quite like poetry or philosophy and that are simultaneously accused of both obfuscation and pandering populism. Scholarly defenders of both Emerson and Moore distinguish between their serious, difficult, and philosophically oriented writings and those aspects of their public personas that made them each, in their different ways, immensely popular. This separation, while it has done much to repair the scholarly reputations of both writers, misses the way in which the confrontation between world and idea is a necessary condition of thought for both Emerson and Moore.

Conclusion: Giving Up Ground

Rereading and revising this chapter, I realize that the narrative I have suggested — in which Emerson and Moore both advance a vision that effectively dismantles the polarization of real and ideal, poetry and philosophy — is only one of many possible narratives. Might not the dualities of their work just as plausibly be accounted for as evidence of compromise or fragmentation? Consider the following counter-narratives.

In his essay "Emerson, Individualism and the Ambiguities of Dissent," Sacvan Bercovitch portrays Emerson as "the inventor of a mode of individualistic dissent . . . that remained part of the American consensus even in its will to stand radically apart, because individualism was already part of that consensus" (Buell, "Introduction," 7–8). Distinguishing between the "individuality" privileged by socialist and other radical social critics and the "individualism" enshrined by the advocates of laissez-faire capitalism, Bercovitch traces Emerson's ambiguous relation to both terms. While the early Emerson insisted on marking the distance between the real and ideal Americas, Bercovitch argues,

> Increasingly through the 1840's, Emerson drew out the liberal underpinnings of his dissent — i.e., the premises of his commitment to America in its full bi-polar implications, ideal *and* (not or) actual. And increasingly through the decade, in journals, lectures, *Dial* reviews, and Transcendentalist "Conversations," he engaged in a pointed, persistent, and eventually vehement polemic against socialism. (11)

Having realized that socialism was incompatible with his ideal of "individuality," the later Emerson allowed that term to become conflated with the "individualism" of bourgeois liberalism. In Bercovitch's view, Emerson's commitment to the "ideal *and* (not or) actual" represents not, as I have suggested, liberation from the confines of a polarized discourse, but rather an intellectual and political limitation. By wedding "individuality" to "individualism" and the real to the ideal, Bercovitch suggests, Emerson foreclosed the possibility of a more radical (socialist) critique, one that "denied . . . the prophetic myths of manifest destiny, and the typology of the open, regenerative West" that he ultimately embraced (111). Moreover, in Bercovitch's view, this rhetorical move (the union of the real and the ideal Americas) more or less permanently circumscribed the place of dissent within the American ideology: "the ambiguities [the traditions of individualism] have spawned, concerning subversion and/or co-optation, subjectivity as agency of change and/or agent of social control, protest as counter-culture and/or as cultural counter-dependence, remain the central problematic of American literary and political dissent" (129). Bercovitch thus shares my understanding of the way Emerson's writing yokes the ideal and the real, but finds here a deadly compromise, rather than liberation from an ossified discourse.

Conversely, Moore's poetry may be understood not, as I have argued, as a delicate balancing act between the imagined and the real, but rather as a testament to that which *resists* union or coherence. Victoria Bazin, for example, argues that in "Part of a Novel, Part of a Poem, Part of a Play," the sequence of which "The Steeple-Jack" is a part, Moore's playful, difficult language poses a challenge to the economic and social order, enacting "resistance to the efficacy of a linguistic system which passively reflects the experience of the 'real' rather than disrupting it" (439). In poems like "The Steeple-Jack," Bazin writes, "the repeated emphasis upon surface, form and play" undermines "the logic of the acquisitive ethic. Poetry becomes not a reflection of the material world, but an inversion of the relations of production, a site of non-production" (440). The very strength of Moore's language, in Bazin's view, lies not, as I suggest, in its ability to balance seemingly disparate elements, but rather in its very off-centeredness, its *refusal* to reach equilibrium.

Given the strength of these counter-narratives, why do I persist in portraying Emerson and Moore as officiates at the happy wedding of nature and spirit?

*

It is remarkable to me the way it sounds — re-reading these pages — as if a single voice is speaking, at a single point in time. Writing, or scholarly writing, at any rate, is deceptive in this way. When I began this chapter, I lived in Brooklyn, and used to watch each morning at six as the garbage men tossed bags from the curb into the open jaws of still-moving trucks. Now I live in small town in Maine, and in the mornings I watch the old pickups pull up in front of the phone-booth-sized post office, and I listen to the Temple Stream rush toward larger waters. I have had two children since I started work on this chapter and have witnessed, through the remote and clouded lens of a computer screen, unmanned drone airplanes, "piloted" from the Nevada desert, drop missiles on villages full of children in Pakistan and Afghanistan.

My interest in what I have described here as Emerson and Moore's epistemology is that it allows me to understand both how the mind works on the world — the way ideas, about America, say, work on the world — as well as how the world, with its crying babies and rushing waters, works on the mind. On the most mundane and personal level, I am invested in Emerson and Moore's attempts to disassemble the mind/

world binary because it mirrors my own deconstructive efforts: only insofar as it is possible for these writers to bring together the life of the world and the life of the mind does it seem to me possible to reconcile the physical facts of my life and the life of the planet with my writing and thinking.

Given the plausibility of other readings of Emerson and Moore, and my own interestedness in the question, on what ground do I defend the critical narrative I have fashioned? This question haunts my thinking about Emerson and Moore, and my thinking about what it means to engage in writing about texts generally. The only plausible answer seems to me, on *no* ground: for it is precisely groundedness that Emerson, in his commitment to onwardness, deprives us of. In "Self-Reliance," he declares: "I would write on the lintels of the door-post, *Whim*. I hope it is somewhat better than whim at last, but we cannot spend the day in explanation." Stanley Cavell notes the implications of this gesture:

> We hope it is better than whim at last, as we hope we may at last seem something better than blasphemers; but it is our poverty not to be final but always to be leaving (abandoning whatever we have and have known): to be initial, medial, American. What the ground of the fixated conflict between solipsism and realism should give way to — or between subjectivity and objectivity, or the private or the public, or the inner and the outer — is the task of onwardness. (*Emerson*, x)

My reading of Emerson and Moore is located on no ground, then, but along the horizon of my engagement with their language, a horizon that (in our onwardness) is both the most constant feature of the landscape and the least stable. Other readings are indeed possible; I choose this one because of what it allows me to do. Every critical response to a text is the byproduct of an interaction — even when one half of the interaction is suppressed. As Thoreau reminds us, "it is, after all, always the first person that is speaking" (*A Week*, 325). To confess as much is to cede the possibility of neutral ground and to find oneself, instead, describing a particular relation. James writes that trying to look steadily at what he calls the "transitive parts" of our thinking — the part having to do with relations between things rather than with things by themselves — is like trying to catch a snowflake in your warm hand. Just by holding it, it ceases to be itself (*Writings*, 244). Describing relations, as James's turn to figurative language demonstrates, is poetic work. It involves the continual search for a form.

Notes

[1] Richard Poirier calls this tendency in Emerson "superfluity," and convincingly relates it to the pragmatist tradition, which he considers "a form of linguistic skepticism" (*Poetry*, 4).

[2] I am grateful to Joan Richardson for drawing my attention to Cavell's important observation along these lines in his essay "Emerson's Constitutional Amending": "the Emersonian sentence is philosophical in showing within itself its aversion to (turning away in turning towards) the standing confirmation of its words, as though human thinking is not so much to be expressed by it as resurrected with it" (*Emerson*, 31).

[3] John Michael has noted this tension in Emerson's early work, arguing that

> *Nature* is — at least at crucial moments — an attempt to overcome skepticism by means of an ideal theory that distinguished between consciousness and phenomenon, mind and matter, self and others. But instead of the resolution and triumph that critics have habitually found in it *Nature* dramatizes an unresolved conflict between the poles of Emerson's dualism. (35)

[4] Grace Schulman's 2003 edition of Moore's poems, which I have used here, disregards the poet's final wishes about several of her most famous poems, including "Poetry," which Moore had famously reduced to three lines for the 1967 *Complete Poems*. Whatever one may think of Schulman's editorial decisions, however, Moore scholars can only be grateful that Schulman included so much of the textual history of the poems in the Editor's Notes. My discussion of the textual history of "The Steeple-Jack" relies on versions of the poem that can be found in Schulman's volume, as well as manuscript versions housed at the Rosenbach Library and Museum in Philadelphia.

[5] See Lisa Steinman's "Modern America, Modernism and Marianne Moore" for a discussion of "The Student" as a defense against accusations of American materialism.

[6] Bonnie Costello notes that "In 'The Student' Moore draws from Emerson's 'American Scholar' more directly than she owns. The essay can tell us a great deal about her art, particularly her concreteness, which for the average literal-minded American is dead fact, but for the superlative American is poetry" (249).

3: Robert Frost, Charles Sanders Peirce, and the Necessity of Form

Ruins

IF YOU BELIEVE HIS OWN ACCOUNT (which some biographers do more than others), by the time Robert Frost sold the farm bequeathed to him by his grandfather and left Derry, New Hampshire, with his family, he had run the place almost into the ground. His official biographer, Lawrence Thompson, writes that the farm was so "badly neglected" that Frost was "unable to find a buyer who would pay anything like the original price" (148). I imagine it as a ruin: the hen cages broken and abandoned, the barn roof collapsing, pastures overgrown with young trees. It is an often-noted irony that Frost, whose poems frequently celebrate the arduousness and discipline of rural life, was a near-total failure as a farmer, mocked by his neighbors for his laziness and carelessness with money. While it's true that, as Jay Parini points out, this image of Frost as a failed farmer comes largely from Frost's own exaggerated stories about himself, it is also the case that until Frost began teaching at Pinkerton Academy, the family lived entirely on an annuity left by his grandfather, and that as the years passed, the farm was less and less plausible as an economic enterprise (74–75). It is the farm as Frost left it I like to imagine — half-wild, the old stone walls crumbling — and not as it appears on the Robert Frost Farm website: pristine clapboard on a well-kept lawn. Many of Frost's best-known poems, written later, were set on the Derry farm. He abandoned it (first by neglect and later by leaving) only to return again and again in poems, in accordance with his Thoreauvian sense of economy: "strongly spent is synonymous with kept" (*Poetry*, 401). The abandoned farm was the ground on which he built his poetic, like the phoebes nesting in the barn of the burned house in "The Need of Being Versed in Country Things." And if domestic order and the discipline of labor is part of this poetic, so too is wildness and disrepair, that which is "burned, dissolved, and broken off" (*Complete Poems*, 520).

No website invites one to visit Charles Peirce's ruined house, Arisbe, although the Pike County Historical Society notes that the house still stands on route 209 in Milford, Pennsylvania, housing the administrative offices of the National Parks Service. Like Frost's farm, it was a place more imagined than realized, the shingled skeleton of a dream of wholeness. Peirce's "The Architecture of Theories," which outlines the basis for his vast theoretical system, draws an analogy between the construction of a philosophy and the building of a house:

> When a man is about to build a house, what a power of thinking he has to do, before he can safely break ground! With what pains he has to excogitate the precise wants that are to be supplied! What a study to ascertain the most available and suitable materials, to determine the mode of construction to which those materials are best adapted, and to answer a hundred such questions! Now without riding the metaphor too far, I think we may safely say that the studies preliminary to the construction of a great theory should be at least as deliberate and thorough as those that are preliminary to the building of a dwelling-house. (*Essential*, 1:286)

Like his architectonic philosophical system, sketched out but never completed, Peirce's continually evolving design for the grand house outpaced its execution: builders were hired but never paid, renovations begun but never finished. In the meantime, despite the best efforts of William James and others to secure Peirce an income, the Peirces' financial situation became desperate. They lived their final years at Arisbe in illness and sometimes hunger, without running water or heat. The lilacs grew so high and thick they hid the house from view (Brent, 321).

A ruin offers itself to the imagination in a way a monument or a museum does not. Because it is broken, partial, it begs our participation, our mental reconstruction not only of the house as it must have stood, but also of the events that must have led to its ruin. The fragmentary nature of Peirce's philosophical papers have long prompted the kind of imaginative reconstruction that I imagine Arisbe, at least as it was when its contents were sold at auction to the people of Milford, must also have elicited. Josiah Royce and Fergus Kernan, referring to Peirce's metaphysics, wrote in the *Journal of Philosophy, Psychology and Scientific Methods* in 1916, two years after Peirce's death,

> Peirce's thoughts on this subject are fragmentary. Indeed his entire life work may be in a certain sense called fragmentary. Yet it is my belief that his ideas will repay study. As he himself says in the conclusion to that brilliant essay, "The Architecture of Theories," — "may some future student go over this ground again and have the leisure to give his results to the world." (703)

As for Frost, if the poems have become a museum of his thinking — so carefully preserved by critical and popular attention that it becomes difficult to see the sharp edges that still beg imaginative engagement, Robert Faggen's recently edited *Notebooks of Robert Frost* may provide a necessary corrective. This massive volume of undated, often half-articulated thoughts reminds us of the contradiction and darkness beneath the clean surface of so many of the poems. The readings of Frost's poems that follow have been influenced greatly by *The Notebooks*, and I am indebted to Faggen for the painstaking editorial work that has made them available.[1]

Peirce, Frost, Pragmatism, Temperament

> For the philosophy which is so important in each of us is not a technical matter; it is our more or less dumb sense of what life honestly and deeply means. It is only partly got from books; it is our individual way of just seeing and feeling the total push and pressure of the cosmos. (James, *Writings*, 487)

Frost's acquaintance with pragmatism and deep indebtedness to James have been well documented,[2] and no doubt some of what I see as the Peircean nature of Frost's thinking comes second hand by way of James. But to read James is to inhabit a decidedly different world that that of Frost's poems. The particular shade and texture of darkness in a poem like, for example, "The Subverted Flower," is nowhere evident in James's prose, not even in his descriptions in *The Varieties of Religious Experience* of life for the "sick soul," a category in which he placed himself.[3] If, as James contends, our philosophy is less a matter of intellectual position than it is of temperament, Frost's philosophy is closer to that of Peirce, whose writings are inflected with the sense of a struggle never fully transcended. Peirce knew the impact of his personal suffering on his thought, writing to James in 1897,

> I have learned a great deal about philosophy in the last few years, because they have been very miserable and unsuccessful years, — terrible beyond anything that the man of ordinary experience can possibly understand or conceive. . . . Much have I learned of life and the world, throwing strong lights upon philosophy in these years. (in Brent, 341)

At the heart of Peirce's epistemology is a vivid sense of conflict: "Doubt is an uneasy and dissatisfied state from which we struggle to free ourselves and pass into a state of belief" (*Essential*, 1:114). This struggle, for Peirce, is unending, and represents one iteration of the greater struggle, between design and chance, in which the world is locked.

For Frost, too, conflict is central to "what life honestly and deeply means" (James, *Writings*, 487). The ties of love and domestic duty are strained by the impulse toward boundlessness and freedom. In poems like "Storm Fear" and "The Hill Wife," wildness assaults the familiar and the domestic. In poems like "A Late Walk" and "Stopping By Woods . . ." the pull of domestic ties proves more powerful than the lure of wildness. The two forces are never reconciled, but like Peirce's doubt and belief, define each other reflexively through struggle. This chapter will trace the way that conflict and struggle shape both Peirce and Frost's understanding of form, and in doing so, demonstrate how the search for form becomes one of the central motives for pragmatist thought. Given this focus, my readings of Frost's poems are particularly attentive to formal choices. In examining these choices, I wish to follow Peirce's particular brand of pragmatism into the realm of action, to observe pragmatic thinking about form in its concretion within poetic practice. My claim here, as elsewhere, is that the formal choices of Frost and others represent a bringing-to-life of pragmatic thinking, giving us a picture of this thought working itself out in practice: in this case, the unique practice of writing a poem.

In the first of the series of lectures that comprise *Pragmatism,* James writes:

> The history of philosophy is to a great extent that of a certain clash of human temperaments. . . . Of whatever temperament a professional philosopher is, he tries, when philosophizing, to sink the fact of his temperament. Temperament is no conventionally recognized reason, so he urges impersonal reasons for his conclusions. Yet his temperament really gives him a stronger bias than any of his more strictly objective premises. It loads the evidence for him one way or the other, making for a more sentimental or a more hard-hearted view of the universe, just as this fact or that principle would. He *trusts* his temperament. Wanting a universe that suits it, he believes in any representation of the universe that does suit it. (*Writings,* 488)

My attempt to reconstruct what was, for Peirce and for Frost, "a way of seeing and feeling the total push and pressure of the universe" relies a great deal on my sense of the temperament of these two writers, a sense which comes both through the facts of their biographies and through the tone and feeling of their language. The ruined farm and the ruined house are central to my thinking about these two figures, for the ruins not only evoke the sense of darkness and disquiet in both men's work, but also speak to the dynamic relations between order and chaos, growth and decay the perception of which marked their thinking and writing.

To hypothesize a relationship between Peirce and Frost is to make an implicit argument about a relationship between philosophy and poetry. James's definition of philosophy in its broadest sense, "our more or less dumb sense of what life honestly and deeply means," and his insistence on the role of temperament in shaping this sense, opens a door between the seemingly disparate regions of philosophical and poetic thinking. Frost's poems and Peirce's architectonic, as different as they are in language, are each "representations of the universe" as it is inflected by a combination of temperament and experience (James, *Writings*, 488). In her description of the evolution of pragmatism from its origins in the experiences of the European settlers in America, Joan Richardson highlights the pragmatist insight that all thinking — whether philosophical or poetic — is "subject to the same processes of growth and change as all other life forms" (1). Poetries and philosophies are evolving structures of thought and language, and function to adjust our individual and collective relationship to our world. Richardson writes,

> It is important to keep in mind the continuity of successful forms of expression in the evolution of thinking, and more particularly to consider this feature in the context of language as an organic form as well, as natural and necessary to the survival of human beings as the honeycomb to bees, the structure in and by which transformations essential to the life of the community are made. (6)

From this perspective, in which linguistic forms serve, first and foremost, to provide us with a way of understanding and so negotiating our environment, the practice of philosophy and the practice of poetry begin to look like mirror images, approaching the same point from different directions. Frost, beginning in local and particular experience, especially the experience of sound as it operates in a spoken sentence, approached the same questions about the relationship of chaos to order and self to others to which Peirce, beginning in the cosmos, devoted his life.

An Inky Blackness

A certain elusiveness was central to the temperaments of both Peirce and Frost. Both had ways of stymieing a reader's attempts at interpretation, a reflection of a broader tendency to resist being absorbed by others. Frost was particularly guarded about the details of his life, and frequently worried that his biographer, Lawrence Thompson, was ferreting out his "secret." In a letter to Thompson in 1959, Frost struck a conciliatory tone, but betrays his ambivalence about Thompson's enterprise.

> I've meant to give you all the advantages, supply you with all the facts, and keep nothing back, save nothing out for my own use even in case I should ever write my own story. And I have left entirely up to your judgment the summing up and the significance. You've had a long time to turn me over in your mind looking for some special phrase or poem to get me by. By now you may think you have plucked the heart out of my secret and I don't care if you have. (*Selected Letters*, 584)

More than a character trait, Frost's evasiveness was a consistent poetic strategy. In a letter to Louis Untermeyer, Frost explained,

> You get more credit for your thinking if you restate formulae or cite cases that fall easily under formulae [but] all the fun is outside saying things that suggest formulae but won't formulate — that almost but don't quite formulate. I should like to be as subtle at this game as to seem to a casual observer altogether obvious. (*Collected Poems, Prose and Plays*, 692)

As I will demonstrate in the pages that follow, Frost's poems frequently find ways to resist formulation; lines that seem as placid and steady as proverbs ("We love the things we love for what they are," "good fences make good neighbors," etc.) begin to give under the slightest pressure, and the poems take on darker tones. As Priscilla Paton documents in her essay "Apologizing for Robert Frost," contemporary scholars, defending Frost against his reputation as "the genial, chatty American institution . . . middlebrow and 'anti-modern,'" have identified what I am here calling Frost's "evasiveness" as the source of the critics' misappraisal of his work (73). "The difficulty in Frost's poetics," Frank Lentricchia writes, "is not the absence of depth and modernist sophistication, but too much subtlety" (*Robert Frost*, 3). Similarly, John Hollander, in his introduction to Richard Poirier's *Robert Frost: The Work of Knowing*, asserts that "Frost's particular greatness as a poet had confused a whole generation" (xi–xii).

Frost's elusiveness is most clear in poems like "Hyla Brook," in which one's initial reading is complicated, if not cancelled, by subsequent ones.

> By June our brook's run out of song and speed
> Sought for much after that, it will be found
> Either to have gone groping underground
> (And taken with it all the Hyla breed
> That shouted in the mist a month ago,
> Like ghost of sleigh-bells in a ghost of snow)—
> Or flourished and come up in jewel-weed,
> Weak foliage that is blown upon and bent
> Even against the way its waters went.
> Its bed is left a faded paper sheet
> Of dead leaves stuck together by the heat —
> A brook to none but who remember long.
> This as it will be seen is other far
> Than with brooks taken otherwise in song.
> We love the things we love for what they are.
> (*Complete Poems*, 149)

At first glance, the poem seems like a tribute to the familiar and easily over-looked. Like the aptly named "jewel-weed," the brook, Frost seems to insist, is not romantic. Unlike "brooks taken otherwise in song," Hyla brook remains local and particular, a real brook, loved for its own sake, and not as a lyric trope. Upon closer examination, however, this reading of the poem proves untenable, or at least incomplete. For the summer heat does not simply diminish the brook, making it less grand and thus less romantic, it actually makes the brook cease to be a brook at all. This Heraclitian body of water is transformed so completely that it emerges only as "weak foliage that is blown upon and bent / Even against the way its waters went." In the perplexing logic of this sentence, the brook takes on a new form, not just different from but opposed to its original being. This sense of the transformation of things into their opposite is echoed in the eerily elusive line "like ghost of sleigh-bells in a ghost of snow," an evocation of the vanished season. The final line thus leads us to paradox: how can we "love the things we love for what they are" if things, like the brook, have no stable essence? Perhaps it is this lack of essence that we must accept when we say we "love" something?

The poem's seemingly clear anti-romantic statement is also complicated by second and third readings. Frost insists that his own brook "will be seen," presumably by future readers, as different from or "other" to romanticized brooks "taken otherwise in song," yet this very formulation carries its own appeal to posterity and subtle suggestion of the immortality of poetry. Similarly, this poem about a brook that is also about the unstable nature of identity can't help but make us think of Heraclitus, an allusion that belies the poem's apparent desire to banish figuration in deference to the real and particular. Frost's is an allegorical brook as much as it is an actual one. Like the Hyla Brook, Frost's poem seems to cancel itself, evading the reader's attempt to capture its essence.

Though less deliberately tricky, Peirce is similarly elusive in his writings. Many of Peirce's late essays and lectures give so little consideration to readers unfamiliar with his new categorical system (which nearly all of his contemporary readers were) that even William James, his most consistent and important supporter, could not make sense of them (Brent, 291). In his introduction to his "A Guess at the Riddle," Peirce seems both apologetic for and proud of his obscurity:

> But before all else, let me make the acquaintance of my reader, and express my sincere esteem for him and the deep pleasure it is for me to address one so wise and patient. I know his character pretty well, for both the subject and the style of this book ensure his being one out of millions. (*Essential*, 1:247)

Like Peirce's supporter, James, Josiah Royce, whom Brent calls "probably the only philosopher to . . . grasp the kernel of Peirce's thinking in Peirce's lifetime" recognized Peirce's obscurity as a fact of his temperament (328). In an essay coauthored by Fergus Kernan, Royce, seeking to introduce Peirce to a wider readership within the philosophical community, writes,

> It is not always easy to understand Peirce. He never regretted the fact that most people found it hard to follow his ideas. He deliberately chose that most of his research should be concerned with highly technical topics and should be secure from the intrusion of the uncalled. Upon occasion he could be brilliantly clear in his expressions of highly complex and recondite problems, although this clearness was a capricious fact in his life and in his writings, and was frequently interrupted by a mode of expression which often seemed to me to be due to the fear that, after all, in case mediocre minds found themselves understanding too many of his ideas, they would be led to far too high an impression of their own powers. One finds this tendency toward what might be called "impenetrability" especially evident in his manuscripts. Too often the reader meets with a thought of surpassing brilliancy only to have it disappear like the cuttlefish in an inky blackness of its own secretion. (707)

For Peirce as for Frost, the urgent desire to communicate, to make his ideas clear, was balanced by a refusal to compromise his intense idiosyncrasy of vision.

Strained Relation

Given both Peirce and Frost's resistance to absorption[4] and insistence on individuality, it is striking that both writers also insist, in the strongest possible terms, on the importance of community. Frost writes,

> It has been said that recognition in art is all. Better say correspondence is all. Mind must convince mind that it can uncurl and wave the same filaments of subtlety, soul convince soul that it can give off the same shimmers of eternity. At no point would anyone but a brute fool want to break off this correspondence. It is all there is to satisfaction; and it is salutary to live in fear of its being broken off. (*Poetry*, 347)

This belief in the importance of "correspondence" lay behind Frost's rejection of many of the innovations of poetic modernism, and his commitment to bringing "the very regular preestablished accent and measure of blank verse" and "the very irregular accent and measure of speaking intonation" into a "strained relation" (Thompson, 172). "Strained relation" may be, in fact, as good a gloss as any for the dynamic at the heart both of Frost's life and his poems. Like Peirce, Frost was highly dependent on, and often intensely alienated from, those closest to him. His particularly (and famously) strained relation with his biographer, Lawrence Thompson, may serve as a representative example.[5]

Frost's early poem "The Tuft of Flowers" illustrates the way an internal division between a desire for "correspondence" and an insistence on independence evolves into a dynamic poetic structure that appears again and again in his poems. The poem's speaker, out to "turn the grass once after one / Who mowed it in the dew before the sun," looks around for the mower, and, realizing that his fellow laborer has "gone his way," concludes that

> ... I must be, as he had been, — alone,
>
> "As all must be," I said within my heart,
> "Whether they work together or apart."

As the speaker continues his labor in the field, he comes upon "A leaping tongue of bloom the scythe had spared / Beside a reedy brook the scythe had bared," and feels an instant kinship with the mower who has left this tuft of flowers "to flourish, not for us." The speaker concludes his imaginary dialogue with the mower with an inversion of his earlier statement: "'Men work together,' I told him from the heart, / 'Whether they work together or apart'" (*Complete Poems*, 32). Correspondence seems to have won the day, but it is worth noting that the speaker's interlocutor is absent, and that the togetherness posited in the poem is wholly dependent on the speaker's ability to imagine it.

A similar sense of solidarity with physically absent others dominates Peirce's epistemology, in which community plays a central role:

> The real, then, is that which, sooner or later, information and reasoning would finally result in, and which is therefore independent of the vagaries of you and me. Thus, the very origin of the conception of reality shows that this conception essentially involves the notion of a COMMUNITY, without definite limits, and capable of an indefinite increase of knowledge. (*Essential*, 1:52)

For Peirce, the community of knowers was of such overriding importance that, as Joseph Brent explains, "the individual man, since his separate existence is manifested only by ignorance and error, so far as he is anything apart from his fellows, and from what he and they are to be, is only a negation" (Brent, 337). In fact, Brent argues that Peirce's apparent inability or unwillingness to make his behavior conform to the expectations of others may have been the result of precisely this dismissal of the role of the individual. Peirce "believed his own and anyone else's behavior as an individual separate from the congregations of science to be incorrigible. [Thus] he acted as he wished," seemingly blind to the potential consequences of his actions (337). At the same time, the centrality of evolution to Peirce's thought meant that he valued the variations between one mind and another. It is only through such mutations in thinking and perception, Peirce believed, that we move toward what we call "truth." As Louis Menand writes in *The Metaphysical Club*, "Peirce's first rule as a philosopher of science was that the path of inquiry should never be blocked, not even by a hypothesis that has worked for us in the past" (276). Peirce's view of progress depended, in other words, on the contributions of unique individual minds to collective knowledge. His own habit of writing in a manner seemingly designed to keep his ideas "secure from the intrusion of the uncalled" reflects the powerful strain of individualism that ran counter to Peirce's vision of collectivism (Royce and Kernan, 707).

Interestingly, the deep division in both Peirce and Frost between, on the one hand, the impulse toward connection and "correspondence," and, on the other, toward individualism and independence, led them to occupy opposing positions on the political spectrum. In "Evolutionary Love," Peirce condemned the nineteenth century for its emphasis on greed and individual success: "Political economy has its formula for redemption, too," he wrote bitterly, "it is this: Intelligence in the service of greed ensures the justest prices, the fairest contracts, the most enlightened conduct of all the dealings between men, and leads to the *summum bonum*, food in plenty and perfect comfort. Food for whom? Why, for the greedy master of intelligence" (*Essential*, 1:354). Frost, on the other hand, was wary of any government policy that he saw as impinging upon the rights of the individual, and felt that Roosevelt's New Deal "tended . . . to weaken the human capacity to shape life by proposing the negligible power of individual enterprise" (Poirier, *Frost*, 24). Frost was especially critical of Marxism for what he saw as its ambition to eliminate conflict: "A nation is not meant to be harmonious as a family. . . . Here lies the noble seeming fallacy of the socialists. . . . A nation should be just as full of conflict as it can contain, physically mentally, financially. . . . But of course it must contain. The strain must be short of the bursting point — just short" (*Notebooks*, 455).[6]

Equally important is the fact of the nearly opposite reception Peirce and Frost's writing received in their lifetimes. Professionally, Peirce was, in his own estimation, a failure. Deeply alienated from many in the scientific and academic communities, Peirce was unable to secure a permanent academic appointment or even, toward the end of his life, a viable means of supporting himself and his wife, Juliette. In spite of the persistence of "a small company who respected Peirce's genius and were inspired by it," much of Peirce's work remained unpublished for decades (Brent, 8). Frost, on the other hand, was so lionized in his lifetime that Lionel Trilling speculated, on the occasion of Frost's eighty-fifth birthday, that archaeologists of the future would regard him not as "an historical individual but rather . . . a solar myth, a fertility figure" (375).

The difference between Frost's public reception and Peirce's seems to have been in part Frost's ability to construct a persona, within and outside of his poems, which covered and compensated for his "difficulties," both temperamental and poetic. The profound resonance of this persona, and its effectiveness in concealing the darker and more difficult aspects of Frost's poems, can be seen in the public outcry following the speech referred to above in which Trilling called Frost "a terrifying poet" (378). While the darker, more philosophically complex Frost has been acknowledged by many critics in recent decades, at the time, Trilling's characterization was met with intense hostility on the part of many of Frost's readers, who cherished the poet's cultivated image as a benign dispenser of folksy wisdom. Peirce, in contrast, was apparently unwilling or unable to make himself and his work conform, at least outwardly, to the expectations of others. Frost's stubborn emphasis on independence and belief that "nine tenths should be in and individual and one tenth out and social" was tempered by a populist image and a (seemingly) accessible writing style (*Notebooks*, 270). Peirce, on the other hand, while a populist in politics and a believer in the primacy of communal over individual knowledge, was nevertheless, as Royce pointed out, stubbornly uncompromising in the expression of his ideas, resisting at every step James's attempts to popularize them.

For both writers, the relationship between the individual self and any larger collective was essentially a relationship of conflict. Peirce and Frost's difficulty with others, their struggles to integrate their recognition of the importance of community with the fierce idiosyncrasy and independence of their thought, is reflected in the centrality of conflict to all of their thinking.

Head Above the Deluge

In "The Architecture of Theories," Peirce proposes a "Cosmogenic Philosophy" that would

> suppose that in the beginning, — infinitely remote, — there was a chaos of unpersonalised feeling, which being without connection or regularity would be properly without existence. This feeling, sporting here and there in pure arbitrariness, would have started the germ of a generalizing tendency. . . . Thus, the tendency to habit would have started; and from this with the other principles of evolution all the regularities of the universe would be evolved. At any time, however, an element of pure chance survives. . . . (*Essential*, 1:297)

In a letter to *The Amherst Student*, Frost writes,

> There is at least so much good in the world that it admits of form and the making of form. . . . When in doubt there is always form for us to go on with. . . . The background in hugeness and confusion shading away from where we stand into black and utter chaos; and against the background any small man-made figure of order and concentration. (*Selected Letters*, 418–19)

Both Peirce and Frost saw their particular modes of inquiry (science and poetry, respectively) as advances of order upon chaos. "There is nothing quite so composing as composition," Frost writes in his notebook. "Putting anything in order a house a business a poem gives a sense of sharing the mastery of the universe" (*Notebooks*, 281). It is striking, however, that in both Frost and Peirce's descriptions of order, chaos is dominant, the constant background against which form may temporarily emerge. Thus for both writers, the idea of *absolute* knowledge or certainty is an illusion.[7] Science is "not standing upon the bedrock of fact," Peirce writes. "It is walking upon a bog, and can only say, this ground seems to hold for the present. Here I will stay till it begins to give way" (*Collected*, 5:589). Frost uses a remarkably similar figure in his notebooks: "Expect to keep head above the deluge not by finding a solid peak underfoot by luck but only by treading the forever failing metaphors" (*Notebooks*, 282). As these images vividly convey, both Peirce and Frost possessed a sense of their disciplines as "forever failing" and offering only the most temporary refuge from the bog or deluge of chaos. At the same time, both comparisons simultaneously evoke the absolute necessity of such "momentary stay(s) against confusion," the centrality of our construction of temporary stability to our very survival (Frost, *Poetry*, 394).

For Peirce, creating order, or arriving at new knowledge, always entails engagement with the unknown. As Cheryl Misak explains,

> Peirce's picture is not one of placing indubitable building blocks upon each other as we progress toward the truth. Rather, the picture is one of doubt (recalcitrant experience) forcing us to inquire until we reach another tentative doubt-resistant belief. The ground on which inquiry walks is tenuous and it is only the danger of losing our footing that makes us go forward. Doubt and uncertainty provide the motive for inquiry. (15)

Order exists only in relation to chaos, knowledge to the unknown.[8] Peirce insists that "the *desire to know*, or philosophia, . . . carries with it the confession that we do not know already," and that "nothing can be more completely contrary to a philosophy the fruit of a scientific life than infallibilism, whether arrayed in its old ecclesiastical trappings or under its recent 'scientific' disguise" (*Collected*, 8:282). Key to Peirce's understanding of the function of science is his characterization of it as "*walking* upon a bog" rather than "*standing* upon the bedrock" (*Collected*, 5:589; my emphasis). Scientific and philosophical inquiry never arrives at a stable resting point, but involves continual venturing into the unknown. "Infallibilism," or the acceptance of earlier truths as indisputable, breaks Peirce's "First Rule of Science," that "in order to learn you must desire to learn and in so desiring not be satisfied with what you already incline to think," and its boldface corollary, "Do not block the way of inquiry" (*Essential*, 2:48).

By undercutting the perceived strength of inherited wisdom operating in his poems ("Mending Wall" is perhaps the clearest example), Frost demonstrates his own skepticism about the stability of knowledge and the directness of our access to it. "We have mastered a realm of thought or all but mastered it," Frost writes in his notebooks, but "there is that one almost negligible part that refuses to be brought into knowledge. That is because that little negligible part [is] part of a real adjacent that we haven't touched at all and didn't expect the existence of" (*Notebooks*, 115). In "For Once, Then, Something," Frost foregrounds the experience of doubt that, for him as for Peirce, underlies any provisional belief.

> Others taunt me with having knelt at well-curbs
> Always wrong to the light so never seeing
> Deeper down in the well than where the water
> Gives me back in a shining surface picture
> Me myself in the summer heaven godlike
> Looking out of a wreath of fern and cloud puffs.
> *Once,* when trying with chin against a well-curb,
> I discerned, as I thought, beyond the picture
> Through the picture, a something white, uncertain,
> Something more of the depths — and then I lost it.
> Water came to rebuke the too clear water.
> One drop fell from a fern, and lo, a ripple
> Shook whatever it was lay there at bottom,
> Blurred it, blotted it out. What was that whiteness?
> Truth? a pebble of quartz? For once, then, something.
>
> (*Complete Poems*, 276)

Here, the speaker's vision — a standard romantic figure for lyric genius, wisdom, and power — is shown to be hopelessly superficial, the "picture" of the "godlike" poet shown to be nothing but "surface" illusion. The word "picture" appears three times in the poem, the repetition enacting the poet's inability to get past the limits of his own perception and access "something more of the depths," the "truth" that exceeds our capacity to know. This truth is so tenuous, so unknowable, that the poet's words for it — "a something," "that whiteness," "it" — speak of nothing but their failure to adequately name. The godlike power of the romantic poet-as-seer (complete with symbolic "wreath of fern") is shown to be a "shining surface picture," that simultaneously hides and suggests the failure of the poet to perceive "truth." The poem's uneven anapestic rhythm, its odd, eleven-syllable lines and lack of end rhyme seem also to point to a kind of lyric failure or breakdown. Even the power that Frost felt to be at the heart of his poetry, the power of metaphor, seems undercut, brought into question by the repetition of nouns like "water" and "picture." Lines like "I discerned, as I thought, beyond the picture, / Through the picture," and "Water came to rebuke the too clear water" frustrate the possibility of metaphorical relation by replacing it with mere identity — the picture is a picture, water is water, surface is surface. Here, as in "The Most of It," knowledge of anything wholly independent of the self is a possibility glimpsed but never achieved. Frost suggests that while we may *sense* that we do not "ke[ep] the universe alone," all that we perceive with any certainty is a "shiny surface picture" of ourselves (451, 276).

Both Peirce and Frost ascribe to an essentially evolutionary model of knowledge, in which truth has no permanent foundation but rather emerges continually from our incorporation of new experience into old stores of information. The inherent dynamism of this model is reflected in the dialectical modes of thought employed by both writers.

The Sacredness of Three

For Peirce, an understanding of the limits of knowledge is fundamental not only to his original formulation of pragmatism, but also to his cosmology and metaphysics. Central to the pragmatic method Peirce describes in "How to Make Our Ideas Clear" is his understanding of the evolutionary function of inquiry. In his 1877 paper "The Fixation of Belief," Peirce writes,

> The irritation of doubt is the only immediate motive for the struggle to attain belief. It is certainly best for us that our beliefs should be such as may truly guide our actions so as to satisfy our desires; and this reflection will make us reject any belief which does not seem to have been so formed as to insure this result. But it will only do so by creating a doubt in place of that belief. With the doubt, therefore, the struggle begins, and with the cessation of doubt it ends. Hence, the sole object of inquiry is the settlement of opinion. We may fancy that this is not enough for us, that we seek, not merely an opinion, but a true opinion. But put this fancy to the test, and it proves groundless; for as soon as a firm belief is reached we are entirely satisfied, whether the belief be true or false. (*Essential*, 1:114–15)

The struggle between doubt and belief, in Peirce's view, reflects the human being's engagement with his or her environment. This struggle does not cease with any arrival at "truth," but merely pauses, to be taken up again in a new direction when new information disrupts formerly settled beliefs. The idea of continual change, struggle and growth is also the basis of Peirce's "evolutionary cosmology, in which all the regularities of nature and mind are regarded as products of growth" (1:312). Peirce maintains that laws themselves, and particularly the law of causation, are subject to evolution. In his lecture on "Design and Chance," Peirce outlines a cosmology in which "all known laws are due to chance" (Brent, 175).

Intimately connected to Peirce's vision of the evolution of the lawfulness of the universe from an origin of pure chance and spontaneity is his development of new philosophical categories which he called First, Second and Third. Peirce describes these categories in "A Guess at the Riddle":

> The First is that whose being is simply in itself, not referring to anything nor lying behind anything. The Second is that which is what it is by force of something to which it is second. The Third is that which is what it is owing to things between which it mediates and which it brings in relation to each other. (*Essential*, 1:248)

These categories, which correspond to elements within Peirce's semiotics as well as his cosmology, illustrate the centrality of change driven by triadic relations to all of Peirce's thinking.

Frost, too, believed in what he called "the sacredness of three" (*Notebooks*, 98). As Richard Poirier has repeatedly shown, many of Frost's poems illustrate the relation between "home" and "away" that corresponds to the form/freedom dynamic of his poetics. Here, poetry itself becomes the equivalent to Peirce's category of "Third," mediating and bringing into relation the first and second terms. For both Peirce and Frost, wildness or freedom (Peirce's "First") is an enticing but ultimately evasive possibility, bound as it always is to our experience of Secondness, the already-familiar and domesticated. "Stop and think of it," Peirce writes of Firstness, "and it has flown!" (1:248). Frost's early poem, 'Into My Own," illustrates the structural relation between freedom and domesticity central to so much of his work.

> One of my wishes is that those dark trees,
> So old and firm they scarcely show the breeze,
> Were not, as 'twere, the merest mask of gloom,
> But stretched away unto the edge of doom.
>
> I should not be withheld but that some day
> Into their vastness I should steal away,

> Fearless of ever finding open land,
> Or highway where the slow wheel pours the sand.
>
> I do not see why I should e'er turn back,
> Or those should not set forth upon my track
> To overtake me, who should miss me here
> And long to know if still I held them dear.
>
> They would not find me changed from him they knew —
> Only more sure of all I thought was true.
>
> (Complete Poems, 5)

The speaker's "wish" is for a wildness that would be truly wild, "stretch[ing] away unto the edge of doom." Even in this formulation, however, wildness is limited, bounded by an "edge." More importantly, the speaker's vision of himself "steal[ing] away" from that which would "withh[o]ld" him at home is immediately followed by, and indeed seems to demand, a vision of being "overtake[n]" by the familiar and domestic. The final lines underscore this paradox, for what kind of wildness confirms that which is already known? It is worth noting, too, what a neat little sonnet this paean to freedom is, though within the strict metrical pattern Frost, as always, finds room for the play of the unexpected. The first two lines establish the relation of freedom to restraint that dominates the rest of the poem. The loosely iambic first line, "One of my wishes is that those dark trees," possesses the casual, rambling rhythm of natural speech, while the second "So old and firm they scarcely show the breeze," introduces a stricter iambic meter, closing with a neat rhyme.

Perhaps the clearest statement of the relation of freedom to form in Frost's poetics is his essay "The Figure a Poem Makes." "The possibilities for tune from the dramatic tones of meaning across the rigidity of a limited meter are endless," Frost writes, balancing within the sentence the freedom implied by "possibility" and "endless" with the restraint signaled by the words "rigidity" and "limited" (*Poetry and Prose*, 394). While Frost's statements about poetry, particularly the famous quip about "tennis with the net down," are often taken to be clear-cut defenses of form, looked at more closely his poetics seem rather to seek to preserve the "strained relation" between freedom and form that he saw as central to the function of poetry. Peirce's remark about true philosophical inquiry carrying "the confession that we do not know already" (*Collected*, 8:282) finds its echo in Frost's insistence that "it is but a trick poem and not a poem at all if the best of it was thought of first and saved for the last. It finds its own name as it goes. . . . No surprise for the writer, no surprise for the reader" (*Poetry and Prose*, 394).

Evolution and Design

As W. David Shaw has argued, Frost's theism relates closely to a pragmatic conception of God, one that remains, in James's sense, "unfinished," open to human participation. Drawing upon his readings of Frost's *A Masque of Reason* and *A Masque of Mercy*, Shaw points to a key similarity in Peirce and Frost's conceptions of the divine: their insistence upon the vague. "Vagueness, as both Peirce and Frost conceive it," Shaw writes, "is a form of indeterminacy. The mysteries of indefinition are one means of keeping the universe open and limitless" (185). Frost's "vague" conception of God is driven by a dynamic conflict between the justice, aligned with law, order, and form; and mercy, associated with freedom and openness. In *A Masque of Mercy*, Jonah and Paul, representatives of the new and old testament, argue over the "mercy-justice contradiction," a seemingly irresolvable conflict between opposing visions of God as representative of law and of love (*Complete Poems*, 615). It falls to the Keeper (short for "My Brother's Keeper," and here a representative of humankind) to find the balance between these opposing forces in his final statement; "nothing can make injustice just but mercy" (642).

In spite of this understanding of the necessity of human participation in religious experience, part of Frost's conception of the "vagueness" of God is an insistence on the irreducibility of the divine to human dimensions. In *Robert Frost and the Challenge of Darwin*, Robert Faggen writes that, for Frost, "the fullness of life does not conform to a human sense of purpose or improvement" (246). Nowhere is this incommensurability between human thinking and the workings of the world more clearly manifest than in Frost's poems about God. In "The Most of It," Frost highlights the limits of human perception, which can recognize the presence of God, but cannot decipher the meaning of this presence.

> He thought he kept the universe alone;
> For all the voice in answer he could wake
> Was but the mocking echo of his own
> From some tree-hidden cliff across the lake.
> Some morning from the boulder-broken beach
> He would cry out on life, that what it wants
> Is not its own love back in copy speech,
> But counter-love, original response.
> And nothing ever came of what he cried
> Unless it was the embodiment that crashed
> In the cliff's talus on the other side,
> And then in the far distant water splashed.
> But after a time allowed for it to swim,
> Instead of proving human when it neared
> And someone else additional to him,

> As a great buck it powerfully appeared,
> Pushing the crumpled water up ahead,
> And landed pouring like a waterfall,
> And stumbled through the rocks with horny tread,
> And forced the underbrush — and that was all.
>
> (*Complete Poems*, 451)

The poem's juxtaposition of the solitary man's echo and the appearance of the buck suggests Frost's vision of the unique loneliness of human beings in the universe. In this vision, there are two kinds of experience: experience of that which we are able to know in human terms (ultimately, experience of ourselves, our "own love back in copy-speech"), and experience of that which is so radically non-human that we cannot comprehend it. Clearly, experience of the divine belongs in the second category. The buck, God's "embodiment," arrives as if in response to the man's appeals for "original response," and its presence suggests the erroneousness of the man's belief that "he kept the universe alone." However, the buck does not provide any recognizable "counter-love," but merely "powerfully appear[s]," and just as mysteriously vanishes. The man is given an immediate, overwhelming sense of the presence of a powerful otherness, but is utterly unable to make sense of this presence, or to be comforted by it.

Like Frost's, Peirce's God is both powerfully apparent and unknowable. As Douglas Anderson has argued, in Peirce's conception of the divine, "religious belief is directly experiential and therefore bears the strength of immediacy; it is what Peirce sometimes called 'practically indubitable'" (176). "Where would one find such an idea, say as that of God, if not from direct experience?" Peirce writes, "Would you make it the result of some kind of reasoning, good or bad? . . . No: as to God, open your eyes — and your heart, which is also a perceptive organ — and you see him" (*Collected*, 6:493). While Peirce believed experience of the divine to be direct and indubitable, he also held that "the contents of such beliefs are necessarily vague, general and unfinished" (Anderson, 178). Frost's poem echoes this sense both of the indubitability of God's presence and of its vagueness.

Central to the mystery of God for both Peirce and Frost is the problem of the existence of evil, and the difficulty of reconciling the idea of a loving, omnipotent God with the existence of suffering. In his chilling poem, "Design," Frost juxtaposes images of innocence and destructiveness, the natural and the unnatural, leaving unanswered the question of God's role in the seemingly cruel design of nature.

> I found a dimpled spider, fat and white,
> On a white heal-all, holding up a moth
> Like a white piece of rigid satin cloth —

Assorted characters of death and blight
Mixed ready to begin the morning right,
Like the ingredients of a witches' broth —
A snow-drop spider, a flower like a froth,
And dead wings carried like a paper kite.

What had that flower to do with being white,
The way-side blue and innocent heal-all?
What brought the kindred spider to that height,
What steered the white moth thither in the night?
What but design of darkness to appall? —
If design govern in a thing so small.
(Complete Poems, 396)

The whiteness of the ordinarily blue wildflower, the heal-all, is here associated with darkness, rather than innocence, and flower, spider, and moth are removed from their natural context and reimagined as "ingredients of a witches' broth," implicated in supernatural evil. As Frost turns from the descriptions of the octave to the musings of the sestet, the sentences switch from the declarative to the interrogative mode, marking a shift between the known, observable world and the unknown realm of supernatural (divine or satanic) design. The initial two questions, "What had that flower to do with being white . . .?" and "What brought the kindred spider to that height?" are answered not with a statement but with a third question: "What but design of darkness to appall . . .?" qualified by the "If" (which is emphasized by the inversion of the iambic pattern in the line's initial foot) of the final line. The poem's structure and rhyme scheme — a standard Petrarchan octave followed by a less typical *acaacc* structure in the sestet — seems designed to maximize binary relations. The poem consists of two stanzas, each containing two repeating end-rhymes (as opposed to the more traditional three end rhymes — *cde, cde* — of the Petrarchan sestet). Within the poem's own careful design, nature and the supernatural, light and darkness, innocence and evil, God and the devil become inseparable elements of single structure. While Frost leaves unanswered the questions posed in the sestet about the nature and origin of the universe's design, the poem seems to insist upon the essential interconnectedness of good and evil. As Frost observed in his notebook, "we can't think of good without evil. Neither can come to an end without the other" (282).

Both Peirce and Frost, basing their visions of the universe on an evolutionary model, perceive evil, death, and waste to be essential components of change and so of life. In "Evolutionary Love," Peirce writes,

> Thus, the love that God is, is not a love of which hatred is the contrary; otherwise Satan would be a coordinate power; but it is a love which embraces hatred as an imperfect stage of it, as Anteros — yea,

even needs hatred and hatefulness as its object. For self-love is no love; so if God's self is love, that which he loves must be defect of love; just as a luminary can light up only that which is dark. (*Essential*, 1:353)

Joseph Brent argues that Peirce's understanding of the place of suffering in an evolving world "trivializes evil," an objection that was raised against Frost's view of human pain, as well. Brent's description of Peirce's view of the relationship between good and evil applies remarkably well to the vision of design in Frost's poem:

> A metaphysics which encompasses and justifies in one perfectly harmoniously evolving universe the pink spider crab camouflaged in the attractive blossoms of the rose; the orchid which successfully copies the pheromones and genitalia of the female species of a wasp to accomplish its own fertilization ... is an immensely appealing solution to the problem of evil and pain. (339)

A reporter, responding to a remark of Frost's about the inevitability of famine, war, and disease after periods of human overpopulation, raised a similar objection to this view: "How simple. The great world war was nothing to be regretted, but simply God's way of thinning us out! Poor, ignorant man may think he blundered, but Mr. Frost doesn't think so. The black plague, tuberculosis, gripp[e], smallpox, scarlet fever — these must be looked upon as God's blessings in disguise...." (Thompson, 268).

Similar criticisms have dogged pragmatism since its inception, and at bottom reflect the fear that the only alternative to theories in which truth, good, and evil are absolute is a theory in which such terms become absolutely relative, emptied of all value. As Richard Rorty illustrates in *Philosophy and the Mirror of Nature,* such objections amount to an insistence on an immovable foundation for all knowledge. As we will see in the section that follows, both Frost and Peirce questioned the existence of such a foundation, yet preserved the ideal of an objective reality, a world independent of human perception.

The Sweetest Dream

An understanding of thought as a continual struggle between known and unknown corresponds, in both Peirce and Frost, to a complex epistemology that seeks to establish both the existence of an objective reality "out there" and the shaping power of human perception. Frost's difficult vision of the relation between fact and truth can be seen in the early poem, "Mowing."

> There was never a sound beside my wood but one,
> And that was my long scythe whispering to the ground.
> What was it it whispered? I knew not well myself;
> Perhaps it was something about the heat of the sun,
> Something, perhaps, about the lack of sound —
> And that was why it whispered and did not speak.
> It was no dream of the gift of idle hours,
> Or easy gold at the hand of fay or elf:
> Anything less than the truth would have seemed too weak
> To the earnest love that lay the swale in rows,
> Not without the feeble-pointed spikes of flowers
> (Pale orchises), and scared a bright green snake.
> The fact is the sweetest dream that labor knows.
> My long scythe whispered and left the hay to make.
> (*Complete Poems*, 25)

Despite the poem's reference to Sydney's *Astrophel and Stella* and echoes of Wordsworth's "Solitary Reaper," which seem to elicit critical commentary (Faggen, "Pastoral," 255–57), the poem ends in enigma, resisting interpretation. The poem's central images — the scythe, the grass, the flowers, the snake — seem irreducible, mere "facts" that can't easily be translated into a readily digestible "truth." The poem seems to propose both the stubborn independence of facts from mind ("What was it it whispered? I knew not well myself;") and their inexorable involvement in the human processes of "labor" and "love." These processes result in a truth to which the speaker seems to gain access by the end of the poem by virtue of his deeper involvement with facts. The truth itself, however — that "The fact is the sweetest dream that labor knows" — is an utterly enigmatic one, seeming merely to reinforce the sense that there are *only* facts, and our (human) attempts to divine their truth may amount to mere dreaming or storytelling (about, for example, "easy gold at the hand of fay or elf"). The poem seems to insist simultaneously upon truth as a product of human processes and on its ultimate elusiveness and independence.

Elsewhere, Frost seems to question the existence of an objective reality, or at least the possibility of objective knowledge.[9] In "Education By Poetry," Frost insists that "unless you are at home in the metaphor, unless you have had your proper poetical education in the metaphor, you are not safe anywhere. Because you are not at ease with figurative values. . . . You are not safe in science; you are not safe in history" (*Poetry*, 334). Arguing that all thinking is metaphorical, Frost suggests that those who have received their "education by poetry" have the advantage of knowing when a particular governing metaphor, whether it is operating in physics or in sociology, has been exhausted and a new figure needs to be employed. As Guy Rotella points out, "these ideas about analogy go far toward implying a radical subjectivity that would make human knowing a matter of imposition rather than of discovery" (171).

The uncertainty about our access to truth in Frost's "Mowing" echoes Peirce's simultaneous belief that "knowledge is constituted as the final outcome of inquiry" and insistence that there exists a reality independent of human thinking (Pihlström, 81). Peirce's famous pragmatic maxim, formulated in his 1878 paper "How To Make Our Ideas Clear," places human activity at the center of any picture of reality. "Consider what effects, which might conceivably have practical bearings, we conceive the object of our conception to have. Then, our conception of these effects is the whole of our conception of the object" (*Essential*, 1:132). The strong implication of the shaping power of thought in this formulation (note the repetition of the word *conception*) is difficult to square with Peirce's insistence, in "The Fixation of Belief" (1877), that "it is necessary that a method should be found by which our beliefs may be caused by nothing human, but by some external permanency — by something upon which our thinking has no effect" (*Essential*, 1:120). In "Peirce's Place in the Pragmatist Tradition," Pihlström describes not only the important divergence of James from Peirce with regard to the possible existence of anything "upon which our thoughts have no effect," but also the way both Peirce and James resist categorization as realists or idealists (or, in the terms of the more recent debate between neo-pragmatists, realists or anti-realists). "What makes pragmatism philosophically interesting is its tendency to result in fruitful albeit not easily resolvable struggles between realism and idealism" (50). The complexity and ambiguity of Peirce's position may be seen in Josiah Royce's comment about Peirce's 1877 and 1878 papers: "He seems to regard reality as for us merely the representative of our determination to act so or so. . . . Yet [he] is not content with this, but continually appeals to the transcendent reality as justifying our determination and our expectation" (Pihlström, 52). Peirce's insistence on both the independence of things and the intimate community of mind and nature which "imparts to our guesses a tendency toward the truth" (in Brent, 205) is echoed in an observation from an entry in Frost's notebook: "Every thing that is a thing is out there and there it stands waiting under your eye till someday you notice it" (*Notebooks*, 89). Objective reality is both really "out there," and at the same time "stands waiting" for the shaping power of human perception.

Peirce, Frost, Darwin

In the sections above, I have argued that both Peirce and Frost's thinking is essentially evolutionary in nature, modeled on an understanding of organic growth and change. Peirce and Frost were careful readers of

Darwin, and the significance of Darwinian evolution for both writers can hardly be overstated. As early as 1916, Royce and Kernan classed Peirce as an "evolutionist" (702). Robert Faggen in *Robert Frost and the Challenge of Darwin* argues that "much of the tension and power in Frost's poetry derives from his lifelong engagement with the implications of science in general and of Darwin in particular" (1). As we have seen, both Peirce and Frost saw struggle as essential to life and viewed knowledge as a continually evolving by-product of an ongoing engagement with the unknown. It is important to note, however, that while Peirce and Frost were most certainly "evolutionists," each was critical of Darwin, and each developed his own paradigm of evolution, differing in significant ways from the Darwinian model.

As Royce and Kernan point out, the imprint of evolution on Peirce's thought is not surprising, given his context. "His education was finished, and his maturer scientific work begun, in the great decades of the modern evolutionary movement" (702). The authors argue, however, that Peirce's interest in the concept of evolution led beyond Darwin's biological model. Peirce "wanted to know not merely about the evolution of any one group of physical phenomena, whether stellar or terrestrial, organic or inorganic. He wanted to know about how the laws of nature came to be what they are now" (703). Royce and Kernan summarize Peirce's evolutionary cosmology as follows:

> There is reasonable inductive evidence that the laws which nature follows are themselves only approximately true and are subject to evolution, so that Newton's law of gravitation is presumably very nearly true at the present time for the present moon and planets, the present stellar systems. But it is equally probable that this law is even now only a close approximation, not an absolutely necessary order of things. For similar inductive reasons, it becomes probable that, in so far as Newton's law of gravitation now holds true, it did not always hold true, and that this, like all other laws of nature, is a product of evolution. (704)

By extending the concept of evolution to the laws of nature, Peirce removed it from the exclusively biological context of selective reproduction in the Darwinian model.

Peirce further challenged the Darwinian model in his 1913 paper "Evolutionary Love." Here, Peirce distinguishes between three types of evolution: tychastic, anacastic, and agapastic, representing "evolution by fortuitous variation, evolution by mechanical necessity, and evolution by creative love," respectively (*Essential*, 1:362). Peirce classes Darwin's version as tychastic, driven by chance, and deterministic theories as anacastic, driven by mechanism. His own model is that of agapasm, "which teaches that growth comes only from love." In the following illustration,

Peirce once again removes evolution from its biological frame and applies it instead to ideas.

> Suppose, for example, that I have an idea that interests me. It is my creation.... I love it; and I will sink myself in perfecting it. It is not by dealing out cold justice to the circle of my ideas that I can make them grow, but by cherishing and tending them as I would the flowers in my garden. The philosophy we draw from John's gospel is that this is the way the mind develops.... Love, recognizing germs of loveliness in the hateful, gradually warms it into life and makes it lovely. (1:354)

Peirce's model of agapasm thus reconciles an evolutionary model of change with what he sees as the fundamental principle of Christianity.

Like Peirce, Frost read Darwin intensely, and often engaged him combatively. Frost's biggest objection to Darwin seems to have been that the theory of evolution is subject to popular misinterpretation: "As for Darwin look at the harm he had done to the mob by giving them reason to think everything in general and particular must be growing infinitely," he writes in his notebook (318). For Frost, no growth can be without limit, for growth and limit are terms that define one another reflexively. Like everything else in our experience, growth is not absolute, but is tempered by its opposite. "We know no growth that doesn't round out and come to an end. Everything has counter sides that come up opposed like the sides of a vase to complete a symmetry" (318). In Frost's view, Darwin's explanation of natural selection allows for a fantasy of uninterrupted progress, even perfectibility, which in turn leads to utopian fantasies (like Marxism) that endanger human freedom. "The danger in the word evolution as used is that it stealthily introduces the idea of eternity into the idea of growth" (486).

In contrast to this idea of progress ("much confusion comes from confusing progress with evolution," one notebook entry observes), Frost developed his own, characteristically dialectical model of evolutionary change. "The medium in which alone life can flourish is perished matter. The little organized lives in a bath of broken down organisms — disorganisms." In the same notebook entry he observes, "The tree stands growing in its own waste — the bark it sheds the branches and the bark it sheds" (486).

Frost's understanding of the evolution of life out of waste is most dramatically illustrated in "The Need of Being Versed in Country Things," in which the poet describes phoebes nesting in a burned-down house. After reflecting on what has been lost — the deserted barn, still standing, no longer "opened with all one end / For teams that came by the stony road / To drum the floor with scurrying hoofs / And brush the mow with the summer load" — the speaker notes the presence of the phoebes.

> Yet for them the lilac renewed its leaf,
> And the aged elm, though touched with fire;
> And the dry pump flung up an awkward arm;
> And the fence post carried a strand of wire
>
> For them there was really nothing sad.
> But though they rejoiced in the nest they kept,
> One had to be versed in country things
> Not to believe the phoebes wept.

For Frost, being "versed in country things" means seeing beyond the limited human perspective from which the remnants of a burned house evokes a feeling of sadness and loss. For the phoebes, who have nested in the house, it is spring, the season of reproduction and renewal. The shell of the burned house is the locus of new life. The poem suggests that we mourn loss only because our perspective is limited. The persistently melancholy tone of the poem — the birds' "murmur" sounds less like a song and "more like the sigh we sigh / From too much dwelling in what has been" — suggests that the speaker, though able to see the broader perspective from which loss and death signal the beginning of new life, remains bound by the human tendency to mourn individual losses (*Complete Poems*, 300).

The human perspective and the broader perspective of nature thus define and limit each other, just as life is defined and limited by waste and loss. In both cases, the seemingly opposed terms serve as "counter sides that come up opposed like the sides of a vase to complete a symmetry" (*Notebooks*, 318). Frost's vision of evolution is one of a continual alternation between growth and limitation, rather than linear progress. "Growths," he writes in a notebook entry, "is a better idea than growth (sing.)" (486).

The assimilation of Darwin's discoveries was arguably the single greatest challenge faced by the late nineteenth- and early twentieth-century European and American imagination. The writings of Peirce and Frost provide us with evidence of how this new and disorienting information reacted, as in a chemical experiment, with the dispositions and energies of two highly sensitive minds. If we look at poetries and philosophies as distinct but related means for negotiating our environment, for literally *making* sense out of the world we inhabit, our critical attention may begin to be engaged by a new question: what would it mean to inhabit this way of thinking, this mode of interacting with the world?[10] In the case of Peirce and Frost, the answer to this question involves a re-examination of the relationship between self and non-self, what Emerson calls the "NOT ME" (*Writings*, 8). For both Peirce and Frost, evolution involves an interaction between opposite (or seemingly opposite) terms. Love gradually acts upon and converts hatred, habit emerges from a world of pure chance and establishes order, new growth emerges out of waste. Such engagements with otherness are not always happy, as the biographies of both writers attest. Both Peirce and Frost insist on both the difficulty and the necessity of such encounters, the way any mind both participates in and is eluded by the reality outside it. Their descriptions of the struggle between self and non-self, and the way this struggle shapes the forms of human thought, represent an important current in the pragmatist stream, one that looks back to Emerson and forward to John Dewey.

Other Ruins

There's a great deal to say that I haven't said about Peirce and Frost. I have elided, in my attention to my own vision, a great many very important differences between the two. Most obvious of these is the fact of Peirce's insistence on the "method of science" as our most reliable means to arrive at knowledge of our world. In "Education by Poetry" and elsewhere, Frost, implying the relativity of all knowledge, gives the upper hand to poetry, claiming that "education in the metaphor" is central to a correct understanding of any subject, including science and history (*Poetry and Prose*, 334). Indeed, at times Frost seems particularly skeptical, if not hostile, toward the claims of science. A second, and equally important difference may be found in the relationship of these two writers to language itself. Whereas for Frost, the sound of a sentence was constitutive of its meaning and sentence-sounds were the very basis of poetry, Peirce was uninterested in style, and knew himself unable to compete with William James when it came to felicity of expression. I mention these key differences here, at the end of this chapter, to stand for the many ways in which Peirce and Frost remain more complex than my or any reading of them can allow. Reading, too, is an encounter with the non-self, and I am struck by the way these writings resist being corralled into a too-easy, or too-complete, framework.

Out my driveway and a thirty minute walk northeast on paved and unpaved roads, a small overgrown graveyard marks the center of what was once a town, Eminence, with two churches, a store, and a post office. On my old map (1866) the houses are marked with small squares and identified by family name: Wood, Eller, Pinder, Coon, Vandeusen. The worn gravestones, barely legible, bear the same names. There are still a few houses, now part of the towns of Summit or Blenheim (depending on their placement on the street), but the place is mostly woods and crumbling walls and old cellar holes.

What are such places to us, or we to them? What do we make of the ruins of the past? I imagine these men and women squeezing their subsistence from the rocky dirt, fencing in their cattle with stone walls, burying their children, year after year, in the graves marked by the smallest stones. It is a dim picture, glimpsed like Frost's whiteness at the bottom of the well, only grazing the edge of the strange reality of the gravestones and the sunken ground beneath them.

Frost's farm and Peirce's house must bear a similar strangeness, the concrete otherness of a past we can imagine but cannot inhabit. This feeling of strangeness, of a not-quite-traversable distance between ourselves and the past, has, I believe, a place in literary scholarship. The stubborn otherness of texts, their refusal to conform fully to any critical story we may wish to tell, is what gives any reading experience its difficult pleasure, what makes it more than just talking to ourselves.

Notes

[1] In recent months, two critics — William Logan and James Sitar — have attacked Faggen's transcription of the notebooks as "untrustworthy" and error-ridden (Rich, "Editing . . ."). Despite such criticisms, I continue to see the widespread availability, in however imperfect a form, of Frost's notebooks as a gift of enormous value to students and readers of Frost.

[2] For discussion of the connection between James and Frost, refer to Poirier's *Poetry and Pragmatism* and Shaw's "Poetics of Pragmatism."

[3] I do not mean to imply that James possessed a particularly sunny disposition. John Jay Chapman once observed that "there was, in spite of his playfulness, a deep sadness about James. You felt that he had just stepped out of this sadness in order to meet you and was to go back into it the moment you left him" (R. Richardson, *James*, 236). However, as one can sense from his remarkable solicitude for the audiences of his lectures, James was an essentially sociable person. Friends and family, Richardson notes, "almost always describe him as active, vivacious, humorous, playful and, said Royce, 'eternally young'" (420). This portrait stands in stark contrast to descriptions of both Peirce and Frost, as should become clear in the pages that follow.

[4] Peirce's rejection of the popularized "pragmatism" and renaming of his own approach "pragmaticism," a term he hoped would be "ugly enough to be safe from kidnappers," is a typical example of what I refer to here as "resistance to absorption" (*Essential*, 2:335).

[5] For an account of the relationship between Thompson and Frost, see Sheehy, 393–410.

[6] As Stephen Collis observes, this is, of course, a misreading of Marx, who understands class conflict as the animating force of history.

[7] As Nathan Houser has pointed out, Peirce occasionally envisioned "an infinitely distant future" in which the world would become "an absolutely perfect, rational and symmetrical system," devoid of the operations of chance (Peirce, *Essential*, 1:297). At other times, however, he insisted that the progress of the universe tended not toward the elimination of chance but toward an equilibrium between chance and law (1:iii). For the practical purposes of the present (and foreseeable future), however, Peirce insisted upon the necessary coexistence of chance and law, doubt and belief.

[8] Stephen Collis pointed out to me the very close parallel of Peirce's notion of the centrality of uncertainty to thought to Keats's concept of "negative capability." Indeed, Dewey notes the latter concept's similarity to pragmatist thought in *Art As Experience*, saying that the letter in which the concept is announced "contains more of the psychology of productive thought than many treatises" (*Later Works* 10:40).

[9] As Guy Rotella has shown, Frost's knowledge of contemporary physics was considerable, and confirmed his sense of both an objectively existing reality and of that reality's elusiveness for human observers. Rotella notes Frost's delight at the fact that "in shifting emphasis from certitude to probability, modern physics has made room again for freedom in a world of determined chance" (176).

[10] Note that this question is a reformulation of Peirce's maxim, "Consider what effects, which might conceivably have practical bearings, we conceive the object of our conception to have. Then, our conception of these effects is the whole of our conception of the object" (*Essential*, 1:132).

4: "As Much a Part of Things as Trees and Stones": John Dewey, William Carlos Williams, and the Difference in Not Knowing

Discovery

*S*HE SAID, DO YOU HAVE ANY INCOME? *I said nope! hahaha I did! I just lied to 'em.* I have finished my pancakes and tea. From my booth in the front of the Summit Country Store I watch the cars on route 10 and listen to the old men at the back table. It is Columbus Day, and the weekend people are headed back to the interstate. The old men are gearing up for hunting season. *The only reason they even make 'em is to keep Remington in business.* I have left my baby for the first time and with this separation bought myself two hours to write. But the world is clouded and there are no words, nothing to express. My transgender neighbor, Katherine, comes in and sits at her customary table, telling the waitress, *today's the day the Native Americans discovered Columbus and got killed for it.* The waitress, used to this kind of talk from Katherine, smiles with crooked teeth. The waitress's kids are with her at work today — no school. *I got a doggie bone! I got a doggie bone!* the boy shouts to a customer. *I eat these!* I think that I can hear the baby crying, four miles away. I cannot imagine ever having written anything. I start typing up the old men's talk. *I tell you what, I learned a lot off him. He wasn't perfect, far from it, but I learned a lot off him.* On the wall in front of me a giant buck, head cocked to the side, stares unblinkingly in my direction, at nothing. *That's a big one he bought. From the road it looks big.*

I have a chapter to write. I am thinking about Dewey teaching five-year-olds to bake and Williams delivering babies in dingy apartments, and what relation these activities bore to their writing. *You ever go over to Brownsville, on the water there? Spend any time over there? They got the monument, the guys were fishing on the jetty or whatever the hell?* I am thinking about what writing is, and what relation it bears to a crying baby. I am thinking about the old men's talk, and what relation it bears to philosophy.

What difference does it make to the writing of a sentence not to know how the sentence will end? Not to be pulled along by a period, or an end rhyme? What difference does discovery make?

Thoughts/Words

"Philosophy," Wittgenstein famously suggested, "ought really to be written only as a *form of poetry*" (Perloff, xviii). Like many of Wittgenstein's statements, this one has the quality of a gnomic utterance, in part because it suggests the proximity of poetry and philosophy, the way one may shade into the other, while at the same confirming their separateness. The "ought" reminds us that philosophy is *not* written as a form of poetry; it would not be recognizable as philosophy if it were.

The writings of both John Dewey and William Carlos Williams emerge from a new understanding of experience, one in which the subject is part of, inseparable from, the experienced event. The different ways that Dewey and Williams bring this new understanding to the act of writing is the subject of this chapter. It is a difference more easily felt than defined, and such difficulties of definition touch the heart of the matter. I am tempted to write that it is the difference between *thoughts first* and *words first*, that Dewey, as a philosopher, sought to translate an ordered set of philosophical ideas into language, while Williams, the poet, was always improvising, letting language lead him to new thoughts. Williams writes in the foreword to his autobiography, "Thought was never an isolated thing with me; it was a game of tests and balances, to be proven by the written word" (xiii).

I am tempted by this characterization, but it will not quite do, for the splitting up of words and thoughts ignores the critique of language implied by Dewey's work and made explicit in Williams's: ideas are not separate from the words that embody them, the life of a thought is the life of language, and to imagine otherwise is to misunderstand the relationship between ourselves and our world.

John Dewey's thinking about the inherited categories of philosophy — subject and object, existence and essence, etc. — posed a challenge to philosophical thinking that philosophical writing, even his own, could not answer. Meanwhile, in Rutherford, New Jersey, between patients, William Carlos Williams improvised, scratching words on prescription pads in a way that suggested a dissolution of the inherited ontology Dewey sought to "reconstruct." "A writer," Williams writes in *The Embodiment of Knowledge*,

> is a person whose best is released in the accomplishment of writing — perhaps it is a good variant to say — in the act of writing. He does not necessarily think these things — he does not, that is, think them out and then write them down: he writes and the best of him, in spite even of his thought, will appear on the page even to his surprise, unrecognized or even sometimes against his will, by the proper use of words. (7)

One difference between philosophy and poetry — the difference Williams saw — is the greater space for improvisation in the later. It is in Williams's improvisatory approach to writing that Dewey's call for a reconstruction of philosophy is most fully answered.

Dewey's Critique

Dewey's critique of philosophy derives from his contention that "our inherited philosophical traditions arose out of and have failed to advance beyond the assumptions and habits of a prescientific worldview" (Burke, Hester, and Talisse, xi). Among such assumptions is the idea that the mental and the physical occupy separate "realms." This idea was derived, in Dewey's view, from the separation between theory and practice which was the natural result of the economic organization of Ancient Greece, in which physical labor was allocated to slaves, leaving non-slaves the leisure necessary for contemplation (*Middle*, 12:258–59). As a result of the persistence of the idea of an opposition between thought and practice, Western philosophy of both the rationalist and the empiricist varieties adopted a "spectator view of knowledge," in which "knowledge is the passive beholding by an extranatural or 'internal' mind of a complete and fixed 'external' world" (Burke, Hester, and Talisse, xii). As a consequence of the separation of realms implicit in this view, our claims to "know" anything, as well as the relations between mind and body, self and others, etc. become "problems" which it has been philosophy's self-appointed task to solve.

Dewey contends that these "problems" arise not from the real nature of our experience of the world but from the outmoded assumptions and vocabulary of philosophy itself. Rather than solve these "problems," which have become increasingly remote from the practical concerns of daily life, philosophy should instead address itself to a reconstitution of its method and vocabulary to account for the insights of modern science. As Burke, Hester, and Talisse point out in their introduction to *Dewey's Logical Theory*,

> The insight driving Dewey's reconstructive program is that the spectator view of knowledge is untenable in the light of the successes of modern science. As even the most cursory examination will show, scientific inquiry is premised on the idea that knowing and acting are intimately related. The practice of pursuing knowledge by means of deliberate experimentation, a mode of directed and controlled action, constitutes a rejection of the spectator conception. On the scientific model, a knower as such is an agent within the world that is known, not a ghostly beholder of an antecedent and alien Reality. (xii)

In place of the traditional "problem" of the relationship of an independent consciousness to the objective world outside of it, Dewey posits a "dynamic interaction of two physical agents in producing a third thing, an effect — an affair of precisely the same kind as in any conjoint action, say the operation of hydrogen and oxygen in producing water" (*Middle*, 10:31). In essence, Dewey argues that the subject-object "problem," which had dominated philosophical thinking for centuries, is not solved but rather dissolved by a new paradigm, one that "begins from a Darwinian premise of interaction" (Burke, Hester, and Talisse, xiv). Experience, according to this view, is "an *exchange*, a *transaction* between an organism and the physical and social factors within its environment" (xiv).

Predictably, the aspect of Dewey's program that met with the greatest resistance was its reevaluation of the function of philosophy: in particular, Dewey's suggestion, most clearly expressed in "The Need for a Recovery of Philosophy," that philosophy "surrender all pretension to be peculiarly concerned with ultimate reality, or with reality as a complete (i.e., completed) whole: with *the* real object" (*Middle*, 10:38). Rejecting the assumption underlying much of Western philosophy, "that experience centres in, or gathers about, or proceeds from a centre or subject which is outside the course of natural existence, and set over against it" (*Middle*, 10:22), Dewey reiterates and expands William James's earlier claim that "the trail of the human serpent is . . . over everything"; that there can be no extra-human or absolute knowledge (*Writings*, 515). As Richard Rorty writes in *Philosophy and the Mirror of Nature*, Western philosophy since Plato has been preoccupied with its own status as the arbiter of knowledge-claims, forever attempting to shore up its own authority on the basis of its special access to the unchanging foundations of knowledge. Dewey calls for philosophy to abandon "the quest for certainty" (as he phrased it in the title of his 1929 Gifford lectures). But as Dewey himself points out, the "surrender" of claims about the foundations of all knowledge

> is not easy of achievement. The philosophical tradition that comes to us from classic Greek thought and was reinforced by Christian philosophy in the middle ages discriminated philosophical knowing from other modes of knowing by means of an alleged peculiarly intimate concern with the supreme, ultimate, true reality. To deny this trait to philosophy seems to many to be the suicide of philosophy. (*Middle*, 10:38)

For Dewey, then, one of the main challenges implicit in the writing of philosophical texts is to find a way to preserve the radical nature of his call for a "reconstruction in philosophy" without committing philosophical suicide: without, that is, ceasing to be legible as a philosopher.

Dewey's attempt to preserve philosophy while laying siege to its conception of itself demanded a compromise in the presentation of his ideas. Much of the famed "difficulty" of Dewey's prose, can, I believe, be attributed to this simultaneous desire to dismantle and to preserve the old systems. For John Beck, this position is common to Dewey and to Williams, and is representative of a larger desire "to preserve the good without falling into nostalgic conservatism" (3). While my own reading of Williams differs from Beck's (as will become clear in subsequent sections, I find Williams to have been significantly *less* ambivalent than was Dewey about the need for radical change on the level of language), I concur with his assessment as it applies to Dewey. Dewey's desire to "attain a middle ground" (3), to challenge the bedrock of traditional philosophy while preserving its significance, can be seen most clearly in his attempt to reclaim certain key philosophical terms (among them, "Logic," "Experience," and "Metaphysics") as well as in his effort to rebuild philosophy on a new foundation of scientific thought.

The Burden of Vocabulary

Dewey's theory of inquiry represented such a significant break from the traditional conception of logic as existing prior to and independent of the objects of inquiry to which it was applied that many, including Charles Peirce, questioned whether it could properly be called a "logic" at all.[1] In *Logic: The Theory of Inquiry*, Dewey argued that rather than existing permanently outside of experience, "all logical forms (with their characteristic properties) arise *within the operation of inquiry* and are concerned with the control of inquiry so that it may yield *warranted assertions*" (*Later*, 12:11). Logical forms, that is, do not govern inquiry from without, but rather have their origin within inquiry itself. Moreover, they do not yield absolute certainty (as purely logical or mathematical judgments were believed to do), but only "warranted assertability." Like other elements of Dewey's philosophy, this theory of inquiry, as Larry Hickman observes, is rooted in Dewey's understanding of Darwinian evolution.

> Dewey identified inquiry as the primary means by which reflexive organisms seek to achieve stability through adaptation. It is by means of inquiry that humans are able to exert control over their own habit formation, thereby creating new instruments. In the short run, these instruments enable us to improve conditions that we deem unsatisfactory. In the long run, they enable us to influence the course of our own evolution. (167)

This definition of logical inquiry as always directed toward a special end and embedded within a particular environmental context strips logic of its neutrality and permanence, the very attributes for which it has historically been valued.

Along with his redefinition of logic, Dewey ascribed new meanings to several of its key terms. "A priori," in the Deweyan sense, refers not to preexperiential categories imposed onto experience, but rather to "directive principles, regulative limiting ideals" that are themselves the products of prior inquiry (*Later*, 12:345). Similarly, unlike traditional logicians who assume the subjects of propositions to be "given in a determinate fashion to the senses," Dewey posits that both "subject and predicate are determined in correspondence with each other in and by the process of 'thought,' that is, inquiry" (*Later*, 12:128). Dewey attempts a similar rehabilitation of the word "necessity" in his 1893 essay "The Superstition of Necessity." As Ralph Sleeper contends, Dewey "was trying to work out a conception of logical necessity that would accord with our actual experience in the natural sciences, one that would not evoke the transcendental at all" (35). Here again, Dewey's approach is to retain the vocabulary of the tradition (in this case idealist) while transforming its basic meaning. In the Kantian and Hegelian systems, the principle of logical necessity is transcendental — it exists apart from experience and is applied to it. As Sleeper observes, in "The Superstition of Necessity," Dewey concludes that "the concept of necessity arises from the practice of inquiry, that it is, in a sense, the a posteriori product of thought rather than its a priori principle" (35).

Perhaps the most well-known instance of Dewey's attempt to transform the language of philosophy is his use of the word "experience" throughout his writings. In the opening chapter of *Experience and Nature*, Dewey sets forth his unique, transactional definition of the term.

> Experience is *of* as well as *in* nature. It is not experience which is experienced, but nature — stones, plants, animals, diseases, health, temperature, electricity and so on. Things interacting in a certain way are experience; they are what is experienced. Linked in certain other ways with another natural object — the human organism — they are *how* things are experienced as well. Experience reaches down into nature; it has depth. It also has breadth and to an indefinitely elastic extent. It stretches. (*Later*, 1:12–13)

Late in his life, Dewey recognized that his redefinition of the word had been widely misunderstood and proposed changing the title of *Experience and Nature* to *Culture and Nature*.

> The historical obstacles are now so conspicuous that I can at times but wonder how they came to be overlooked. There was a period in modern philosophy when the appeal to "experience" was a thoroughly wholesome appeal to liberate philosophy from dessicated

abstractions. But I failed to appreciate the fact that subsequent developments inside and outside of philosophy had corrupted and destroyed the wholesomeness of the appeal — that "experience" had become effectively identified with experiencing in the sense of the psychological, and the psychological had become established as that which is intrinsically psychical, mental, private. My insistence that "experience" also designates *what* is experienced was a mere ideological thundering in the Index for it ignored the ironical twist which made this use of "experience" strange and incomprehensible. (*Later*, 1:362)

Missing Dewey's radical redefinition of *experience*, some readers of *Experience and Nature*, including Santayana, assumed that Dewey's investment in the term reflected a basically idealist metaphysics, one that denied "the reality of objects apart from experience" (Sleeper, 113). As Sleeper argues, the later Dewey was not an idealist but a "transactional realist." "Unlike traditional realists," Sleeper contends, "he is not arguing against nominalism, but, in Hegelian fashion, for the role of the knower in determining the character of the known. He is arguing for a transaction between the knower and the known — in a word, for a kind of transactional realism" (23). In spite of Dewey's attempts to redefine *experience* to reflect this transactional model and encompass both *how* experience is had and *what* is experienced, many readers continued to understand *experience* in opposition to *existence* — as a shorthand for an idealist ontology.

Finally, as Richard Rorty observes in his essay on "Dewey's Metaphysics," Dewey, though persistently critical of the metaphysical tradition, sometimes referred to his book *Experience and Nature* as containing his own "natural" or "empirical metaphysics." "For better or worse," Rorty writes, Dewey "*wanted* to write a metaphysical system. Throughout his life, he wavered between a therapeutic stance toward philosophy and another, quite different, stance — one in which philosophy was to become 'scientific' and 'empirical'" (46). In response to Santayana's criticism that "naturalistic metaphysics" was an oxymoron, Dewey claimed that his method would use the scientific method to arrive at "a statement of the generic traits manifested by existences of all kinds without regard to their differentiation into mental and physical" (*Later*, 1:308). This ambition sounds, to Rorty, suspiciously like the quest of traditional philosophy for an absolute foundation for all knowledge that Dewey spent so much of his life critiquing. Rorty summarizes Dewey's attempt to resolve the contradiction as follows:

> There must be a standpoint from which experience can be seen in terms of "generic traits" which, once recognized, will make it impossible for us to describe it in these misleading ways which generate the subject-object and mind-matter dualisms that have been the dreary

topics of traditional philosophical controversy. This viewpoint would not be *sub specie aeternitatis,* since it would emphasize precisely the temporality and contingency which Augustine and Spinoza used the notion of "eternity" to exclude. But it would resemble traditional metaphysics in providing a permanent neutral matrix for future inquiry. (59–60)

The difficulty, as Rorty identifies, manifests itself in Dewey's desire to preserve the idea of certainty implied by the term "metaphysics," while simultaneously insisting on a historicist critique of all preceding attempts to provide such certainty. Some of the confusion inherent in Dewey's "naturalistic metaphysics" stems from what Rorty contends are his contradictory allegiances to both Hegel and Locke:

> Dewey, in short, confuses two ways of revolting against philosophical dualisms. The first way is to point out that the dualism is imposed by a tradition for specific cultural reasons, but has now outlived its usefulness. This is the Hegelian way — the way Dewey adopts in "An Empirical Survey of Empiricisms." The second is to describe the phenomenon in a non-dualistic way, which emphasizes the "continuity between lower and higher processes." This is the Lockean way — the way which led Locke to assimilate all mental acts to raw feels, thus paving the way for Humean skepticism. (62)

The second kind of revolt, in other words (and the one which Rorty clearly rejects), seeks to eliminate philosophical dualisms not simply because they have outlived their cultural "usefulness," but because experience *really is* non-dualistic. This "Lockean way" of challenging the tradition is grounded in science, a grounding Rorty rejects as simply one more attempt to elevate philosophy by providing a "permanent neutral matrix for future inquiry": in other words, a foundation.

The Exception: Science as Foundation

Reading with Rorty's critique in mind, it is easy to find moments when Dewey does indeed seem to have "c[o]me down with the disease he was trying to cure" (72). In an introduction written for the 1948 edition of *Reconstruction in Philosophy,* Dewey claims a special kind of "universality" for the method of science, "a method of inquiry so inclusive in range and so penetrating, so pervasive and so universal, as to provide the pattern and model which permits, invites, and even demands the kind of formulation that falls within the function of philosophy" (*Middle,* 12:270). The scientific method itself, this passage suggests, may provide a new "universal" foundation for philosophic thought. By setting science apart from other kinds of thinking in this way, Dewey replicates the split it was his project to repair.

In his account of the origins of philosophic thought, Dewey describes early or "natural man" as living "in a world of dreams, rather than facts."

> To treat the early beliefs and traditions of mankind as if they were attempts at scientific explanation of the world, only erroneous and absurd attempts, is thus to be guilty of a great mistake. The material out of which philosophy finally emerges is irrelevant to science and to explanation. It is figurative, symbolic of fears and hopes, made of imaginations and suggestions, not significant of a world of objective fact intellectually confronted. It is poetry and drama, rather than science, and is apart from scientific truth and falsity, rationality or absurdity of fact in the same way that poetry is apart from these things. (*Middle*, 12:83)

By insisting on the strict separation of "objective fact" and subjective "imaginations," Dewey isolates the kind of knowledge called science from other ways of conceptualizing experience, notably literary ways. More significantly, he assumes that the criteria of "objectivity" and "truth" are applicable to scientific thought. Dewey's own explanation of the impact of Darwinian thought in *Democracy and Education* (published in 1916, four years before *The Reconstruction in Philosophy*) would seem to dismantle this very assumption.

> For the doctrine of organic development means that the living creature is a part of the world, sharing its vicissitudes and fortunes, and making itself secure in its precarious dependence only as it intellectually identifies itself with the things about it, and, forecasting the future consequences of what is going on, shapes its own activities accordingly. If the living, experiencing being is an intimate participant in the activities of the world to which it belongs, then knowledge is a mode of participation, valuable in the degree in which it is effective. (*Middle*, 9:347)

According to the logic of this earlier statement, *no* kind of knowledge can claim objectivity, or freedom from human perspective and participation.

Dewey's implicit claim about the exceptionalism of science reflects a widespread and longstanding belief in the ideal of a purely objective standard for what constitutes scientific knowledge. As Thomas Kuhn established in *The Structure of Scientific Revolutions*, however, the criteria governing the choice between competing scientific theories are often values rather than rules, and thus open to "subjective" interpretations. Kuhn argues that "the choices scientists make between competing theories depend not only on shared criteria — those my critics call objective — but also on idiosyncratic factors dependent on individual biography and personality. The later are, in my critics' vocabulary, subjective" ("Objectivity," 388). Particularly noteworthy here is the way Kuhn questions the very terms — "objective" and "subjective" — of the discussion. Kuhn's recognition of the influence of the idiosyncratic nature of individual scientists' experience on the selection of scientific theories — and thus on the general progress of science — can be read as an extension of Dewey's principles to the one area of thought to which Dewey himself failed to apply them: the field of scientific inquiry.

Dewey's Theory of Language

Dewey's dissolution of the dualisms of philosophy — knower and known, mind and body, subject an object — have radical implications for the use of language. While Dewey took a first step toward realizing these implications in his attempts to redefine the inherited terms of philosophy, his desire to remain philosophically legible prevented him from fully embodying his own ideas in his writing. One of the reasons Dewey's writing has left so many readers cold is that it fails to participate in the dynamism of his thought.

Paradoxically, Dewey was, in my view, limited less by lack of imagination or facility with language than by the particular stress placed on communication in his philosophy. For Dewey, "mind" and "meaning" are the products of language, rather than essences that precede it. Raw events are not, properly speaking, objects of knowledge — they have no intrinsic meaning until "they are readapted to meet the requirements of conversation; whether it be public discourse or that preliminary discourse termed thinking." It is during this process that "Events turn into objects, things with a meaning" (*Later*, 1:132). The ancient Greeks, Dewey writes, "overlooked the fact that the import of logical and rational essences is the consequence of social interactions" (135). In fact, Dewey contends, the Western assumption of a split between permanent essences and empirical existence stems from philosophy's failure to grasp the way language functions.

> Meanings, under the name of forms and essences, have often been hailed as modes of Being beyond and above spatial and temporal existence, invulnerable to vicissitude. . . . Yet there is a natural bridge that joins the gap between existence and essence; namely communication, language, discourse. Failure to acknowledge the presence and operation of natural interaction in the form of communication creates the gulf between existence and essence and that gap is factitious and gratuitous. (133)[2]

The central role of language as the bridge between facts and meanings, existence and essence in Dewey's philosophy raises the stakes for communication. And, as Sleeper points out, in Dewey's view, "communication is as perilous an undertaking as it is wonderful. Because it is existential, it illustrates the same generic traits as human beings and other things. Because it involves human beings in their immediate uniqueness and attempts to link such individuals in a common undertaking of cross-reference, success is elusive" (123). This double sense of the centrality of communication to meaning and of its capacity to fail underlies Dewey's linguistic conservatism, his reluctance to abandon the established vocabulary of philosophy. In the introduction to the second edition of *Experience and Nature*, Dewey describes the work as an attempt "to establish working connections between old and new subject-matters. We cannot," he insists, "lay hold of the new, we cannot even keep it before our minds, much less understand it, save by the use of ideas and knowledge we already possess" (*Later*, 1:3). Here, Dewey echoes William James's contention in *Pragmatism* that "the most violent revolutions in an individual's beliefs leave most of his old order standing," and that "new truth is always a go-between, a smoother-over of transitions" (*Writings*, 513). Knowing that the work he prescribed for philosophy was contingent upon a successful act of communication, Dewey retained the inherited vocabulary of philosophy, even when this vocabulary pulled against the grain of his thought. Dewey's strategy of "employing, as one must do, a body of old beliefs and ideas to apprehend and understand the new," would allow, he hoped, for a kind of compromise, a "way by which we can be genuinely naturalistic and yet maintain cherished values" (*Later*, 1:4).

Dewey's view of meaning as a product of language rather than an essence that precedes it approaches Wittgenstein's position in *Philosophical Investigations* that "the meaning of a word is its use in the language" (43). While both philosophers challenged the notion of words as stable signposts for pre-existing meanings, however, Wittgenstein took the critique a step farther in his interrogation of the way philosophers have traditionally used language. Given that language has no essence, whatever meaning it has is located within the context of its collective use by a community of speakers. By removing words from the language games in which they are ordinarily used and assigning them limited, specialized, and static meanings, Wittgenstein contends, philosophers generate artificial philosophical problems. In Wittgenstein's terms, then, Dewey, despite his radically anti-essentialist view of language, continued to use language in the way philosophers always have: by removing words from their various contexts in ordinary, public use and assigning them special and limited meanings within their own systems. This way of using language has allowed philosophers, Dewey included, to imagine that words like "experience" may serve as stable foundations for philosophical theories.

Other scholars, most notably Joan Richardson and Richard Poirier, have observed the distance between the view of language implied by Dewey's philosophy and his actual linguistic practice. Expanding on a point previously made by Poirier, Richardson applies this critique to both

Dewey and Charles Sanders Peirce. Alluding to a line by Wallace Stevens, Richardson writes, "their writing is not 'part of the res,' but *about* it. . . . Reading Emerson, William and Henry James, Stevens or Stein against Peirce or Dewey makes abundantly clear the difference between language that is pro-*vocative* and language that is not" (141). To Richardson's list of provocative writers, I would add William Carlos Williams.

One way of understanding the differences and similarities in Dewey and Williams's approaches to language is to see them in relation to a long line of writers struggling against writing, aware of the cultural and ontological burdens carried by syntax and grammar and wanting to circumvent these while retaining the communicative function of the written word. As Richard Poirier and Stanley Cavell have demonstrated, this dilemma is common to Emerson, who "lets his language reveal the pathos of discovering in his own sentence how words resist his efforts to represent what he believes to be the flow or stream of his experience" (Poirier, *Poetry*, 27) and Thoreau, who attempts to "free us and our language from one another, to discover the autonomy of each" (Cavell, *Senses*, 63). It is the same dilemma that prompts Derrida to attempt to evade the limitations of language by inventing and defining a word — différance — which he paradoxically insists "is neither a word nor a concept" (385). The question for writers whose work embodies what Poirier calls "linguistic skepticism," is how to use written language without gesturing toward some prior presence, how to liberate language from the need to authorize itself by pointing to a disembodied thought (or otherworldly "foundation") while at the same time preserving its communicative function. As I have tried to show above, Dewey's belief in the urgency and perilousness of communication led to a conservatism in his use of language that cuts against his own theory of the way language works. Lacking any such coherent theory, Williams embodied the new, anti-essentialist understanding of how words work in the language games of his poems.

Spring and All: Two Language Games

In a 1934 letter to Marianne Moore, responding to her review of his *Collected Poems: 1921–1931*, Williams writes that he is glad she has observed the "inner security" of his poems.

> The inner security though is an overwhelmingly important observation. I am glad to have had you bring it up. . . . It is something which occurred once when I was about twenty, a sudden resignation to existence, a despair — if you wish to call it that, but a despair which made everything a unit and at the same time part of myself. I suppose it might be called a kind of nameless religious experience. . . . Things have no names for me and places have no significance. As a

reward for this anonymity I feel as much a part of things as trees and stones. (*Selected Letters*, 147)

In a profile of Dewey in the *Atlantic Monthly*, Max Eastman describes a remarkably similar "mystical experience" the philosopher had as a young man teaching high school in Oil City, Pennsylvania. Dewey paraphrased this experience to Eastman. "What the hell are you worried about anyway?" Dewey had asked himself, "Everything that's here is here, and you can just lie back on it. I've never had any doubts since then, nor any beliefs. To me faith means not worrying. . . . I claim I've got religion, and that I got it that night in Oil City" (Eastman, 673).

The relationship between self and world at the heart of both Dewey's philosophy and Williams's poems seems to have come independently to both writers as young men, as a kind of epiphany. For both, the moment consisted of the abandonment of traditional notions of religious faith and the acceptance of a new kind of faith in the objects of everyday life. Most importantly, it established for each of them a new ontological starting point in which "subject" and "object" are not discrete categories but continuous with one another, a worldview in which human beings are "as much a part of things as trees and stones." While there is some evidence — notably in the references to Dewey in *The Embodiment of Knowledge* — that Dewey's work influenced Williams, I agree with John Beck's assessment of the connection as essentially one of intellectual confluence, rather than influence. While Beck attributes this confluence to their shared inheritance of "the moral values of the Victorian middle class," my own sense is rather that Dewey and Williams shared a propensity for the interrogation of received ideas, and that for both, a background in modern science contributed to a new conception of human beings' relationship to their environment. In spite of Williams's sometimes antagonistic stance toward science, his writing derives much of its power from the insight that originates with Darwin and finds its echo in the discoveries of modern physics: that human beings are part of the knowledge they produce, that "knowing and acting are intimately related" (Burke, Hester, and Talisse, xii). Williams writes,

> How can we accept Einstein's theory of relativity, affecting our very conception of the heavens about us of which poets write so much, without incorporating its essential fact — the relativity of measurements — into our own category of activity: the poem. Do we think we stand outside the universe? Or that the Church of England does? Relativity applies to everything, like love, it applies to anything in the world. (*Selected Essays*, 238)

Williams understood the essential lesson of modern science to be that we do not "stand outside the universe" but within it, "as much a part of things as trees and stones."

The *Selected Letters of William Carlos Williams* contains two references to John Dewey. The first, in a letter dated January 26, 1933, is a response to Kenneth Burke's observation of Williams's debt to Dewey in *The Embodiment of Knowledge*: "If I could convince myself or have anyone else convince me that I were merely following in the steps of Dewey I'd vomit and quit — at any time. But for the moment I don't believe it — and the poetry is offered not too confidently as proof" (*Letters*, 138). The second reference occurs in a May 5, 1944, letter to Horace Gregory, and refers to Williams's longstanding argument with T. S. Eliot about the significance of the local. "In fact, there can be no general culture unless it is bedded, as he says, in a locality — something I have been saying for a generation: that there is no universal except in the local. I myself took it from Dewey. So it is not new" (*Letters*, 224). Taken together, these two remarks give an indication of Williams's ambivalence about Dewey and his relation to Williams's own work. While Williams adopted some of Dewey's positions, he saw the *form* of his own writing, "the poetry," as "proof" that he was not "merely following in the steps of Dewey" (138).

In the letter to Kenneth Burke quoted above, Williams distinguishes between poetry, or "knowledge in the flesh" and the "body of knowledge called science or philosophy."

> From knowledge possessed by a man springs poetry. From science springs the machine. But from a man partially informed, that is, not yet an artist, springs now science, a detached mass of pseudo-knowledge, now philosophy, frightened acts of half-realization. Poetry, however, is the flower of action and presents a different kind of knowledge from that of S. and P. (*Letters*, 173)

Williams's claim for poetry is that it enacts an "embodiment of knowledge," a claim that explicitly challenges "the value of any 'body of knowledge' that is distinct from its expression; that is to say, any knowledge that is conveyed by words but claims to be different from the words themselves." As Alec Marsh explains, "ordinarily, a fund of knowledge, such as moral rules, scientific 'laws,' or historical 'facts,' is supposed to exist in the absence of any expression of its existence; its just out there, inhuman information that can be lost and rediscovered" (Marsh, 171). The special legitimacy of poetry, in Williams view, is that "its meaning *is* the words" — there is no extra-human beyond or independently existing knowledge to which words refer (171). While Williams's conception of a purely human knowledge, knowledge that is "a mode of participation," is striking in its similarity to Dewey's anti-foundationalism, Williams took the premise a step farther (Dewey, *Middle*, 9:347). As the readings below will show, in *Spring and All*, in particular, Williams enacts his ontological premises on the level of the words themselves, allowing the implications of the pragmatic understanding of the relation between self and world to be felt in his language, to become part of the experience of the poems.

Both Williams and Dewey struggled with the inherited structures of language and understood these structures to be the consequences of an outmoded ontology. Dewey believed the old lexicon could be rehabilitated, the words redefined. Williams, on the other hand, was a utopian about language:

> He felt that if he could himself somehow be primal at the process he could in his own writing bring off instances in which the poetry would live like the thing or the person or the event that occasioned it, would live not as a mock-up but as a manifestation of the actual, would live naturally, organically with the words and the form of the words proceeding out of the actual like a living, growing thing. (Whittemore, 223)

Williams's linguistic radicalism, his desire for poems to be not mere representations but "manifestations of the actual," pulled him in several directions. In the text of *Spring and All* it pulls him in at least two: toward an understanding of words as intensely involved in and allied with things, and toward a competing vision of words as independent of and separate from things. His biographer writes:

> He kept insisting that the art side was first — that poetry was words first and painting was paint first — and though he also wanted the other, wanted the words or the paint to be kissing cousins of the immediacies of perception they were meant to evoke, he could never get around the difficulty that the words or the paint were not the same as the immediacies but approximations. (Whittemore, 181)

Williams's desire for words to be "both free of things and related to them" generates the tension that drives much of his most experimental work (Miller, *Poets*, 308).

To a student familiar with the anthology Williams of simple, direct language and stripped-down imagism, the sheer strangeness of the opening pages of *Spring and All,* with its rapid shifts of address and modality, its out-of-sequence and upside-down chapter headings, its violent, inflated rhetoric, comes as a shock. The selective reprinting of lyric passages such as "By the Road to the Contagious Hospital" and "The Red Wheelbarrow," divorced from their context, has given to most students of American poetry a partial picture of Williams's work, devoid of the tension that animates a text like *Spring and All.* In his attempt to eliminate the boundaries between words and things — or, more accurately, to write from a position from which such boundaries simply do not exist — Williams employs two distinct, seemingly contradictory strategies. The first of these, for which he is popularly known, is the anti-romantic presentation of the particulars in which "one by one objects are defined," an insistence on "clarity, outline of leaf," that is closely aligned with Pound's imagism and appears most clearly in the verse sections of *Spring and All* (*Poems*, 1:183). The second strategy, most vividly demonstrated in the prose passages, is the use of words in a deliberately, even ostentatiously, anti-mimetic way. Here, in a method comparable to Gertrude Stein's, Williams draws the reader's attention not to the objects named or evoked by language, but to the words themselves as objects in nature. "The work will be in the realm of the imagination as plain as the sky is to a fisherman — A very clouded sentence. The word must be put down for itself, not as a symbol of nature but a part" (189). The result of the interplay between these two approaches is a text that enacts Williams's Deweyan conception of embodied knowledge.

In the influential introductory essay to the *Twentieth Century Views* volume on Williams, J. Hillis Miller accounts for the first of these strategies as it applies to the poem "Young Sycamore" from the 1927 volume *Poems*. "The tree," Miller writes, "does not stand for anything, or point to anything beyond itself. Like the red wheelbarrow, or the seatrout and butterfish, or the flowering chicory in other poems by Williams, the young sycamore is itself, means itself. It is an object in space, with its own sharp edges, its own innate particularity" (3). This attention to the particularity of objects as objects, rather than symbols, characterizes much of the recognizably "poetic" sections of *Spring and All*. In the first verse section, marked only by the Roman numeral I and beginning "By the road to the contagious hospital," Williams describes the landscape in decidedly anti-romantic terms:

> All along the road the reddish
> Purplish, forked, upstanding, twiggy
> stuff of bushes and small trees
> with dead, brown leaves under them
> leafless vines —

Though it is also an invocation of spiritual renewal, spring here is primarily a literal phenomenon, touching "now the grass, tomorrow / the stiff curl of wildcarrot leaf" (1:183). In his attention to the details of objects for their own sake — "the red paper box / hinged with cloth / . . . lined inside and out / with imitation leather" — Williams enacts the Deweyan connection between self and world (210). As Miller writes, the "concentration on a single object or group of objects so habitual to Williams confirms his identification with all things. . . . A primordial union of subject and object is the basic presupposition of Williams's poetry" (6).

Williams's second strategy in *Spring and All*, most evident in the "prose" passages, provides a stark contrast to these lyric, imagistic passages.

Among other things, *Spring and All* is a treatise, the announcement of a new, anti-symbolic poetics.

> Crude symbolism is to associate emotions with natural phenomena such as anger with lightning, flowers with love . . .
> Such work is empty. It is very typical of almost all that is done by the writers who fill the pages every month of such a paper as. Everything that I have done in the past — except those parts which may be called excellent — by chance, have that quality about them. (1:188)

In place of "crude symbolism," Williams advocates a new way of writing poems, in which "excellence" will be measured by "an identity with life since [the poems] are as actual, as sappy as the leaf of the tree which never moves from one spot" (189). In these and other statements of the poetics of *Spring and All*, Williams articulates a principle that will become the basis for the objectivist poetics of Zukofsky, Oppen, Olson, and others. Charles Altieri defines the objectivist approach in contrast to the symbolic mode of romanticism.

> On the most general level, there are probably two basic modes of lyric relatedness — symbolist and objectivist styles. The former stress in various ways the mind's power to interpret various events or to use the event to inquire into the nature or grounds of interpretive energies, while objectivist strategies aim to "compose" a distinct perceptual field. . . . Where objectivist poets seek an artifact presenting the modality of things felt or seen as immediate structure of relations, symbolist poets typically strive to see beyond the seeing by rendering in their work a process of meditating upon what the immediate relations in perception reflect. (26)

The objectivist approach amounts to a renunciation of any poetic strategy that relies, implicitly or explicitly, on an understanding of poetry as a means to transcend the material world, what Williams calls "the pageless actual" (Williams, *Imaginations*, 275; qtd. in Beck, 49). Instead, Williams insists, a poem must strive to become "not . . . a symbol of nature but a part," an artifact that, like stones and trees, is experienced rather than interpreted (*Spring and All, Poems*, 1:189). This new poetics, as Altieri observes, must overcome a deeply entrenched romanticism that has long reinforced the split announced by Kant between ideal and empirical, metaphysical and material realms. In place of the romantic poetics of transcendence, Williams advocates a Deweyan poetics, one in which self and world, mind and object exist within a single field. In this paradigm, meaning is not generated through the mind's power to transcend nature but arrived at collectively, through the shifting relations among writer, reader, words, and objects. The poem is not a vehicle for access to any beyond, but rather a "field of action" in which relations generate meaning (*Essays*, 280).

Spring and All begins with a series of prose paragraphs apparently addressed to the reader. After two short paragraphs of what we presume to be the poet's voice, a new voice is introduced, critiquing the work we are about to read:

> What do they mean when they say: "I do not like your poems; you have no faith whatever. You seem neither to have suffered nor, in fact, to have felt anything very deeply. There is nothing appealing in what you say but on the contrary the poems are positively repellent. They are heartless, cruel, they make fun of humanity. What in god's name do you mean? Are you a pagan? Have you no tolerance for human frailty? Rhyme you may perhaps take away but rhythm! why there is none in your work whatever. Is this what you call poetry? It is the very antithesis of poetry. It is antipoetry. It is the annihilation of life upon which you are bent. Poetry used to go hand and hand with life, poetry that interpreted our deepest promptings, poetry that inspired, that led us forward to new discoveries, new depths of tolerance, new heights of exaltation. You moderns! It is the death of poetry that you are accomplishing. No. I cannot understand this work. You have not yet suffered a cruel blow from life. When you have suffered you will write differently"? (*Poems*, 1:177)

Williams introduces this long quotation as if it is merely a generic complaint, a paraphrase of what "they say." The introductory tag and the question mark following the final quotation marks seem to indicate that the quotation is subordinate to the author's own question. The sheer length and rhetorical charge of the quotation, however, create the sense that the critic's voice has taken over. The question of who in the text is speaking to whom is further complicated by the paragraphs that follow.

> I love my fellow creature. Jesus, how I love him: endways, sideways, frontways and all the other ways — but he doesn't exist! Neither does she. I do, in a bastardly sort of way.
>
> To whom then am I addressed? To the imagination. (178)

Here, the authorial "I," undercut by the voice of the critic, reasserts itself as the shaping power of the work. Any sense of the primacy of this voice is undermined again, however, by the concluding paragraph of the introductory section, in which the reader comes to the fore as a full partner in the construction of the text's meaning. "In the imagination, we are from henceforth (so long as you read) locked in a fraternal embrace, the classic caress of author and reader. We are one. Whenever I say 'I' I mean also 'you.' And so together, as one, we shall begin" (178).

The cumulative effect of these shifts of voice and address is a uniquely open text, in which writer, reader, and others move in and out of what Williams calls the "field of action" and Altieri refers to as "a distinct perceptual field." The instability generated by these movements brings the act of meaning-making to the fore, making the poem into a site of activity, a "flower of action" rather than a static artifact.

Together, the two poetic strategies I have outlined above generate a text that participates in both the chaos of experience and the clarity provided by language. In the post-Darwinian paradigm that both Dewey and Williams announce, perceiver and perception, subject and object become part of a single field, such that

The day

All that enters in another person
all grass, all blackbirds flying
all azalea trees in flower
salt winds —

are part of the picture (190). It is a vision of things that at once defies inherited ways of using language and insists upon the kinds of connection that language can forge. Williams both condemns the "falseness" of representation and insists on the power of naming: "the only means we have to give value to life is to recognize it with the imagination and name it" (202). In his essay "William Carlos Williams Between Image and Object," Tom Orange points to the tension in Williams's understanding of the artist's relation to the world, a tension reflected in the two modes of *Spring and All*. "The artist," Williams writes, "is (not) limited to the range of his *immediate* contact with the objective world." As Orange remarks, "The 'is (not)' construction effectively holds subjective perception and objective world *sans rature*: contact both is and is not a limit for artistic creation. He mounts a case for each side of the argument, and at the height of his epistemological and aesthetic abstraction, Williams derails one train of thought only to send us off on another" (143). Williams's dual approach in *Spring and All* reflects the dilemma in which all of us as users of language are caught, both limited by the world we seek to describe and desiring to transcend that limit, wishing simultaneously to communicate our experience to others in recognizable terms and to be true to the idiosyncratic, form-defying nature of that experience. By stressing both the proximity of words and objects and their profound separateness, Williams touches both sides of our often-contradictory relation to language. By alternately foregrounding the perceived object and perceiving subject in the text of *Spring and All*, he stages the performance of their interdependence.

"The *Kinetics* of the Thing": Williams's Improvisations

The analysis above highlights what I have called the two poetic strategies of *Spring and All*. This phrase may serve as a representative of my analysis as a whole in its overstatement of Williams's intent. I doubt very much that Williams "strategized" as much as my description suggests about the placement and effect of the words that comprise *Spring and All*. Rather, as I suggested at the beginning of this chapter, his approach was largely improvisatory. Paul Mariani describes the spontaneity of Williams's method:

> It was only in the heart of actual composition that he knew what was satisfying, even if he could not say really how he had come to make that poem out of the prose surrounding it or why he had made most of the thousand machine-calibrated adjustments necessary to the finished poem. (199)

As Reed Whittemore documents in his biography of Williams, the improvisatory method came from Kandinsky, via Marsden Hartley.

> By 1913 Kandinsky in Germany had done a good many paintings that he called improvisations. Only one of these made it to the Armory Show (Stieglitz bought it) but the improvisations notion got firmly planted in Hartley's head in 1913 or thereabouts when he was in Germany and studied under the man. As a result he took up improvisations himself — written ones — and came back to New York full of the theory of improvisations. In 1918 WCW decided to call his own *Kora in Hell* "improvisations." (123)

Like *Kora in Hell*, *Spring and All* was written during Williams's most experimental period and exemplifies a method Whittemore characterizes as "the insistent juxtaposing of the happened-on" (124). In both the lyric mode of the "poetic" sections and the anti-mimetic mode of the prose passages, Williams allows language to unfold "in spite even of his thought" (*Embodiment*, 7).

Kandinsky's treatise, *Concerning the Spiritual in Art* (to which Williams alludes in the prologue to *Kora*) describes three modes of expression:

1. A direct impression of nature, expressed in purely pictorial form. This I call an "Impression."
2. A largely unconscious, spontaneous expression of inner character, non-material in nature. This I call an "Improvisation."
3. An expression of slowly forged inner feeling, tested and worked over repeatedly and almost pedantically. This I call "Composition." Reason, consciousness, purpose play an overwhelming part. But of calculation nothing appears: only feeling. (77)

As Mike Weaver argues, "Williams, like his friends, worked in all three modes, singly, successively, and at times combining them" (39). By the time he arrives at *Spring and All*, however, the formal deliberations of Composition have been largely abandoned in favor of the energetic spontaneity of Impressions and Improvisations. The movement between these modes highlights the essentially fluid, kinetic quality of each. As its placement between a smiling Gypsy and a tirade against the artificial categorization of knowledge suggests, the red wheelbarrow is not a static emblem of everydayness, but an object glimpsed by a moving eye, recorded by a working mind. In the context in which Williams placed it, the red wheelbarrow is a *moving* picture, a spontaneous impression.

Both Williams's movement away from the inherited forms of English poetry and toward the rhythms of American speech, and his commitment to an organic form particular to each poem and inseparable from its content reflect an underlying and abiding interest in movement, a preference for the energy of present over the polish of the past. It is this sense of energy, this notion of poetry as a "flower of action" that becomes the germ of Charles Olson's 1950 manifesto "Projective Verse" and the basis of the new, process-oriented poetics (*Selected Letters*, 173). Olson's description of Projective Verse may be read as, among other things, a theorization of what it was Williams (and to a limited extent, Pound) had been up to.

> A poem is energy transferred from where the poet got it (he will have some several causations), by way of the poem itself to, all the way over to the reader. Okay. Then the poem must be a high energy-construct and, at all points, an energy discharge. ("Projective," 240)

Olson's prescription for achieving this level of energy — "ONE PERCEPTION MUST IMMEDIATELY AND DIRECTLY LEAD TO A FURTHER PERCEPTION" — captures the essence of Williams's technique in much of *Spring and All*. In section VIII, the poet moves from image to idea, from Greek myth to the industrial age, with a fluidity that defies the kind of new-critical exegesis promoted by Eliot and others. Indeed, rather than disclosing any clear, isolatable meaning, these lines seem simply to evoke the energy of a mind in motion, what Olson calls "the *kinetics* of the thing" (240).

> The sunlight in a
> yellow plaque upon the
> varnished floor
>
> is full of a song
> inflated to
> fifty pounds pressure
>
> at the faucet of
> June that rings
> the triangle of the air

> pulling at the
> anemones in
> Persephone's cow pasture —
>
> When from among
> the steel rocks leaps
> J.P.M. (*Poems*, 1:196)

This movement of the perceiving eye and the working mind among the objects of the world reflects the Deweyan belief in the essentially interactive, interdependent nature of subjects and objects, a belief that dissolves any absolute boundaries between them. Olson remarks on the capacity of poetry based on Williams's model to eliminate the

> lyrical interference of the individual as ego, the "subject" and his soul, that peculiar presumption by which western man has interposed himself between what he is as a creature of nature (with certain instructions to carry out) and those other creations of nature which we may, with no derogation, call objects. ("Projective," 247)

Closely related to the energy at the heart of this poetic is the relation that, following both Dewey and Kandinsky, Williams recognizes between the local and the universal. Kandinsky outlines three principles:

> 1. Every artist, as creator, has to express himself (Element of Personality).
> 2. Every artist, as the child of his epoch, has to express what is particular to this epoch (Element of Style — in an inner sense, composed of the speech of the epoch, and the speech of the nation, as long as the nation exists as such).
> 3. Every artist, as the servant of art, has to express what is particular to all art (Element of the pure and eternal qualities of the art of all men, of all peoples and of all times, which are to be seen in the works of all artists of every nation and of every epoch, and which, as the principle elements of art, know neither time nor space. (in Weaver, 38)

Weaver writes that "from these principles Kandinsky developed a fourth; that the first two elements only needed to be practiced for the third to follow of itself" (38). This final principle is echoed by Dewey in a 1920 essay first published in the *Dial*, entitled "Americanism and Localism." Dewey contends that "the [local] newspaper is the only genuinely popular form of literature we have achieved," chiefly because it "hasn't been ashamed of localism" (*Middle*, 12:14). Pushing the American novelist to "dig down in some locality mentioned in the gazetteer till he strikes something," Dewey concludes that "we are discovering that locality is the only universal. . . . We have been too anxious to get away from home"

(15–16). This is the formulation that in 1944 Williams acknowledges borrowing from Dewey, and that informs his work from the 1920s on.

"Like a Woman at Term"

> When and where, after such forays, did I or could I write? Time meant nothing to me. I might be in the middle of some flu epidemic, the phone ringing day and night, madly, not a moment free. That made no difference. If the fit was on me — if something Stieglitz or Kenneth had said was burning inside me, having bred there overnight demanding outlet — I would be like a woman at term; no matter what else was up, that demand had to be met. (Williams, *Autobiography*, xiii)

Upon surveying the anarchic landscape of Williams's vast output, a first thought: there is relatively little that lends itself to neat analysis or reproduction in anthologies. A second thought: perhaps we are better off regarding this writing not as a collection of discrete literary objects but rather as the product of an interaction between a moving mind and its environment. If, as Dewey insists, we live in the same world as the objects we observe, and are not separated by a wall dividing "subjective" and "objective" experience, then this intimacy applies to our relation to texts as well, and the "woman at term" becomes an appropriate figure for writers of all kinds.

The idea of a writer's output as his or her progeny is certainly not new. Mary Shelley, for one, exploited this figure to great effect in *Frankenstein*. Newer, though, at least as new as our relatively recent absorption of Darwin's lessons, is our sense of what it means to be a living organism. The fundamental shift from a teleological to an evolutionary model of artistic production is one that marks much of the writing we call modern, and it is a particularly useful frame for understanding Williams's work. In this context, it is worth recalling Joan Richardson's characterization of pragmatism as entailing "the realization of thinking as a life form, subject to the same processes of growth and change as all other forms" (1).

What difference does it make to regard the objects of our attention (in this case, literary texts) as forms of life?[3]

Conclusion: The Difference in Not Knowing

The old men have come and gone again this morning from the Country Store, where I am sitting now with cold coffee, watching the first snow of the year, unpredicted by our local meteorologist, turn the air to slow crystal. On the other side of these hours, my daughter has been sleeping, crying, living. My absence for these intervals — a few hours, twice a week, the first separations of her life — will or will not have made a difference to her. To live in the presence of a child whose self is still a wordless flux of feeling pulls one in the direction of dangerous weather. I am the waitress's only customer now, and she leaves me alone, my check — $3.49 — left discretely, upside-down on the corner of the table. This time has cost something. I cannot separate the thinking that writes itself in these pages from the snow, from the waitress, from my daughter, whose future is a story I can't tell.

It may be nothing more than these circumstances that suggest to me the significance of a commitment to — or better, a recognition of — our not knowing the ends of things. But if it is the case that we are part of what we know, that as Dewey says, "experience reaches down into nature," that "it stretches" to include both mind and the world, then our circumstances, where we find ourselves, become a relevant part of the picture (Dewey, *Later*, 1:12–13). In light of such an understanding, one task for literary studies might be to redefine our relation to texts, re-engaging with the aspects of our selves and our language that don't yet know where they're going.

Notes

[1] In a 1904 letter responding to *Studies in Logical Theory*, authored by Dewey and others, Charles Sanders Peirce writes, "You propose to substitute for the Normative Science [of logic] which in my judgment is the greatest need of our age a 'Natural History' of thought or experience" (in Colapietro, 45). Such a "Natural History" of thought, because descriptive rather than normative, could hardly be considered "logic" in Peirce's view.

[2] This passage also serves as an illustration of Dewey's problematic strategy of recuperating philosophical terms. Claiming that "essences" are actually just "meanings" generated by human communication, rather than existing "beyond and above spatial and temporal existence" (*Later*, 1:133), Dewey strips the term of its very definition in the philosophical lexicon.

[3] The poet and essayist Joan Retallack vividly engages the idea of writing as a form of life in her book *The Poethical Wager*, in which she articulates the value of improvisational writing:

> To get lost in the writing can be a way out of officially charted territory. Gertrude Stein says this, enacts this emphatically in her own essays — to act out of one's unprecedented contemporariness is to be able to tolerate, even enjoy, not knowing where one is going even in sustained forays. Stein's essays — in a tradition that continues through John Cage, Rosemarie Waldrop, Leslie Scalapino, and others — literally compose (live) their way through the necessary uncertainty that transforms language according to one's sense of the active principles of change in one's time. This is to enter the event of literature (as writer/reader) most directly as a "form of life" in Wittgenstein's sense. (57)

5: Henry Thoreau, Charles Olson, and the Poetics of Place

> *Shall I not have intelligence with the earth? Am I not partly leaves and vegetable mould myself?*
> — Thoreau, *Walden*, 432

MUCH OF THE THINKING about Thoreau and Charles Olson that follows had its beginning in a failed experiment.[1] Struck by the intensity of attention to place in both *Walden* and Olson's *Maximus Poems*, I decided to visit these writers' respective neighborhoods, hoping, I suppose, to find them at home, still part of the texture of their towns.

It is just under an hour from Gloucester, Massachusetts, to Concord, and most of it is highway. Route 128, expanded in the 1950s to facilitate access to the suburbs outside of Boston, takes you almost the whole way. Gloucester marks the end of this circular highway, on which clockwise is always "north," whatever your compass may tell you. Charles Olson hated the idea of 128, which arrived in Gloucester in 1951 and brought the nation with it.[2]

Much of Gloucester's history — its old houses, its thriving fishing wharves — has been improved or renewed away, a fact from which Olson never recovered. *The Maximus Poems* may be read as, among other things, a tirade against the ongoing demolition of the old and well-made by the new and the cheap. It takes a little hunting to find 28 Fort Square — the building where Olson lived in a second-story apartment during the final years of his life and where he composed many of *The Maximus Poems* — but it still stands, looming above the eastern arc of Fort Point and the harbor. The woman at the tourist information center has never heard of Charles Olson. There are seagulls, still, and fishing boats, and a shelf devoted to local writers in the library, but it is hard to find much else of Olson here, among the cars and the vinyl-sided seaside houses crammed in along the shore.

> But that which matters, that which insists, that which will last,
> that! o my people, where shall you find it, how, where, where shall
>   you listen
>
> when all is become billboards, when, all, even silence, is spray-
>   gunned?

when even our bird, my roofs,
cannot be heard

when even you, when sound itself is neoned in? (*Maximus*, 6)

About forty miles southwest of Gloucester, Concord is a museum town. There's the Emerson House, the Alcott house, the Old Manse, the site of the battle of Lexington and Concord, and the Concord Museum. In this last, you can see Thoreau's furniture from Walden behind a velvet rope.

It is a rare house in Concord that does not bear a plaque celebrating its age. In the museum, an informational video presents images of the sites in their autumnal New England glory, punctuated by passages from *Walden* and Emerson's *Nature* read aloud by an actor with the pitch and diction that the producers of such videos associate with Great Men. It is at least as hard to find Thoreau here, among the coffee mugs emblazoned *simplify, simplify, simplify!* as it is to find Olson in Gloucester.

Both Olson and Thoreau have more or less disappeared from the places in which they invested themselves so thoroughly — Olson into relative obscurity, Thoreau into an obscuring celebrity. My impression of this disappearance stuck with me, haunted my thinking about both writers, and called to mind other conspicuous absences. In particular, I returned to Stanley Cavell's question in *The Senses of Walden*, "Why has America never expressed itself philosophically?" (33).

"Men Have Been There Before Us"

The extant biographies and critical works about Olson contain a few, sparse references to Thoreau, in which the latter is almost always grouped with the other figures of the American Renaissance. Olson's Master's thesis, for example, includes the sentence "the position of Melville with Whitman, Thoreau, Hawthorne, Emerson and Poe is assumed" (Maud, *Olson's*, 26). A few more substantive remarks are to be found in Olson's correspondence with Frances Bolderoff, but here Olson is largely dismissive, expressing his distaste for "a mixing of god with nature," and comparing Thoreau, Payne and Keats unfavorably with Blake and Rimbaud (Maud and Thesen, *Modern*, 343).[3] I had more or less given up on finding evidence of a historical link between Olson and Thoreau when I contacted Peter Anastas,[4] a Gloucester-based writer and Olson scholar who had been Olson's friend. Anastas, who was himself a Thoreau scholar as a graduate student at Tufts between 1964 and 1967, wrote to me that, while working on his thesis, he had discussed Thoreau's *A Week* with Olson.

Our discussions centered around Thoreau's descriptions of the places he and John had traveled through on their two-week water and land excursion, particularly the accuracy of those descriptions and Thoreau's use of available town histories, gazetteers, maps, land surveys and other texts to ground those descriptions in history, geography and topography. During those discussions we both fixed on Thoreau's remark in the Thursday chapter, "Go where we will on the surface of things, men have been there before us." And Olson suggested that in my work on Thoreau I should pay close attention to the way he situated himself in place and time. (Anastas)

For reasons that I hope will become clear, it is fitting that the evidence I'd been searching for that Olson had absorbed Thoreau's radical commitment to place came not from the available scholarship about Olson's reading, but rather from a living person, in Gloucester. "Go where we will on the surface of things, men have been there before us" (*A Week*, 248). I imagine Olson, counting the paces between points on a human-scaled map of his own making, following Thoreau.

Like Thoreau's *Walden* and his unpublished, incomplete Kalendar project, Charles Olson's epic *Maximus Poems* may be read as a record of the writer's engagement with a particular philosophical problem: the relation between subject and environment — what Olson describes as the "stance toward reality" (*Special*, 17). In spite of their very different philosophical commitments, both Thoreau's and Olson's engagements with their surroundings led them to a similar epistemological stance toward writing and the world. For both writers, writing was less an art that culminates in the creation of an object than a mode of interaction with the environment.

In *Walden* and the Kalendar, Thoreau explores the relation between self and environment by keeping a record of his encounters with particular places. It is my contention that the rigor of his approach — the degree to which Thoreau committed himself to a lived investigation of his relationship to place — led him away from the dualism of subject and object implicit in nineteenth-century idealism, toward a new epistemology in which the self is finally inseparable from its surroundings, part of the processes of nature it describes.

In *The Maximus Poems*, Charles Olson builds a modern epic on the foundation of Alfred North Whitehead's conception of reality as process and the interrelatedness of subject and object that this conception entails.[5] Taking from Whitehead the belief that the individual subject "has truck with the totality of things," Olson records his investigations into the history, geography, and economy of Gloucester, Massachusetts (Whitehead, *Process*, 18). Like Walden Pond for Thoreau, Gloucester is Olson's sometime-home, a place to which he comes to live and write. Olson's commitment to presenting self, place, and world as interrelated parts of the same process can be seen in volume two of the *Maximus Poems,* at the end of a poem dated November 21, 1961: "I am making a mappemunde. It is to include my being. / It is called here, at this point and point of time...." (257).

My reading of Thoreau has been shaped by the significant reevaluation of the philosophical significance of Thoreau's work initiated, as H. Daniel Peck observes, by the publication of Staley Cavell's *Senses of Walden* in 1972. Cavell's book "identified *Walden* as an epistemological project that, he said, should be taken absolutely seriously as philosophy, and as a distinctively American contribution toward philosophical thinking" (Peck, "Thoreau's," 85). In the wake of Cavell's reassessment, several philosophical treatments of Thoreau have emerged, including Sharon Cameron's *Writing Nature* and Lawrence Buell's *The Environmental Imagination.* The most significant for my purposes is Peck's *Thoreau's Morning Work.* Through his analysis of *Walden, A Week on the Concord and Merrimack Rivers* and especially Thoreau's Journal, Peck concludes that "Thoreau is a writer who, because of a unique mixture of predilection and ideas, stands on the threshold of an objectivist, process-oriented philosophy, even though he did not fully comprehend the radical implications of his work" (xi). Another significant (and related) shift in Thoreau studies reflected in this chapter is the reevaluation of Thoreau's later work, including the later volumes of the Journal and manuscripts unpublished during his lifetime, undertaken by Bradley Dean, Rochelle Johnson, William Howarth, Laura Dassow Walls, and others. The traditional view of Thoreau's later work as inferior to *Walden* because more "scientific" than "literary," has been challenged by these scholars, who, like Peck, have suggested the "incipient modernism" and/or scientific value of the later work (*Thoreau's,* 74).

Walden

In the chapter entitled "House-Warming," we learn that Thoreau has put off plastering his house at Walden Pond until winter is underway, after he has built his chimney and for some time has been warming his house in the evenings with a fire. Given Thoreau's pride in his house and his economy, this is a curious fact. "Yet I passed some cheerful evenings in that cool and airy apartment, surrounded by the rough brown boards full of knots, and rafters with the bark on high overhead. My house never pleased my eye so much after it was plastered, though I was obliged to confess it was more comfortable" (*A Week,* 515). Thoreau's preference for permeable walls, his reluctance to solidify the boundary between inside and outside space, echoes throughout *Walden.* After completing his house, he writes, "I did not need to go out doors to take the air, for the atmosphere within had lost none of its freshness. It was not so much within doors as behind a door where I sat, even in the rainiest weather" (390). Thoreau welcomes the many animals that penetrate the walls of his house, bringing the outside world in. Of the wasps that come to his house "as to winter quarters," he writes, "I did not trouble myself much to get rid of them; I even felt complimented by their regarding my house as a desirable shelter. They never molested me seriously, though they bedded with me" (513). Thoreau shows equal pleasure in seeing his household effects pass outside the bounds of his cabin when he is cleaning his floor.

> They seemed glad to get out themselves, and as if unwilling to be brought in. I was sometimes tempted to stretch an awning over them and take my seat there. It was worth the while to see the sun shine on these things, and hear the free wind blow on them; so much more interesting most familiar objects look out of doors than in the house. A bird sits on the next bough, life-everlasting grows under the table, and blackberry vines run round its legs; pine cones, chestnut burs, and strawberry leaves are strewn about. (413)

In the context of Thoreau's exploration of his relation to Walden, the preference for a porous boundary between inside and outside space takes on particular significance.[6] In his description of his dream house, "a house without ceiling or plastering . . . a house whose inside is as open and manifest as a bird's nest," Thoreau articulates a model for a new understanding of subjectivity, an interior self understood as continuous with exterior nature (516). This gradually evolving epistemological stance emerged, I believe, from Thoreau's careful attention to his experience of the natural world during the time of his experiment at Walden and after, and was confirmed by his 1860 reading of Darwin's *Origin of Species*. As Thoreau wrote shortly after his first reading of *Origin*, "A man receives only what he is ready to receive, whether physically, or intellectually or morally. . . . We hear and apprehend only what we already half know" (*Journal*, 13:77). Thoreau was, in fact, prepared for Darwin's radical rethinking of the relationship between human beings and their environment by his own experience in the natural world, beginning with his time at Walden.[7]

Thoreau's sense of himself as located *within* his surroundings is most evident in the chapter entitled "Solitude": "I was suddenly sensible of such sweet and beneficent society in Nature, in the very patterning of the drops, and in every sound and sight around my house, an infinite and unaccountable friendliness all at once like an atmosphere sustaining me. . . . Every little pine needle expanded and swelled with sympathy and befriended me" (427). This recognition of the self's deep involvement with its environment prompts many of *Walden's* reversals of received sentiment, including this one about the melancholy quality of rain.

> The gentle rain which waters my beans and keeps me in the house to-day is not drear and melancholy, but good for me too. Though it prevents my hoeing them, it is of far more worth than my hoeing. If it should continue so long as to cause the seeds to rot in the ground and destroy the potatoes in the low lands, it would still be good for the grass on the uplands, and, being good for the grass, it would be good for me. (426–27)

Thoreau's epistemological stance — his vision of himself as inextricably bound to Walden — forces a redefinition of each of the key terms he employs. Here, "good" is wrested from its conventional association with sunny weather and redefined in terms of the environment as a whole. Thoreau engages in a similar redefinition of terms throughout *Walden*; words such as "economy," "value," "neighbor," and "harvest" take on new meaning in Thoreau's lexicon because they are written from a new epistemological position. In the conclusion of *Walden*, Thoreau writes, "in proportion as [a man] simplifies his life, the laws of the universe will appear less complex, and solitude will not be solitude, nor poverty poverty, nor weakness weakness" (580). As Stanley Cavell observes, one of Thoreau's ambitions in *Walden is* "to win back from [economics] possession of our words. This requires replacing them into a reconceived human experience" (*Senses*, 92). An obvious danger of this strategy is that people may simply fail to recognize it, may continue to read Thoreau's words according to their conventional definitions. To read *Walden* this way, without engaging in the "redemption of language" that Thoreau intends, is not so much a failure of interpretation as a failure of engagement, the failure to *be* at Walden, to occupy the new philosophical ground that Thoreau has claimed there (92).

Like the *Maximus Poems*, *Walden* aspires to become, rather than to describe, an environment.[8] Central to the experience of inhabiting the text of *Walden* is a sense of disorientation, a feeling of being lost in the density of language, the new and strange use of words. "Every man has to learn the points of the compass again as often as he awakes, whether from sleep or any abstraction. Not till we are lost, in other words, not till we have lost the world, do we begin to find ourselves, and realize where we are and the infinite extent of our relations" (459). It is telling that part of the reorientation that Thoreau would have us undergo is a movement away from "abstraction" and toward a realization of "relations." In this formulation, "abstraction," like sleep, distances us from our real life, which is bound up in, indeed defined by, "the infinite extent of our relations." Removed or "abstracted" from our actual involvement with our environment, language becomes static, designating subjects and objects, discrete selves and monolithic places, denying both the continual flux of nature and our own participation in that flux. A recognition of our intense relatedness to where we live requires a new way of using words, as both Thoreau and Olson recognize.

One of the ways that the experience of reading *The Maximus Poems* is similar to that of reading *Walden* is the sense of a superfluity of information. Despite Thoreau's undeniable tendency in *Walden* to rely on analogies between the physical and metaphysical — the sentence "what I have learned of the pond is no less true in ethics" in the chapter "The Pond in Winter" (554) may serve here as a representative example — one finds long passages in which no metaphor appears, no metaphysical import is assigned. Johnson, Peck, and Cameron have noted Thoreau's tendency to resist, in the Journal (which they contrast with *Walden* in this regard), modes of figuration that use the natural world as a stepping-stone to the metaphysical (R. Johnson, 198–208; Cameron, 15; Peck, *Thoreau's*, 59–60). As Peck points out, Thoreau's analogical tendency in the Journal is "horizontal," linking phenomena to other phenomena, in contrast to Emerson's impulse to link nature "vertically" to the Ideal, an impulse which Thoreau himself indulges in *Walden* (*Thoreau's*, 59–60). While I agree with this characterization of this difference between the two texts, I find numerous passages in *Walden* in which the writer is apparently recording the details of a natural scene for their own sake, rather than "for the sake of tropes and expressions" as he confesses to doing in "The Bean Field" (451). The list of local species of plants and trees at the beginning of "Baker Farm," for example, seems to have no figurative value.

> I paid many a visit to particular trees, of kinds which are rare in this neighborhood . . . such as the black-birch, of which we have some fine specimens two feet in diameter; its cousin the yellow birch, with its loose golden vest, perfumed like the first; the beech, which has so neat a bole and is so beautifully lichen-painted, perfect in all its details, of which, excepting scattered specimens, I know but one small grove of sizable trees left in the township . . .; the bass; the hornbeam; the *Celtis occidentalis*, or false elm. (483)

Walden is full of passages like this, which in Johnson's view mark "a general shift away from metaphor," a shift that would become pronounced in Thoreau's work after 1850 (191). In place of "tropes and expressions," these passages present factual observations about a place, testifying to its real existence. In this way, Walden clearly meets what Buell articulates as the first criterion for an "environmentally oriented work": "*The nonhuman environment is present not merely as a framing device but as a presence that begins to suggest that human history is implicated in natural history*" (*Environmental*, 7; emphasis in original).

The inclusion of factual, non-symbolic observations of the natural world in *Walden* point to Thoreau's interest in nature *as such* — not as symbol or gateway to the metaphysical — an interest that, after *Walden*, becomes increasingly central to Thoreau's work, and that dominates both the late Journal and the Kalendar project.

The Maximus Poems and *The Maximus Poems IV, V, VI*[9]

In his 1950 essay "Projective Verse," Olson heralds the arrival of a new kind of writing: the open form, or "composition by field." As Rosmarie Waldrop explains, "Projective Verse" "is more than a call for a new kind of versification: it is a manifesto of an attitude toward reality" (467). Olson's notion of the poem as a field of energy, a system of relationships rather than a series of artfully arranged statements, derives from an anti-Aristotelian[10] vision of reality as a continuous "going-on":

> What makes most acts — of living and of writing — unsatisfactory, is that the person and/or the writer satisfy themselves that they can only make a form (what they say or do, or a story, a poem, whatever) by selecting from the full content some face of it, or plane, some part. And at just this point, by just this act, they fall back on the dodges of discourse, and immediately they lose me, I am no longer engaged, this is not what I know is the going-on. . . . [I]t comes out a demonstration, a separating out, an act of classification, and so, a stopping, and all I know is, it is not there, it has turned false. ("Human," 157)

A corollary to this vision of reality as process is a recognition of the artificiality of the subject-object distinction. Olson praises objectivism for "getting rid of the lyrical interference of the individual as ego, of the 'subject' and his soul, that particular presumption by which western man has interposed himself between what he is as a creature of nature . . . and those other creations of nature which we may, with no derogation, call objects" ("Projective," 247). Olson' s anti-categorical conception of reality also involves a fierce particularism, a defense of the "self-existence" of things. "This is what we are confronted by," he writes, "not the thing's 'class,' any hierarchy, or quantity or quality, but the thing itself, and its *relevance* to ourselves who are the experience of it" ("Human," 158).

The implications for poetics of such a radical shift in epistemological ground are dramatic, and Olson's principle project in *The Maximus Poems* is to discover them. After Descartes, Olson writes in "A Later Note on Letter #15" of *The Maximus Poems*,

> In English the poetics became meubles — furniture . . .
>
> until Whitehead, who cleared out the gunk
> by getting the universe in (as against man alone
>
> & *that* concept of history . . .
>   The poetics of such a situation
>
> are yet to be found out (*Maximus*, 249)

The Maximus Poems enacts Olson's theory of composition by field, staging in language the relationships between the town's founders and its contemporary inhabitants, its changing topography and economy, its spiritual and social life. In *The Special View of History*, Olson articulates the stance that he adopts in *The Maximus Poems*: "One will get nowhere in catching the traffic of the human universe," he writes, "if one does not recognize that a man is at once subject and object, is at once and always going in two directions" (33). Following Whitehead's conception that "there are no brute, self-contained matters of fact, capable of being understood apart from interpretation as an element in a system" (Whitehead, *Process*, 18), Olson imagines a new poetics that engages simultaneously the personal and the historical, in which the self and place are inextricable. "The skin itself," Olson writes in "Human Universe," "the meeting edge of man and external reality, is where all that matters does happen, that man and external reality are so involved with one another that, for man's purposes, they had better be taken as one" (161). Like Thoreau, Olson conceives of the self as continuous with its environment, part of the process of history.

The Gloucester of *The Maximus Poems* is not merely a geographical location but the site of a continual engagement between Maximus, the poet's persona, and his environment, an engagement that, for the poet, constitutes reality. Olson continually locates Maximus within the scenes of the poems, reminding the reader of the precise location from which the words are written.

>   Dogtown to the right the ocean
> to the left
>   opens out the light   the river flowing
> at my feet
>   Gloucester to my back
>
>   the light hangs
>   from the wheel of heaven
>
>   the great Ocean
>   in balance. (296)

Although this description contains no physical action, it is dominated by a sense of continual process: the river is flowing, the light opening out and hanging. Each of the elements of Gloucester geography exists in precise relation to the body of the speaker, which becomes another element in the constellation. Like Thoreau, Olson rediscovers the points of the compass: left and right hands, feet and back become reference points, measuring direction in human terms.

Similarly, distances in *The Maximus Poems* are measured by counting off steps. "Letter, May 2, 1959" begins by recording the number of paces between landmarks, both contemporary and historical:

> 125 paces Grove Street
> fr E end of Oak Grove cemetery
> to major turn NW of
> road
>
> this line goes finally straight
> fr Wallis property direct
> to White (as of 1707/8)

Toward the bottom of the page, the words begin to fall at odd angles, no longer simply noting distances but topographically representing the relationships between places, so that the poem becomes not merely a record but a map, a means of locating oneself in both space and time (150).

In *The Special View of History,* Olson writes, "Man is forever estranged to the degree that his stance toward reality disengages him from the familiar" (29). *The Maximus Poems* may be read as an attempt to repair this estrangement, to re-engage with that which is most familiar. To this end, Olson presents Gloucester as a city of human dimensions, composed of human stories. Olson juxtaposes Maximus's present with the narratives of Gloucester fishermen and stories of Cape Ann's original settlers. The poems do not confine themselves to a single historical moment, but rather move fluidly between past and present, embracing Whitehead's vision of reality as process. In "Maximus, to Gloucester," Olson juxtaposes Maximus, in the present, who

> sit[s]
> in a rented house
> on Fort Point,
> the Cape Ann Fisheries
>
> out one window,
> Stage Head looking me
> out of the other . . .

with "those men /who saw [Gloucester] / first." In this vision, the present is continuous with the past, as Olson/Maximus is with the original Gloucester settlers. Olson ends the poem by observing that

> the snow flew
> where gulls now paper
> the skies
>
> where fishing continues
> and my heart lies. (112)

Like Thoreau, Olson does not present (or represent) a place so much as build an environment for the reader temporarily to inhabit. In *A New Theory for American Poetry,* Angus Fletcher describes the way "environmental sensitivity" creates a new genre of poetry:

> This I am calling the *environment-poem*, a genre where the poet neither writes *about* the surrounding world, thematizing it, nor analytically represents that world, but actually shapes the poem to be an Emersonian or esemplastic circle. . . . [T]hese poems aspire to surround the reader, such that to read them is to have an experience much like suddenly recognizing that one has an environment, instead of not perceiving the surround at all. (Fletcher, 9)

Although Fletcher does not discuss Olson, his model of the environment-poem applies particularly well to Olson's ambition to construct within language "an actual earth of value" (*Maximus*, 584). Like Thoreau in *Walden*, Olson includes in *The Maximus Poems* an enormous amount of information with no analogical or metaphorical function. Conventional figuration (although Olson does sometimes use it) runs counter to his purpose:

> All that comparison ever does is set up a series of *reference* points: to compare is to take one thing and try to understand it by marking its similarities to or differences from another thing. Right here is the trouble, that each thing is not so much like or different from another thing (these likenesses and differences are apparent) but that such an analysis accomplishes only a *description*, does not come to grips with what really matters: that a thing, any thing, impinges on us by a more important fact, its self-existence, without reference to any other thing, in short, the very character of it which calls our attention to it, which wants us to know more about it, its particularity. ("Human," 157–58)

Like Thoreau, Olson insists on the particularity of his experience of place, using words not to confer symbolic or metaphoric significance on the details of local life, but simply to recognize them, to acknowledge their "self-existence" and the fact of their involvement in his own life. For Olson, a word properly used is characterized by an irreducible specificity, it is "meant to mean not a single thing the least more than / what it does mean" (*Maximus*, 15). In "Letter 3" of *The Maximus Poems,* Olson celebrates a particular local flower, tansy, as it blooms in a specific time and place:

> Did you know, she sd., growing up there
> how rare it was? And it turned out later she meant exactly the long
>   field

                drops down from Ravenswood where the land abrupts,
                this side of Fresh Water Cove, and throws out
                that wonder of my childhood, the descending green does run
                so,
                by the beach
                            where they held the muster Labor Day, and the engine teams
                            threw such arcs of water
                                                    runs with summer with
                tansy. (14)

Here, past and present collide in the seasonal phenomenon of the blooming of tansy. Again, Olson locates the details of the poem within an *active* field of space and time — the land itself "drops," "abrupts," "throws out," and "runs" — placing each element in precise geographical and temporal relation to the others. Olson's placement of himself within this field, and thus within the context of seasonal change, speaks to the centrality of the relation of self to world that links his work to Thoreau's in general, and to the project that dominated Thoreau's last years in particular.

Thoreau's Kalendar

In the final years of their lives, both Olson and Thoreau were immersed in work on large-scale, ambitious projects that were both deeply rooted in the particulars of place and invested in the idea of the eternal. Between 1860 and his death in 1862, Thoreau attempted to consolidate his observations of seasonal change over the years in a variety of lists and charts comprising a project he sometimes referred to as his "Kalendar."[11] Some of the charts record individual seasonal phenomena, such as the flowering of trees, or autumn leaf fall (see fig. 5.1). On these charts, the individual species are listed in a column on the left hand side of the page, with the years (1852–1860) listed in a row along the top. The date of a tree's first flowering is noted in the square corresponding to each year. Other charts depict "general phenomena" for individual months, with the phenomena listed in a column on the left side of the page, and the years along the top (see fig. 5.2). In the spaces of the grid created by these two axes, Thoreau copied observations from the Journal. These monthly charts are of particular interest because they demonstrate Thoreau's desire to create a record, not of the seasons themselves, but of his own experience of the seasons, to place his life in the context of seasonal change. While the monthly charts of general phenomena form only one portion of this enormous incomplete project,[12] I believe they demonstrate Thoreau's use of writing as a way of re-engaging the familiar during these final years.

As Peck argues, the Kalendar project may be understood as the culmination of Thoreau's desire, articulated in the Journal beginning in the

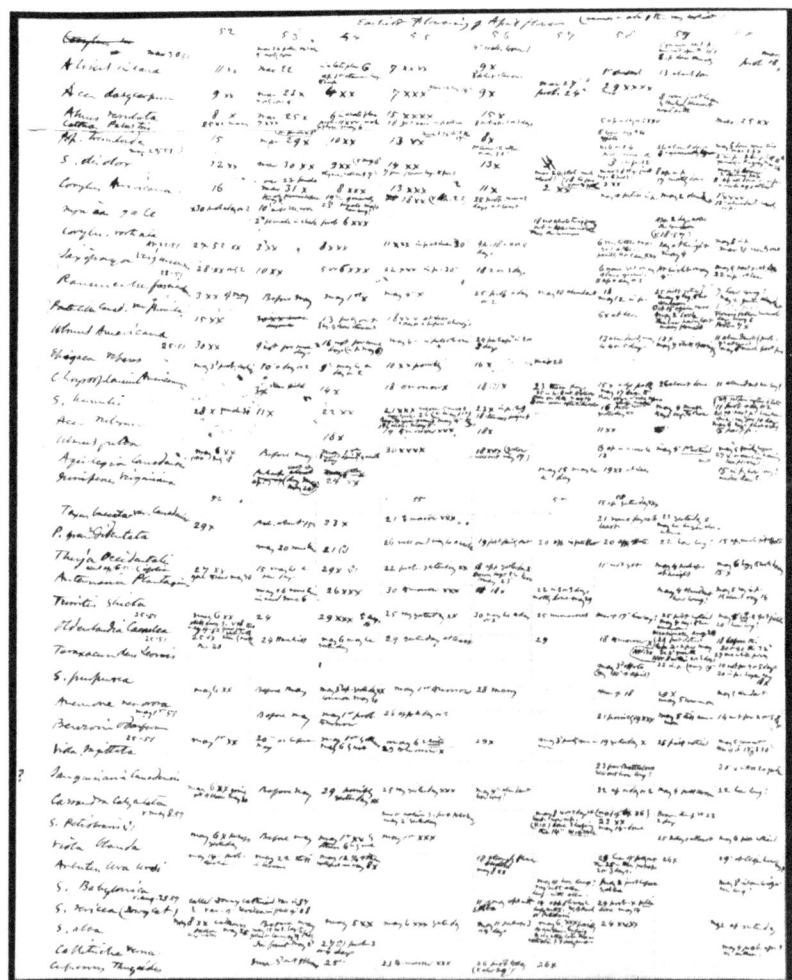

Fig. 5.1. Earliest Flowering of April Flowers, *from Henry David Thoreau, Nature notes, charts and tables: autograph manuscript, 1851–1860. The Pierpont Morgan Library, New York. MA 610, C8. Photograph by Joseph Zehavi, 2004.*

early 1850s, for a comprehensive view of nature. "The Kalendar," Peck notes, "is the most literal expression of [this desire], as well as (from our point of view), the most vivid testimony to the impossibility of its fulfillment" (*Thoreau's*, 108). Most of the squares of Thoreau's grids remain blank — and even if they had been filled, Peck argues, Thoreau, who continually revised his categories of phenomena, redrawing seasonal boundaries to reflect his experience of nature, would have had to create ever-finer and more specific categories under which to file his observations. It was,

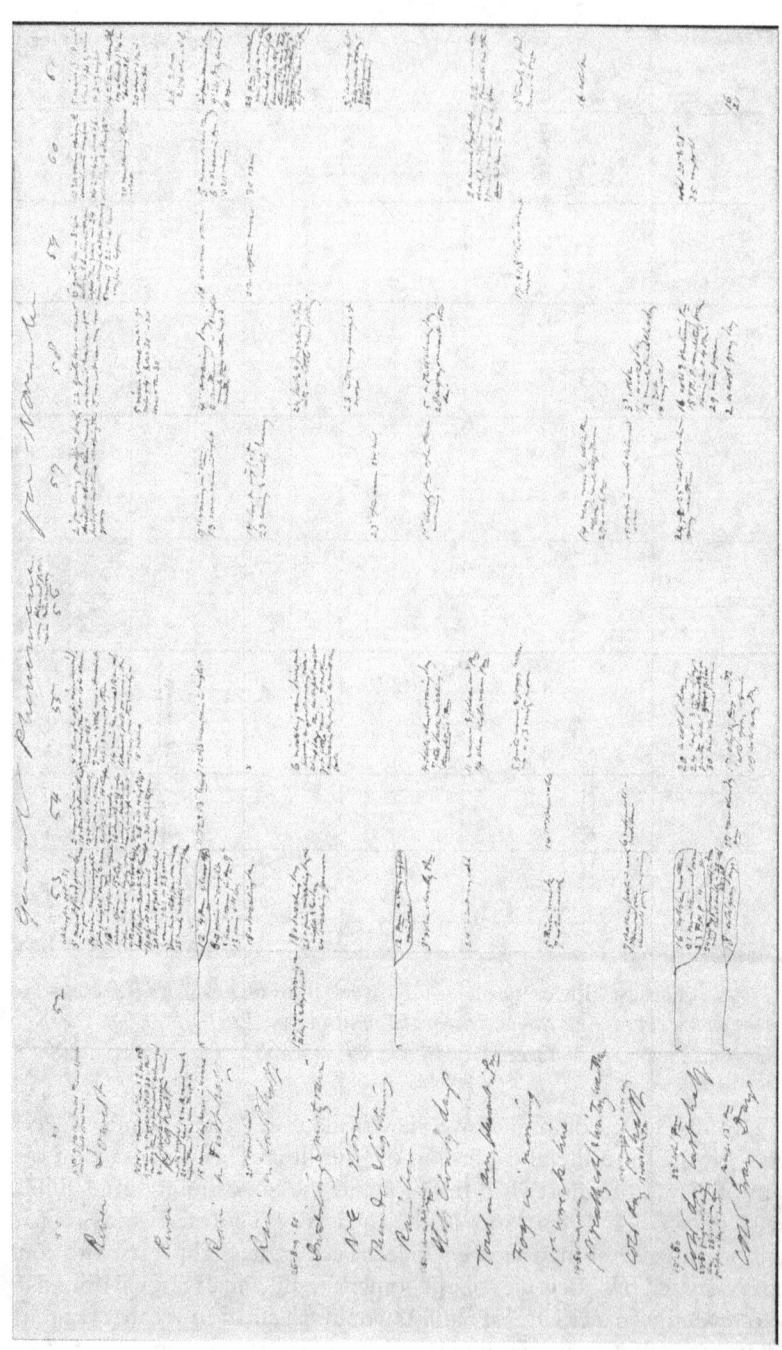

Fig. 5.2. General Phenomena for November, from Henry David Thoreau, *Nature notes, charts and tables: autograph manuscript, 1851–1860*. The Pierpont Morgan Library, New York. MA 610. Photograph by Graham Haber, 2010.

in its very conception, an impossible project, the unrealizable dream of total vision.[13]

Thoreau's desire for a comprehensive view, a complete understanding of the natural world, mitigates, in Peck's view, against the apparent openness and provisional quality of the Journal. For while the method of the Journal in the later years suggests that Thoreau stood "on the threshold of an objectivist, process-oriented philosophy" (*Thoreau's*, 74), the totalizing ambition reflected in the Kalendar project suggests the extent to which he remained bound to the idealizing tendencies of the nineteenth century. Peck notes that

> The unstated assumption of the Journal is that at some future point, a point always receding before the endless work of observation, the picture will be complete. At that moment, the master perceiver will collect his views and integrate them into a coherent vision, which would be nothing less than the world as seen in the mind of God. (75)

While the totalizing ambition of the project seems clear, Thoreau's inclusion of highly subjective categories of observation speaks to a different, and I believe more central function of these charts — that of placing himself within the natural world. These subjective categories — "First shadows noticed," "Washing day," "Sleep with window open" in May, for instance, and "Seek sheltered places," and "End of sauntering walks" in November — are remarkable for their idiosyncrasy, their emphasis on the particulars of Thoreau's experience of nature, rather than on the "objective" observation of nature itself. Peck usefully observes that for Thoreau a "phenomenon" (a word used frequently in the Journal) is "like Whitehead's event,[14] an entity that bridges the gap between subject and object" (*Thoreau's*, 68). Peck notes that "Thoreau's category is a perceptual construct that exists in and of the world, and in this sense dramatizes the relation between self and world" (107). Indeed, tracking his relation to his environment seems to me Thoreau's overriding purpose in the Kalendar project. While an 1851 Journal entry notes Thoreau's desire to attain "a true and absolute account of things — of the evening and the morning and all the phenomena between them" (November 10, 1851; 9:103–4; in Peck, *Thoreau's*, 108), the method of the charts of general phenomena suggests that, at the end of his life, Thoreau was more invested in the interaction between self and world than in an absolute or God-like vision of the world.

One may read in Thoreau's various schemes for organizing the observations recorded in his journal either the attempt to arrive at ever-more comprehensive modes of picturing the world, or a realization that no single mode would ever be complete. Differences between the charts of

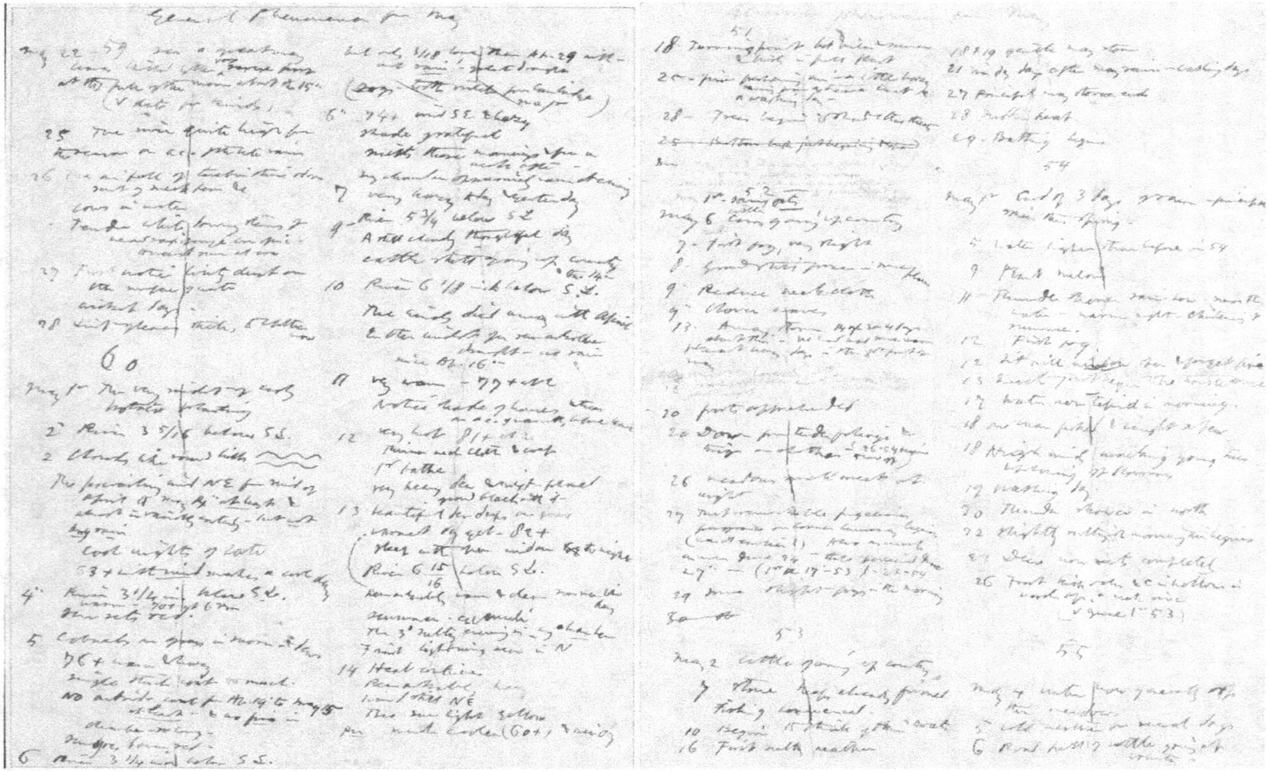

Fig. 5.3. General Phenomena for May, from Henry David Thoreau, Nature notes, charts and tables: autograph manuscript, 1851–1860. The Pierpont Morgan Library, New York. MA 610. Photograph by Graham Haber, 2010.

specific phenomena and the monthly charts of general phenomena suggest that Thoreau may have had different purposes for these two methods of organizing his observations. The charts for the flowering of trees in spring and for leaf fall in autumn are far more comprehensive and exact in their presentation than the monthly charts. They contain no excess information or qualitative observation, simply the names of the species, listed on the left margin, and the dates of the flowering or leaf fall by year. The creation of the monthly charts, by contrast, was a multi-stage and highly subjective process. Thoreau began by copying from his journal relevant observations for each month in list form. The May charts, for example, are accompanied by several pages of observations, listed by date under headings for each year (see fig. 5.3). These lists thus present the relevant material in chronological order, irrespective of the phenomena observed. Though much of this material is difficult to decipher, it appears, based on the sheer volume of the lists, that there is far more information listed here than is ultimately included in the charts. The selection involved in the creation of the charts suggests that Thoreau was less interested in comprehensiveness than he was in tracking certain key phenomena — probably those that captured, for him, the essence of the month. Once Thoreau transferred the selected material to the charts, the organization became more complex, since the charts can be read either down or across, by phenomena or by year.

Thoreau's interest in different methods of displaying information was likely a result of his exposure to Alexander von Humboldt, who, as Laura Dassow Walls has shown, profoundly influenced Thoreau's orientation toward the natural world after 1850. Walls notes a probable connection between "the fashion of tabulating data, as one outgrowth of Humboldtian science, and the 650 separate tables and charts of data which Thoreau assembled in the last years of his life" (81). Even more significant, however, is Thoreau's debt to Humboldt for his emerging understanding of the self and its relation to the natural world. Humboldt's insistence on the mutuality and interconnectedness of man and nature confirms Thoreau's own emerging epistemology, and, as Walls persuasively argues, sparks his resolution "to know the world not through the abstraction of dry and barren systems, but through involvement with it" (126). Indeed, Humboldt's approach to scientific inquiry, which Walls terms "empirical holism," may be seen as a model for the "epistemology of contact" that emerges from the late Journal and the Kalendar (126).

In addition to recontextualizing observations by placing them in a new spatial and temporal organization, the charts form a unique index to the Journal. The chart's cursory observations — often simply a date, or one or two words — correspond to longer, more detailed descriptions in the Journal, presented there in their original context, within the linear flow of time. Thoreau understood and valued this aspect of the Journal, and in 1850 ceased his earlier practice of cutting out passages to use in essays and lectures. On January 27, 1852, he writes,

> I do not know but thoughts written down thus in a journal might be printed in the same form with greater advantage than if the related ones were brought together into separate essays. They are now allied to life, and are seen by the reader not to be far-fetched. It is more simple, less artful. (3:239)

The charts of natural phenomena, I contend, are not meant to replace the Journal, but to complement it, to provide an alternate view of the information Thoreau has amassed, as well as an alternate view of time. In this regard, the charts function like hypertexts — each filled-in square "linking" to the original journal passage. As Peck has observed, the Kalendar, like *Walden*, explores the notion of experience as cyclical (and thus timeless) rather than linear (and temporal). In contrast with *A Week*, which, Peck argues, deliberately engages with loss and the passage of time, *Walden* and the late Journal "reveal an increasingly sure sense of nature's special and temporal coherence" (*Thoreau's*, 47). While I agree that the Journal demonstrates Thoreau's growing interest in the notion of cyclical experience, I see the use of multiple kinds of records — both the Journal in its commitment to linear chronology and the charts with their focus on the recurrence of phenomena over time — as indicative of his abiding interest in both aspects of temporal unfolding. The charts and the Journal, taken together, provide a shifting, dynamic picture of time, experienced both as a cycle and as a stream.

At the center of this inquiry into the nature of time is Thoreau's attempt to place himself within a calendar of seasonal change. As Sharon Cameron has demonstrated in *Writing Nature*, Thoreau's Journal is principally concerned with the relation between the human and the natural. Underlying the project of the Journal, Cameron contends, is Thoreau's recognition of "the ways in which he is separate from the nature that he loves" (46). While I disagree with Cameron's claim that Thoreau believes he can "abandon the human" and "make himself into the alienness [nature] he was forced to confront," I agree that Thoreau was motivated by a sense of alienation from, as well as a sense of connection to, the natural world (48). "Though the frost is nearly out of the ground the winter has not broken up in me," he observes in March of 1852; "It is a backward season with me. Perhaps we grow older & older till we no longer sympathize with the revolution of the seasons — & our winters never break up" (3:363). The prospect of such a progressive loss of "sympathy" with the natural world would have been a terrible one for Thoreau, one he sought to guard against by writing himself *into* the "the revolution of the seasons." By charting the signs of seasonal change in himself — the exact date, each year, that he started making fires in the fall, and ceased making them in the spring, or the night in June that he began to "leave off flannel" — Thoreau sought to place these human events in the context of the natural.

One of the phenomena listed on the chart for the month of November is "Seek sheltered places." Like the headings that surround it — "Wear gloves," "Too cold to paddle" and "End of sauntering walks," this category demonstrates Thoreau's principle interest in these charts — the tracking of his own experience of and in the natural world. Across from this heading, under the year 1857, Thoreau has noted a date, 18, and written two words: "rejoice in." Tracing the notation back to the journal entry for November 18, 1857, one finds the following passage:

> The sunlight is a peculiarly thin and clear yellow, falling on the pale-brown bleaching herbage of the fields at this season. There is no redness in it. This is November sunlight. Much cold, slate-colored cloud, bare twigs seen gleaming toward the light like gossamer, pure green of pines whose old leaves have fallen, reddish or yellowish brown oak leaves rustling on the hillsides, very pale brown, bleaching, almost hoary fine grass or hay in the fields, akin to the frost which has killed it, and flakes of clear yellow sunlight falling on it here and there, — such is November.
>
> The fine grass killed by the frost, withered and bleached till it is almost silvery, has clothed the fields for a long time.
>
> Now, as in the spring, we rejoice in sheltered and sunny places. (10:186)

Here, the two-word notation expands into a lyrical description of a November day, moving from the general, recurring phenomenon marked on the chart to the unique experience of a particular day recorded in the Journal. The description emphasizes the way November combines elements of both winter and summer. Sunlight is accompanied by slate-colored clouds; the grass and the frost are, for this brief season, parts of the same phenomenon. Thoreau ends the description by making explicit the human presence in this landscape, noting that the arrival of the cold weather has the effect of making "sheltered and sunny places" a cause for rejoicing. That Thoreau has chosen this last phenomenon — human rejoicing — as a category for the November chart speaks to the function of the chart as a method of placing the human back into the natural context. The intent is less to document an interaction between man and nature, the inner and the outer experience, than to show that the human exists within, and not separate from, that natural world, that human rejoicing is as much a November phenomenon as frost.

The Maximus Poems: Volume Three

In his final years, Olson devoted himself to the last volume of the *Maximus Poems*, which remained incomplete, or at least uncollected, at the time of his death in 1970. George Butterick, who, along with Charles Boer, undertook the Herculean task of editing the final volume, describes the state of the "manuscript" Olson left behind:

> Some of the poems in the volume under consideration were written on check stubs and recopied, on blank checkbooks or envelopes torn open and spread flat, or on a card from a deaf-mute portraying the hand alphabet of the deaf, undoubtedly handed to him in the street — the only things he might have had in his pocket at the time. In another case, a partially opened letter lay, presumably, at hand on the kitchen or bedside table. He began a poem (III, 190) on the back of the envelope and continued onto the back of the protruding letter, in which position it was found preserved among the papers, like a figure from Pompeii. (1)

The final volume of *The Maximus Poems* combines the focus on local geography and history in the original *Maximus Poems* with the interest in mythology developed in *Maximus IV, V, VI*. In these late poems, Olson/Maximus (it is increasingly difficult to separate the "persona" of these poems from the person of Charles Olson) moves easily between present day Gloucester, the Gloucester of the 1600s, and Gloucester as the stage for a universal, mythological drama.

In tracing Olson's debt to Whitehead's objectivism, Robert von Hallberg notes that in Olson's poetics "the making is more valuable than what is made, because only by activity is man fully human.... This kinetic aesthetic grows out of the metaphysical principle that reality is a process one approaches by enactment" ("Olson," 92). In Whitehead's philosophy, action replaces Aristotle's central notion of substance (93). According to Whitehead, this key substitution "means that the essence of being is to be implicated in causal action on other beings" (*Adventures*, 120). Olson derives his poetics, in part, from this essential principle: being, properly defined, is action.

If what von Hallberg calls the "kinetic aesthetic" applies to the *Maximus Poems* as a whole, it reaches its zenith in volume three, in which the question of a final product, an actual text to be assembled, is continually deferred, until at last, after Olson's death, the task falls to Butterick and Boer. The incomplete volume is, in this way, much like Thoreau's late notes on nature, the integration of which was similarly deferred to "a point always receding before the endless work of observation" (Peck, *Thoreau's*, 75). The third volume of the *Maximus Poems* contains poems written in spiral formation, poems containing diagrams, poems with lines crossing one another on the page. In these poems, the act of writing — writing while walking, writing while eating at a local diner, writing while being in the world — so entirely eclipses writing as means to a textual end that the final text, beautifully and responsibly edited by Butterick and Boer, and revised by Butterick for the single volume, complete *Maximus Poems* in 1983, cannot but feel a bit hollow, drained of the spontaneity that was its life. Even more than its predecessors, the third volume is a tracing of the poem-as-act, a record of the poet's engagement with space and time. Don Byrd writes,

> Of course, we have no way to know what Olson would have done had the time arrived for him to edit the volume himself. His intention is always to bring into existence a new mind, and he has nothing but the present mind to guide him. The engagement with the poem, therefore, inevitably takes place in a blind-spot. The poem is a place of action rather than expression or rhetoric. . . . For Olson, thinking and writing are one. To construct a book is retrospective work, a sorting through of the work done, to see what has accrued. (165)

Like Thoreau, Olson was principally occupied, in his late writings, in charting his place within his environment. The poem "The winter the Gen. Starks was stuck," written on December 21, 1965 — the winter solstice — dramatizes the act of writing as a means of "tak[ing] the marks and bearings" of one's being in the world.

>   the exercise of being with
> a continent or a ocean face or back as will will tell
> me which way to look as the year turns to-day,
> the Sun now in the Southern hemisphere half way
> to that other Pole and life again here in the North saved
> by the tilting of the ecliptic once more in its favor . . .
>
> I turn either left or right or east or west or now
> that there's promise again and the Sun comes back once more
> toward Equator and I can confidently expect the year (481)

In the poems written in the winter of 1965–66, Olson observes the horizon, the tides, the length of evenings and the latitude and longitude of his own position. Like Thoreau's, Olson's observations track the impact of the environment on his person, or, more precisely, mark the point at which person and environment become inseparable. The late poems also seem particularly invested in accuracy of observation for its own sake. On Sunday, January 16, 1966, Olson notes:

> Glow dying by 5:20
>   PM
> 40 minutes after sunset

> light in house now almost
> reduced so I cannot see
> to write
>
> Evening then is
> at the most 40 minutes long. (485)

Olson's commitment to the "kinetic aesthetic" emerges in these poems, as well, as Olson/Maximus repeatedly refers to the act of writing in the present tense:

> In the twilight snow for less than a minute
> less time than I proposed to write
> that the green of the whiting dragger the <u>Santa Lucia</u>
> was, two minutes ago, as worn & exact as the color
> of that Saint's eyes as they lie as, three minutes ago
> the color of the leaden sky too . . . (488)

Olson's insistence on the present, on reality as process, and on the kinetic, did not preclude, and indeed was linked to, an interest in eternity. Like Thoreau, Olson saw the temporal as intersecting with the eternal. As von Hallberg explains, Olson's concept of eternity is derived from Whitehead. "According to [Whitehead's] interpretation of the theory of relativity, no two actual entities [or 'events'] are unrelated; each actual entity 'feels' every other actual entity" ("Olson," 89). In this formulation, past events are connected to present ones, and in this way achieve a kind of dynamic immortality. Thus, late twentieth-century Gloucester is continually overlayed with the Gloucester of the earliest settlers, and both historical moments are juxtaposed with the eternal time of Norse, Hindu, and Greek mythology.

In "Maximus, in Gloucester Sunday, LXV" Olson returns to the figures of Osmund Dutch and John Gallop, mariners active in Gloucester harbor "at a probable date earlier / than 1630," who were first introduced in volume one, along with Abraham Robinson, another early Gloucester fisherman. Olson cites the historical record, a letter concerning the payment of their wages: "[T]heir wages / asked that they be paid to the Dorchester / Co. July 1632." Moving seamlessly from the founding of Gloucester as a fishing community to his own life, Olson writes, "Now date August 1965 returning / Gloucester from as far out in the world as my own / wages draw me" (449). Like the mariners, Olson's wages drew him away from Gloucester; Butterick notes that the poem was written "upon the poet's return from teaching the previous Spring at Buffalo and reading at the Festival of the Two Worlds in Spoleto, Italy and at the Berkeley Poetry Conference that summer" (584). Like Thoreau, Olson saw in the recurrence of phenomena over time — in this case the departure and return of Gloucester laborers — the intersection of the temporal and the eternal. Describing this intersection, Don Byrd writes, "We are, despite our stratagems, finite, and, if the world is not infinite, it is larger than we. In the *Maximus* these two forms play against one another, alternately reinforcing and frustrating one another" (180).

Though Olson was, like Thoreau, invested in the idea of the eternal, it is important to note that his was an earth-bound eternity: "I believe in God / as fully physical," he writes in *Maximus* volume three, a statement that resonates with Thoreau's question in *A Week:* "May we not *see* God? Are we to be put off and amused in this life, as it were with a mere allegory? Is not nature, rightly read, that of which she is commonly taken to be a symbol merely?" (310). As Byrd observes, like Thoreau, "Maximus stakes his paradise on perhaps the most fundamental intuition of Indo-European culture: that the absolute is to be known only through the endless process of resurrection and death which is the turning of the seasons" (186).

The intersection of the finite and the infinite in Olson and Thoreau's work is perhaps best illustrated by the status of their late manuscripts. For both writers, writing became a way of tracking their own being in the world, a way of engaging more closely, more consciously, with their respective environments. Such a practice, committed as it is to "onwardness" (to adopt a word of Emerson's), can have no conclusion other than the end imposed by death. As Don Byrd writes, "The third volume provides a conclusion to the *Maximus* only in the sense that it is an end. The process of the poem and the process of the life had so completely merged that it is difficult to imagine any other ending. Death is, after all, final but seldom conclusive" (166). While this organic function is present in both Olson and Thoreau's earlier writing, in their final projects it becomes so dominant that other basic literary functions — that of communication with a (real or imagined) readership, for example — seem to have become less important. Thoreau's intent for his charts and lists was unclear. In the introduction to his edition of Thoreau's late manuscript *Wild Fruits,* Bradley Dean speculates, "Although his lists and charts have never been studied carefully, they are almost certainly the foundation for a large project. . . . Apparently, [Thoreau] intended to write a comprehensive history of the natural phenomena that took place in his hometown each year" (xi). Olson, we know, did intend publication of the third volume of the *Maximus Poems,* and specified to its editors which poems should appear first and last in the sequence. While the conventional, communicative function of writing reflected in these intentions remained active for both writers, the manuscripts themselves suggest that this function had become secondary to the function of engaging with the environment. Both the manuscripts of Olson's late poems and Thoreau's late notes and charts speak to the primacy of process over product: both sets of documents contain many pages that were very hastily written, on whatever scraps of paper lay at hand, with evidently little thought given to legibility. The appearance of the manuscripts suggests that for both writers the act of writing itself, an act from which observation cannot be separated, was more important than the production of a stable text, a task that, in both cases, was infinitely deferred.

For Olson as for Thoreau, the act of writing became, in his final years, inseparable from the act of living. This new orientation poses a significant challenge to literary scholarship. Inhabiting *The Maximus Poems*, or the world of Thoreau's late notes and charts, entails abandoning traditional concepts of aesthetic integrity and completeness. It also involves departing from traditional strategies of critical reading. As Rosmarie Waldrop writes, *The Maximus Poems* is an open structure:

> Even the balance of forces which tells writer and reader that a poem is finished is temporary. On contact with, in the neighborhood of, another poem, the balance proves to have vectors toward yet further perceptions. The occasions form a nexus of occasions, an event. The single poems form a cycle, *The Maximus Poems,* which becomes the one absorbing, total enterprise which goes on forever until an outside force, death, puts a stop to it. (470)

The Maximus Poems resists close reading. Although I have tried, in the passages above, to look closely at the operations at work in the language of individual poems and passages, such an approach seems hopelessly limited, the kind of "separating out" and "classification" that Olson laments in "Human Universe" (157).

Similarly, "reading" Thoreau's notes and charts one begins to understand why these manuscripts have been so long ignored by literary scholars. Sharon Cameron, describing the Journal, notes "the monotony of a record which focuses for twenty-four years on cyclical change," as well as "the plotlessness and discontinuity of the story of that change," and, perhaps most strikingly "the progressive refusal to interpret the observations recorded, as if the significance of the description of a tree were the description of the tree" (5) — observations that apply equally well to the Kalendar manuscripts. Indeed, the Kalendar, like the Journal, forces a redefinition of the aims of literary criticism, for without plot, and interpretation, and figurative description, what is there to talk about?

A New Relation

Both Thoreau and Olson resist philosophical language in their explorations of the relation between self and place, insisting on the particularity of their experiences of Concord and Gloucester. As a result, both works may be misread as simply and narrowly "about" these places, rather than as records of engagement with them. While philosophers like William James and Alfred North Whitehead describe reality as a process to which human beings actively contribute, Thoreau and Olson position themselves *within* this process, not describing but enacting their participation in the real. This choice, to "hew to experience," to stay within what Olson calls the "human universe," entails for both writers the risk that the philosophical dimension of their work will simply not be recognized ("Human," 157).

Further, the radical commitment to writing as a way of being in the world in Thoreau's charts of general phenomena and Olson's late *Maximus* poems makes these works difficult to talk about in the language of literary scholarship. Sharon Cameron writes that "in the *Journal* [and, I would add, the Kalendar] Thoreau turns his back on the relation between the social and the natural to explore the relation between natural and the human — a relation inhospitable to the values and conventions of critical discourse, social by definition" (47). As Buell notes, the recognition of the self as truly inseparable from its environment

> implies the dissolution of plot and calls into question the authority of the superintending consciousness. . . . But what sort of literature remains possible if we relinquish the myth of human apartness? It must be a literature that abandons, or at least questions, what seem to be literature's basic foci: character, persona, narrative consciousness. What literature can survive under these conditions? (145)

My suspicion is that the curious invisibility of Olson and Thoreau I noticed in their hometowns is at least in part a result of the double challenge, to both philosophical and literary discourse, that their work presents.

Like *The Iliad* lying open on Thoreau's desk during his first summer at Walden, these texts ask not to be read so much as lived with. The relationship between self and environment within the texts becomes a model for the relationship between text and reader; to inhabit *Walden*, the Kalendar, or *The Maximus Poems* is to build one's own mappemunde, to connect that particular history to America's and to find oneself located there, part of the unfolding. In "Human Universe," Olson notes the centrality of our relation to the environment to everything we do:

> The meeting edge of man and the world is also his cutting edge. If man is active, it is exactly here where experience comes in that it is delivered back, and if he stays fresh at the coming in he will be fresh at his going out. If he does not, all that he does inside his house is stale, more and more stale as he is less and less acute at the door. And at his door is where he is responsible to more than himself. ("Human," 162)

Like Thoreau's porous walls and permeable boundaries, Olson's door is where we meet our environment and recognize our contiguity with it. As such, it is the locus of our ethical life.

Reading is a name for one kind of engagement with the world. The challenges these texts pose to traditional ways of talking about philosophy and literature reflect the degree to which they ask to be inhabited rather than merely read. In different ways, *Walden,* the Kalendar, and *The Maximus Poems* make great demands on their readers. Readers of *Walden* and the first two volumes of *Maximus* must renegotiate assumptions about the relationship between self and world, subject and object. Readers of the Kalendar manuscripts and *Maximus Volume Three* must revisit basic questions about the function of literary writing, for both writers and readers. The meaning of these texts, then, resides in the relation of the reader to the textual environment. To regard a text not as an object of inquiry but as a part of a process in which we participate involves an ethical as well as an epistemological shift. It involves a new relation to the world.

Notes

[1] For a compelling alternative view of the relationship between Thoreau's work and Olson's, see Stephen Fredman's *The Grounding of American Poetry*. Brief discussions of the Thoreau–Olson connection may also be found in Sherman Paul's *Olson's Push* and H. Daniel Peck's *Thoreau's Morning Work*.

[2] The appeal of Gloucester, for Olson, was its autonomy — physical, spiritual and economic — from the rest of the country. The choice of Maximus of Tyre as the figure to voice these poems stemmed in part from the similar autonomy of Tyre from Ancient Greece. "The interest," Olson writes, "is not in the local at all as such — any local & the choice of Gloucester is particular — that is the point of interest, particularism itself: to reveal it, in all possible ways and force, against the 'loss' of value of the universal.... Tyre as (with Gaza) the only city which resisted Alexander's universalization" (qtd. in Butterick, 8–9).

[3] For his indispensable help tracing Olson's knowledge of and response to Thoreau, I am indebted to Peter Anastas.

[4] For pointing me to Anastas, as for so much else, I am indebted to Daniel Peck.

[5] See the Stanford Encyclopedia's useful definition of Process Philosophy, which contains the following succinct summary:

> Process philosophy diametrically opposes the view — as old as Parmenides and Zeno and the Atomists of Pre-Socratic Greece — that denies processes or downgrades them in the order of being or of understanding by subordinating them to substantial things. By contrast, process philosophy pivots on the thesis that the processual nature of existence is a fundamental fact with which any adequate metaphysic must come to terms. (Rescher)

⁶ In a footnote, Sherman Paul notes the way Olson, like Thoreau, uses the figure of the open house to signify a self open to the external world. Paul reads Olson's lines

> The flowering plum
> out the front door window
> sends whiteness
> inside my house

in terms of the fluidity of interior and exterior space:

> the movement of the lines and the well-placed initial stressed "out" and "inside," enact interpenetration. ". . . inside my house" recalls the epiphanic moment of renewal in *Walden* ("Suddenly an influx of light filled my house"), house having for Thoreau the sense of bodily being as it has for Olson. The poem is an act of attention, demonstrating the stance called for in "Projective Verse." Outside and inside suggest the separation of self and world; the poet is inside himself and there are things outside himself. But the door does not block the passage because he sees through himself . . . that is, shares — is himself moved by — the forces that move the plum to flower. (Paul, 276)

⁷ As Bradley Dean notes in his introduction to Thoreau's important correspondence with Horace Greeley, "Thoreau was actively involved in what many consider the most important intellectual debate of the nineteenth century — that between progressivism, or special creation, and developmentalism, or evolution." Indeed, even before his 1860 reading of *Origin*, Thoreau had already begun attacking the theory of special creation, whose most prominent proponent was Harvard zoologist Luis Agassiz. By 1856 Thoreau had developed his theory of forest succession as driven by seed dispersal, rather than "spontaneous creation." Thoreau's reading of *Origin* confirmed this view. (Dean, "Letters," 630).

⁸ The concept of literary work as environment, which I discuss at greater length below, is the theme of Angus Fletcher's *A New Theory For American Poetry*. My reading of *Walden* as a textual environment follows Cavell.

⁹ *The Maximus Poems* were originally published in three volumes: *The Maximus Poems* (1960), *The Maximus Poems IV, V, VI* (1968) and the posthumously published *The Maximus Poems: Volume Three* (1975). The complete, single-volume *Maximus Poems*, edited by George Butterick with a revised and expanded *Volume Three*, was published in 1983 by the University of California Press. I have used the complete *The Maximus Poems* (1983) throughout.

¹⁰ "With Aristotle," Olson writes in "Human Universe," "the two great means [of discourse] appear: logic and classification. And it is they that have so fastened themselves on habits of thought that action is interfered with." Olson objected to Aristotle's systems of logic and classification both on the grounds that they "intervene" between human subjects and the "harmony of the universe," and because these systems imply a static, unchanging reality (156).

¹¹ My use of the term "Kalendar" to describe the phenological charts and lists Thoreau drew up between 1860 and 1862 follows Peck's usage in *Thoreau's Morning Work*. For a history of the term as it has been used by other Thoreau

scholars and for a description of the eighteenth- and early nineteenth-century models on which Thoreau based his project, see Peck's footnote 16 on page 48.

[12] The charts and lists comprising Thoreau's Kalendar consist of hundreds of manuscript pages divided among various libraries across the country. I looked at only a small portion of these unpublished manuscripts — those housed at the Pierpont Morgan Library in New York (MA 610).

[13] Thoreau's desire for a "comprehensive view of nature" that would also honor each particular natural phenomenon represents an ultimately unrealizable project, similar, in this way, to Alexander von Humboldt's equally ambitious *Cosmos*, which, as Laura Dassow Walls points out, "was not only unfinished, it was unfinishable" (102).

[14] As Robert von Hallberg explains, "According to Whitehead, 'a nexus of actual occasions,' on the molecular level, results in what is commonly called an 'object,' . . . but which Whitehead prefers to call an 'event,'" because it in fact represents an encounter, not only between active molecular particles, but also between mind and world, subject and object ("Olson" 95).

6: Howe/James

> *In childhood, if we are lucky, Nature furls us in the confidence of her huge harmony. Assimilation into civilization's chronology, its grammatical and arithmetical scrutiny, calls for correcting, suspecting, coveting, corrupting my soul into a devious definition of Duty. I must pursue and destroy what was most tender in my soul's first nature. A poem is an invocation, rebellious return to the blessedness of beginning again, wandering free in pure process of forgetting and finding.*
> — Susan Howe, *My Emily Dickinson*, 98

> *My thesis is that if we start with the supposition that there is only one primal stuff or material in the world, a stuff of which everything is composed, and if we call that stuff "pure experience," then knowing can easily be explained as a particular sort of relation towards one another into which portions of pure experience may enter. The relation itself is a part of pure experience; one of its "terms" becomes the subject or bearer of the knowledge, the knower, the other becomes the object known. This will need much explanation before it can be understood.*
> — William James, *Essays in Radical Empiricism*, 4

Beginnings: America/Howe

LURKING BEHIND OR HOVERING, like a ghost, above this work — the explicit concern of which is the relation of mind to world in the work of a constellation of poets and philosophers — is the particularly fraught designation "American." Tracing a scattered lineage, I have found myself traversing Concord and Cambridge, the terrain of the "American Renaissance" — ground that has been profoundly contested in recent decades, perhaps most visibly by Sacvan Bercovitch. I was well underway in this project before it struck me that eight of the ten writers whose work I explore are, like myself, native New Englanders.

Throughout the writing of this book I have been haunted by the persistence of two facts — the intimate, almost-voiceless reality of motherhood and the (to me) frighteningly distant, dangerously abstract reality of war. The former has made me wonder about the relevance of women's lives to the writings of the mostly canonical, mostly male writers about whom I have written. The latter has made me wary of further enshrining the idea of "America" which has rendered the brutality of the United States all but invisible to its own citizens.

Part of my attraction to the writers who are my subjects is my belief that the germ of pragmatist thinking — the understanding of the self as inextricably linked to the world and to others, and of the mind as inexorably involved in what it knows — constitutes an implicit critique of authoritarian power, whether in the guise of patriarchy or of nationalism, and its absolutist claims. This argument is one version of what Bercovitch somewhat dismissively refers to as "the much-discussed radicalism of our classic writers" ("Problems," 641). In his view, there can be no escape from the all-absorbing power of nationalist ideology.

> American ideology... undertakes above all, as a condition of its nature, to absorb the spirit of protest for social ends.... In this view, our classic texts re-present the strategies of a triumphant middle-class hegemony. Far from subverting the status quo, their diagnostic and prophetic modes attest to the capacities of the dominant culture to co-opt alternative forms to the point of making basic change seem unthinkable, except as apocalypse.... Having adopted the culture's *controlling* metaphor — "America" as synonym for human possibility — and having made this tenent of consensus the ground for radical dissent, they redefined radicalism itself as an affirmation of cultural values. (645)

This view, in which even the notion of an American tradition of protest necessarily reinforces the all-absorbing myth of America, is a compelling one. Indeed, the power of this myth seems self-evident. How else can one explain the willingness of so many Americans to accept that the events of September 11 constituted an "attack on our freedom," or that our military's role in Iraq and Afghanistan is to "spread democracy"? With such evidence before me, I have trod carefully around the question of the "Americanness" of the writers whose work I have examined.

I have not sought, for example, to account for the origins of pragmatism, or to define what it is (if indeed there is anything) about these writers that makes them distinctively American. Rather, I have tried to follow some strains of an overheard, intergenerational, cross-disciplinary conversation about thinking and writing, and have found myself wandering mostly in New England. I take this fact as neither an accident nor an emblem. I am a New Englander. I am drawn to voices that, as Susan Howe puts it, speak "New-Englandly" (*Birth-mark*, ix). In the work of many of these writers I find an uneasy relation to the past, a clear inheritance of literary and philosophical tradition combined with a desire to achieve what Emerson calls "an original relation to the universe" (*Essays*, 7). These texts, wandering in and out of New England, embody the pragmatist description of the mind at work, in which the store of old ideas, continually challenged by clashes with experience, gradually evolves, expanding to accommodate the new.

I have chosen to end with this chapter because Susan Howe, negotiating her own complex relation to the American literary tradition and its archives, has been a model as well as a subject for me. In Howe's writing, such relations are themselves part of the literary landscape. Watching what happens to a text by Dickinson or Melville under Howe's critical eye has been both moving and instructive. I do not hear her particular, antinomian voice in the chorus of Bercovitch's American ideology.

Of course, Emerson and James's work can be and has been used to reiterate nationalist and capitalist ideologies.[1] But in their insight about our relatedness to each other and to the world we know, these writers offer a vision that is essentially incompatible with ideologies of dominance. Indeed, as Frank Lentricchia has observed, pragmatism itself was conceived in part as a response to nascent American imperialism.

> The lectures James delivered in late 1906 and early 1907 in Boston and New York, and then shortly after published as the book *Pragmatism*, bear the mark of a decisive moment in U.S. history: our first fully launched imperial adventure, in the last years of the nineteenth century, in Cuba and the Philippines. Among the prominent protesters against our lurch towards empire, James was then and remains today one of our most distinguished intellectuals. His philosophy of concreteness and action, though inchoately present in his *Principles of Psychology*, knew itself as pragmatism only after he found the political terminus of his thought in his anti-imperialist activism at the end of the nineteenth century. ("Return," 11–12)

Inherent in James's pragmatism is his vision of a "Pluralistic Universe," "a vision of heterogeneity and contentiousness — a vision . . . that never claims knowledge of a single unfolding human drama because it refuses the belief and it refuses the often repressive conduct that comes from the belief in a single human narrative" (Lentricchia, 228). The supreme value of Howe's work, in my view, is that it takes this vision seriously, takes it as a premise.

What follows is a collage of relations. My claim is that Susan Howe's work, in its many iterations, gives us one picture of what writing might look like if we were to absorb fully the implications of James's insight that "the relations between things, conjunctive as well as disjunctive, are just as much matters of direct particular experience, neither more so nor less, than the things themselves" (*Writings*, 826). Reading Howe's work in preparation to write this chapter, I was struck by how completely the refusal to subordinate *relation* to *substance* undermines the conventions of scholarly prose. At the same time, I was struck by how difficult it is to break the habits of language, and how thoroughly my own thinking is bound to conventional forms. In *Process and Reality*, Alfred North Whitehead notes how ingrained our language is with the Aristotelian ontology:

> The simple notion of an enduring substance sustaining persistent qualities, either essentially or accidentally, expresses a useful abstract for many purposes of life. But whenever we try to use it as a fundamental statement of the nature of things, it proves itself mistaken. . . . But it has had one success: it has entrenched itself in our language. (79)

This chapter attempts to trace the effect of allowing normally suppressed (or at least unacknowledged) relations — between texts and events happening outside the text, between text and reader — to shape my critical response. As Howe writes about her essay "Encloser" (later "Incloser"), "the whole problem of writing this piece for me is to write it in a way that *is* the thing I am talking about at the same time I am anchoring it down with certain facts" (189).

Dickinson/Howe

Susan Howe's work on Emily Dickinson in *My Emily Dickinson* and the essay "These Flames and Generosities of the Heart" (in *The Birth-mark*), is also about Robert Browning, The Brontës, Charles Dickens, Mary Rowlandson, Shakespeare, Cotton and Increase Mather, Jonathan Edwards, and Susan Howe, among others. It is about the arrival of European settlers in America and their encounters with native peoples, the legacy of Calvinism in American thought, and the violence of the Civil War. Howe's project is multiple and slippery; like Dickinson's poems, it "escapes the ritual of framing" (*Birth-mark*, 147). In part, it is an answer to the following statement of Thomas H. Johnson, for years the shaping force behind our culture's idea of Emily Dickinson:

> Since Emily Dickinson's full maturity as a dedicated artist occurred during the span of the Civil War, the most convulsive era of the nation's history, one of course turns to the letters of 1861–1865, and the years that follow, for her interpretation of events. But the fact is that she did not live in history and held no view of it past or current. (Johnson, xiv; qtd. in *Birth-mark*, 132)

In an interview, Howe recalls that in writing *My Emily Dickinson* "I was really concerned to show that she didn't write in a rapturous frenzy, that she read to write" (*Birth-mark*, 157). Howe's effort was to restore Dickinson not only to her history, but also to her poetic descendants. "Yes, Dickinson is in the canon. But she is treated as an isolated case, not as part of an ongoing influence" (168). In Howe's view, Dickinson's voice, like that of Anne Hutchinson and Mary Rowlandson, has been isolated, stripped of the roots by which it is connected to American history and culture, and thus of its power. Like much of Howe's work, her writings on Dickinson are about drawing out and making visible these suppressed relations, a theme she announces in *The Midnight*: "All who read must cross the divide — one from the other. Towards whom am I floating? I'll tie a rope around your waist if you say who you are. Remember we are traveling as relations" (146).

Howe's relations are not happy, generally speaking, though they include love. At the center of *The Birth-mark*, the book of essays aptly subtitled "unsettling the wilderness in American literary history," the word "antinomian" is a node from which strains of the text emanate and to which they return.

> The issue of editorial control is directly connected to the attempted erasure of antinomianism in our culture. Lawlessness seen as negligence is first feminized and then restricted or banished. For me, the manuscripts of Emily Dickinson represent a contradiction to canonical social power, whose predominant purpose seems to have been to render isolate voices devoted to writing as a physical event of immediate revelation. The excommunication and banishment of the early American female preacher and prophet Anne Hutchinson, and the comparison of her opinions to monstrous births, is not unrelated to the editorial apprehension and domestication of Emily Dickinson. (*Birth-mark*, 1)

Antinomian, like margin, another nodal term for Howe, names a relation: Dickinson's refusal to publish, her inclusion of alternate words in the manuscripts of her poems, her decision not to title (or number) her poems, her obliteration of letter-writing convention are, in Howe's view, gestures of defiance, aimed at existing social power. Howe sees Dickinson, ensconced within her father's house, as resolute outsider and separatist. Howe's writing on Dickinson is a meditation on a poet's relation to authority, the dance between power and powerlessness, inside and outside, in which Howe, too, participates:

> I am drawn toward the disciplines of history and literary criticism but in the dawning distance a dark wall of rule supports the structure of every letter, record, transcript: every proof of authority and power. I know records are compiled by winners, and scholarship is in collusion with Civil Government. I know this and go on searching for some trace of love's infolding through all the paper in all the libraries I come to. (*Birth-mark*, 4)

Restoring Dickinson to her history and the physical facts of her work, is, in itself, a radical gesture, a vivid contradiction of the Emily Dickinson we have inherited. Still more radical is the gesture tucked into Howe's title, *My Emily Dickinson*. Relation *itself*, not a writer, or a poem, or even a particular patch of historical terrain, is the subject of Howe's writing. The relations between words and things, manuscripts and authorized or edited texts, poetry and scholarship, readers and texts, are always at issue. The relationships are too many and too multifaceted for all such reverberations to be traced or "known" by the reader; rather, the reader experiences what William James calls a "feeling of relation," the rapid and ineffable movement of consciousness between discrete images or thoughts.

*

Sleeping badly. When I turn from side to side to alleviate the pain the weight of its body falls and settles like a stone. I turn, it turns. This morning there are long shadows on the grass. The peonies are almost gone, and the sweet pea, and the purple phlox. There are buds on the hollyhocks and lilies. The first pink climbing roses have opened.

A few days ago, U.S. missiles killed twelve women and children in Afghanistan. There are reports that Taliban fighters knew the building was going to be bombed and forced the children to remain inside the building. The sum of cruelty involved seems only slightly altered by whether these reports are true or not. Either way, the children are dead.

In Democracy and Education, *John Dewey explains that if we take seriously the reality that Darwin describes, if we see ourselves as participants in evolution, the categories of mind and body, self and object, knower and known will dissolve. "For the doctrine of organic development means that the living creature is a part of the world, sharing its vicissitudes and fortunes"* (Middle, *9:347). I cannot, that is, separate myself from the world I look out on from this window: the cut grass and the field behind it, the bird I don't recognize repeating its three-note call, and beyond these, but continuous with them, the dairy farm down the hill, the people in town, the women carrying babies, the women giving birth, the women mourning their dead.*

A Bird's Life

James describes "the stream of our consciousness" as a continual alternation between "substantive" and "transitive parts" — between (relatively) static images and more fluid perceptions of relation. "Like a bird's life," the stream of thought is "made of an alternation of flights and perchings. The rhythm of language expresses this, where every thought is expressed in a sentence, and every sentence is closed by a period" (*Principles*, 1:243). The "transitive parts" of consciousness, the "feelings of relation," are necessarily more difficult to analyze than the "substantive parts." The flights of consciousness, the movements between "substantive parts," are characterized by rapid change and motion; to arrest them is therefore to strip them of their defining characteristic. "As a snowflake crystal caught in the warm hand is no longer a crystal but a drop, so, instead of catching a feeling of relation moving to its term, we find we have caught some substantive thing" (1:244).

"Relation" is a key concept for James, not only in his descriptive psychology, but also in his epistemology. Pragmatism, as James defines it, conceives of knowing as a fundamentally dialogic process. While James posits the existence of "a sensible flux" independent of the perceiving mind, he maintains that "*what is true of it* seems from first to last to be largely a matter of our own creation" (*Writings*, 598; James's emphasis). The active role of the perceiving mind in shaping fact into truth means that we are always part of what we know; knowledge emerges from a relation between subject and object. It is worth repeating James's beautifully succinct passage here:

> In the realm of truth-processes, facts come independently and determine our beliefs provisionally. But these beliefs make us act, and as fast as they do so, they bring into sight or into existence new facts which re-determine the beliefs accordingly. So the whole coil and ball of truth, as it rolls up, is the product of a double influence. Truths emerge from facts; but they dip forward into facts again and add to them; which facts create or reveal new truth (the word is indifferent) and so on indefinitely. The "facts" meanwhile are not *true*. They simply *are*. Truth is the function of the beliefs that start and terminate among them. (*Writings*, 585)

Because, in the pragmatist conception, the objects of our knowledge are by definition bound up with the conditions of our knowing, there can be no object of knowledge that is not marked by what James calls "the trail of the human serpent." "Purely objective truth," he insists, "truth in whose establishment the function of giving human satisfaction in marrying previous parts of experience to newer parts played no role whatever, is nowhere to be found" (*Writings*, 515). Like Heidegger, James challenges the idea of discrete, isolable entities (Aristotle's substances, or the subjects and objects of Cartesian thought) that the Western philosophical tradition had always presumed.

James's sense of the centrality of relation to experience informs his late doctrine of "radical empiricism," a doctrine closely related to his earlier pragmatism.[2] James radicalizes empiricism by redefining the "experience" to which it answers: "The relations between things, conjunctive as well as disjunctive, are just as much matters of direct particular experience, neither more so nor less, than the things themselves" (*Writings*, 826). This restoration of the experience of relation to the concept of experience in general sets the static subjects and objects of ordinary empiricism in motion, gives us a new picture of knowing.

> We live, as it were, upon the front edge of an advancing wave-crest, and our sense of a determinate direction in falling forward is all we cover of the future of our path. It is as if a differential quotient should be conscious and treat itself as an adequate substitute for a traced-out curve. Our experience, *inter alia*, is of variations of rate and direction, and lives in these transitions more than in the journey's end. (69)

I wish to mark here the singularly surreal quality of James's second sentence as an instance of what happens to language when knowledge is reconfigured around relations as opposed to objects: "It is as if a differential quotient should be conscious and treat itself as an adequate substitute for a traced out-curve."

*

William James, "The Thing and Its Relations":

> Prepositions, copulas, and conjunctions, "is," "is n't," "then," "before," "in," "on," "beside," "between," "next," "like," "unlike," "as," "but," flower out of the stream of pure experience, the stream of concretes or the sensational stream, as naturally as nouns and adjectives do. (*Writings*, 783)

Susan Howe, *Souls of the Labadie Tract*:

> *from* into the way that leads *to* (36)

> if I can beginning then
> then before — and then (37)

> with me here between us — of
> our being together even in
> english half english too late (54)

Howe/Peirce

"Arisbe," the first section of Howe's *Pierce-Arrow*, is a cluster of associations. As Peter Nicholls explains, the Pierce-Arrow was a luxury car, popular in the 1920s, produced near Howe's home in Buffalo, New York. Howe is pictured on the book's back cover, against the background of the now abandoned Pierce-Arrow factory. "This image closes a temporal loop opened by the book's front cover photograph of Howe aged eleven playing the part of Astyanax in *The Trojan Women*" (442). Connecting the allusion to the Pierce-Arrow in the title and back cover photograph and the classical allusion of the front cover photograph is the figure of Charles Sanders Peirce, who lived for a time on Arrow Street in Cambridge, and whose principles of firstness and secondness Howe finds at work in Homer's *Iliad*. Howe identifies the *Iliad* as the source for the name of Peirce's house, "Arisbe" (Nicholls, 442; Howe, *Pierce*, 15). Peirce, Howe herself, and Homer/Euripides are the major points in the constellation.

There are other, remoter, connections as well: the quotations from Pope's translation of the *Iliad* prompts an association with Thomas Wentworth Higginson, whose "Letters to a Young Contributor" in the *Atlantic Monthly* encouraged writers to present neat manuscripts, and made a negative example of the "'paper-sparing Pope,' whose chaotic manuscript of the 'Iliad,' written chiefly on the backs of letters, still remains in the British Museum" (in Howe, *Pierce*, 21). Higginson, Emily Dickinson's longtime correspondent, friend, and editor, becomes a bridge between Peirce and Dickinson, both marginalized figures whose stubbornly idiosyncratic manuscripts editors have been, in Howe's view, repressed and sanitized beyond recognition. The train of associations here, as I noted it in the margin of my copy of *Pierce-Arrow,* is: Peirce-Arisbe-Homer-Pope-Higginson-Dickinson. Of course, these terms may be reconfigured, as the associations are always multiple, and move in multiple directions. "Howe" may be added between almost any two of the terms in this chain. (Howe's description of reading Peirce's papers on microfilm viewers at the beginning of her "Arisbe" section recalls her early experience with microfilm, recounted in *Europe of Trusts*: "During World War II my father's letters were a sign he was safe. A miniature photographic negative of his handwritten message was reproduced by the army and a microfilm copy forwarded to us. In the top left-hand corner someone always stamped 'PASSED BY EXAMINER'" [13]).

Howe's texts are webs, intricate networks. "In poetry," she writes, "all things seem to touch so they are" (*Pierce*, 13). The fragments of text and history Howe connects may be related historically (Dickinson/Higginson), thematically (Peirce/Homer), graphically or phonetically (Peirce/Pierce).

Nearly all of Howe's texts, whether they look like prose or like poetry, are dense networks of relation. The quantity and variety of these relations, as well as the rapidity of movement between them, continually draw the reader's attention to the works' construction, the mind making these connections. Returning to the archive, Howe rewrites the narrative of American history, bringing to the fore that which has been suppressed, knowing that "knowledge, no matter how I get it, involves exclusion and repression. National histories hold ruptures and hierarchies" (*Birth-mark*, 45). In constructing her counter-narrative, giving voice to those, like Peirce and his wife Juliette, who have been silenced, Howe illustrates the Jamesian insight that histories are always made.

*

The *New York Times*, July 7, 2008:

> Local officials said Sunday that an American airstrike killed at least 27 civilians in an eastern Afghanistan wedding party, most of them women and children and including the bride. Officials of the American-led coalition disputed the report, saying that the airstrike killed militants and that there was no evidence of women and children at the scene. (Wafa)

I wonder what, for coalition officials, would constitute "evidence of women and children." Particularly if the local inhabitants had chosen to bury their dead.

Susan Howe, "The Captivity and Restoration of Mrs. Mary Rowlandson":

> In the first paragraph of the first published narrative written by an Anglo-American woman, ostensibly written to serve as a reminder of God's Providence, guns fire, a father, mother and suckling child are killed by blows to the head. Two children are carried off alive. Two more adults are clubbed to death. Another escapes — another running along is shot. Indians strip him naked then cut his bowels open. Another, venturing out of his barn, is quickly dispatched. Three others are murdered inside their fortification. The victims are nameless. Specificity is unnecessary in whiplash confrontation. Only monotonous enumeration. (*Birth-mark*, 95)

Incloser/Enclosure

"Incloser," which Webster's 1821 Dictionary defines as "he or that which encloses," is another of Howe's key or nodal terms. In *The Birth-mark*, the Enclosure Acts that transformed the English common lands into private property become an emblem for the sealing off of that wilderness that is rightly public — our literary history in its original, anarchic forms — into inaccessible archives and controlled, authorized editions. As Stephen Collis explains,

> Possession and property [in Howe's work] relate to the issues of inheritance and literary influence. Harold Bloom has long maintained that "priority" — originality in the sense of being first, primary — is the "property" poets traffic in. Howe, like Duncan and Olson before her, stands for another ethics — one where poetry is always governed by "fair use," and where "possibility" — the creation of the new — always supercedes the laws of private ownership and intellectual property. (*Words*, 56)

Howe's turning of the lens of literary scholarship away from individual achievement and toward nodes of intersection and relation entails a critique of the proprietary ethos behind traditional models of literary genius. This critique holds, even when Howe's special interest in a writer hinges on that writer's radical non-conformity, as is the case with Emily Dickinson. "Non-connection," Howe writes in *The Midnight*, "is itself distinct/connection" (17). Howe examines Dickinson not only in relation to the social powers she subverted in her practice, but also in relation to others — Emily Brontë, Anne Hutchinson — who engaged in similar acts of subversion and refusal. Of central relevance to Howe's reading of the Dickinson poem beginning "My Life had stood — a Loaded Gun —" is the fact that "the three most serious threats to the political and religious stability of the Commonwealth of Massachusetts in the seventeenth century — the Antinomian controversy of 1636, the Quaker persecutions of the 1650s, and the Witchcraft hysteria in 1692 — all directly involved women" (*My Emily*, 113).

"If you are a woman," Howe notes in an interview included in *The Birth-mark*, "archives hold perpetual ironies. Because the gaps and silences are where you find yourself" (158). Again and again, Howe raises the question of her own relation to the tradition she finds herself both excluded from and inheritor to. Outside Harvard's Houghton Library Reading Room, where she has come to examine Emily Dickinson's closely guarded manuscripts, Howe (in the antechamber — between inside and outside) describes her sense of unease:

> I wonder if I am clothed in accordance with everyday Harvard University Library usage. I am wearing black slacks from Ann Taylor's, a white cotton Ann Taylor shirt, plain shoes rather than sandals, and I have a new monogrammed black leather Coach briefcase my husband gave me for my birthday because we knew I was making this trip and it seemed professorial. Neither of us has a college degree so we have that feeling of failure in common and are always at war with what we wear. I wish he hadn't asked for a monogram. S.H. in gold is so "Connecticut." I wonder if I am more worried about my appearance than any of the scholars who have already made it into the Reading Room. (*Midnight*, 122)

Howe grew up in Cambridge, the daughter of a Harvard professor. Her mother, an Irish-American actress and writer, directed plays at Harvard and Radcliffe. Her parents socialized with F. O. Matthiessen and Perry Miller. She remembers the latter as "a lecherous character who drank too much. . . . He always wore white socks and black shoes. And the skin on his ankles, always visible above the socks, was like polished porcelain. We were all struck by it. Even my parents" (*Birth-mark*, 160). These figures from her childhood — real people with whom she had real relations — are the scholars whose work is both the foundation upon which she builds and the fence beyond which she trespasses.

> I can't tell you how surprised I was to find, when I was working on Dickinson, that this man [Miller], who in real life was so harsh and coarse, was completely different in his written work. He was and is essential for any real understanding of the early history of New England, of the intellectual and religious history of America. With one major exception. While Matthiessen leaves out women,[3] Miller leaves out Native Americans. How could he have written so many books and essays, one of them called *Errand into the Wilderness* and have left out the inhabitants? Yet after faulting him for that I come back to his work. I am trying to indicate how conflicted the whole thing is in my mind. (160–61)

Howe's conflicted relationship to Houghton library and to scholars like Miller and Matthiessen is, to use one of her favorite words, emblematic of her relationship to the American literary tradition as she has (and has not) inherited it. Howe's pragmatic response to her ambiguous position is to revisit the archives and call up its ghosts. Reframing Melville, Dickinson, Thoreau, and other writers in terms of their relations — to each other, to earlier writers, to voices (like Anne Hutchinson's and Mary Rowlandson's) that have been effaced, edited or forgotten — Howe begins to fill, rigorously, imaginatively, "the gaps and silences" of a field of history too often figured as a line.

Relation is her way in.

*

Time slows down. From the backyard the sun seems still in the sky. The angle of it, silver in the grass, seems permanent. I feel so acutely the presence and absence of this baby: its undeniable existence; the absoluteness of the breech between us. I feel again, too, this sense of solitude, the inviolability of the body's secrecy: words move around the outside of it, but don't come into the circle drawn around us. ("Us" — not quite right; there is no pronoun for this sense of compound being). Yesterday in the café two women and their daughters: the oldest a teenager, beautiful, with dreadlocks and flowered skirt, the youngest, maybe three, had Down Syndrome. They all seemed happy, laughing together over breakfast. When the mother tried to put the little girl in her stroller the girl's body went stiff; she began to moan softly. "Yes — we're going now," the mother said, over and over, bending the little girls knees with her hands.

Susan Howe, *My Emily Dickinson:*

> The recipient of a letter, or a combination of letter and poem from Emily Dickinson, was forced much like [Jonathan] Edwards' listen-

ing congregation, through shock and through subtraction of the ordinary, to a new way of perceiving. Subject and object were fused at that moment, into the immediate *feeling* of understanding. (51)

James/Howe

In *The Principles of Psychology*, James describes the activity of what he calls "the stream of thought," noting that it actively selects from a swarm of sensation certain objects of interest.

> And then, among the sensations we get from each separate thing, what happens? The mind selects again, it chooses certain of the sensations to represent the thing most *truly*, and considers the rest as its appearances, modified by the conditions of the moment. Thus my tabletop is named *square*, after but one of an infinite number of retinal sensations which it yields, the rest of them being of acute and obtuse angles; but I call the latter *perspective* views and the four right angles the *true* form of the table, and erect the attribute squareness into the table's essence, for aesthetic reasons of my own. (1:285)

James's description of how we arrive at the truth illustrates the mind's active role in shaping what we call objectivity or "essence." Howe underscores her pragmatist understanding of truth by calling attention to the role contingency plays in her research:

> My retrospective excursions follow the principle that ghosts wrapped in appreciative obituaries by committee members or dedications presented at vanished community field meetings, can be reanimated by appropriation. Always remembering while roving through centuries that, apart from call number coincidence there is no inherent reason a particular scant relic and curiosity should be in position to be accidentally grasped by a quick-eyed reader in reference to clapping. (*Souls*, 15)

The threads she draws together may indeed have no inherent connection. They are connected, the truth of their relation is *made*, by the mind of the writer. The deeply personal and idiosyncratic nature of Howe's histories point to the pragmatist insight that all histories are the products of human construction and imagination. And that "objective" histories hide motives. "In the cold drama of moral lucidity there is a primitive reason just as in the calm dicta of moral lucidity there is a personal reason," Howe writes in the introduction to *Frame Structures* (6). In Howe's writing the editorial interventions in Dickinson's poems and the consignment of Peirce's papers to a forgotten microfilm reading room are revealed as active attempts to suppress Antinomian voices in American literary history.

*

The *New York Times*, July 7, 2008:

> The governor of Deh Bala district, Hamisha Gul, said the airstrike on Sunday came while a group of women and children were walking from the bride's village, Kamalai, to the groom's home. Tradition holds that women and children walk with the bride separately from the men. (Wafa)

Susan Howe, *Frame Structures:*

> Women and children experience war and its nightmare. Their war-dreams share with dreams of other kinds that they are occurrences full of blown sand seaward foam in which disappearance fields expression. (7)

*

In *The Europe of Trusts*, Howe writes, "I wish I could tenderly lift from the dark side of history, voices that are anonymous, slighted — inarticulate" (14). In her desire to hear and amplify American history's barely audible Antinomian voices, Howe echoes James's advocacy of "a re-instatement of the vague to its proper place in our mental life" (*Principles*, 1:254). The voices Howe listens for exist in what James refers to as the "fringe" of consciousness (or history), and do not speak grammatically (1:259). In the "Stream of Thought" chapter of his *Principles of Psychology,* James makes the connection between philosophy and psychology's exclusion of the realities of feeling and relation and the suppression of these realities in our language.

> We ought to say a feeling of *and*, a feeling of *if*, a feeling of *but*, quite as readily as we say a feeling of *blue* or a feeling of *cold*. Yet we do not: so inveterate has our habit become of recognizing the substantive parts [of thought] alone, that language almost refuses to lend itself to any other use. . . . All *dumb* or anonymous psychic states have, owing to this error, been coolly suppressed; or, if recognized at all, have been named after the substantive perception they lead to, as thoughts "about" this object or "about" that, the stolid word "about" engulfing all their delicate idiosyncrasies in its monotonous sound. Thus the greater and greater accentuation and isolation of the substantive parts have continually gone on. (*Principles*, 1:245–46)

One way of understanding Howe's work is as an answer to this exhortation, a bringing to light of those elements of reality that language "almost refuses" to acknowledge. In her own characterization, Howe's work "involves a fracturing of discourse, a stammering even. Interruption and hesitation used as a force. A recognition that there is an other voice, an attempt to hear and speak it. It's this brokenness," she writes, "that interests me" ("Encloser,"192).

Howe's important modification of the Jamesian insight into the exclusions of grammar and officially sanctioned knowledge is to mark these exclusions as political: "Emily Dickinson and Gertrude Stein also conducted a skillful and ironic investigation of patriarchal authority over literary history," Howe observes. "Who polices questions of grammar, parts of speech, connection and connotation? Whose order is shut inside the structure of a sentence?" (*My Emily*, 11). Grammatical authority is allied to real social power, and in its suppression, so eloquently documented by James, of the realities of experience, this authority also suppresses certain kinds of voices. Uniquely attuned to the realities of relation, excluded from the institutions of authority, and intimately familiar with death, birth, violence and other grammar-defying experiences, women were (and are), as Howe's writing makes clear, prime candidates for this suppression.

*

Language collapses, calendar time collapses; it is strange to speak to people who inhabit separate selves, who "go to work," and "go shopping," and "have coffee." I have started to say "we" for "she" — "we're sleeping now," or "we're having some milk." Philosophy comes undone. The idea of a "self" that doubts or knows the existence of "others," or an "exterior world," dissolves in this doubleness. Such a basic experience for women who are mothers, utterly unaccounted for in hundreds of years of epistemological debate. At the very beginning of modern philosophy, a doubting game mothers cannot play.

The *New York Times* has "airstrike" as a single word, no hyphen. My computer's spell-check function does not recognize "airstrike." I wonder if it has been added to the dictionaries used by copy-editors at the *New York Times* and if so, when.

Howe/James

The portions of Howe's later texts (*Pierce-Arrow, The Midnight, Souls of the Labadie Tract*) that look like poetry are often arranged in blocks of text, one or two short stanzas of short, even lines. They contain dashes but no commas or periods. Removing the boundaries imposed by the rules of grammar, Howe channels the stream of her words into a tight visual form. The result is not lawlessness, but a new law, based, in Antinomian spirit, on internal rather than external authority. "I think a lot of my work is about breaking free: starting free and being captured and breaking free again and being captured again" (*Birth-mark*, 166).

Howe opens *The Midnight* with a description of the interleaf, a translucent tissue placed by bookbinders "between frontispiece and title page in order to prevent illustration and text from rubbing together." In his review of *The Midnight*, Stephen Collis writes,

> The tissue interleaf works its mediating betweenness, becoming the governing figure for a series of interchanges which proliferate like a dreaming logic throughout *The Midnight*: poetry and prose (in alternating sections of which the book is composed), text and textile, waking and sleeping, public park and academic archive, inclusion and exclusion, Ireland and America. ("Drawing")

Indeed, *The Midnight* takes relation as its explicit subject: "The relational space is the thing that's alive with something from somewhere else" (*Midnight*, 58). Particularly alive in this way are the books Howe has inherited, which become not only emblems of what she calls "relational space," but also, as Collis observes, models for the construction of her own text.

> My mother's close relations treated their books as transitional objects (judging by a few survivors remaining in my possession) to be held, loved, carried around, meddled with, abandoned, sometimes mutilated. They contain dedications, private messages, marginal annotations, hints, snapshots, press cuttings, warnings — scissor work. Some volumes have been shared as scripts for family theatricals. When something in the world is cross-identified, it just is. *They* have made this relation by gathering — airs, reveries, threads, mythologies, nets, oilskins, briars and branches, wishes and needs, intact — into a sort of tent. This is a space children used to play in. (*Midnight*, 60)

In *The Midnight,* Howe is interested in the markers of separation — bed hangings, curtains, interleaves, the glass that excludes her from access to the manuscripts in the Houghton library — and equally compelled by their failure to separate fully. As a reproduction of the semi-transparent interleaf and half-visible title page of Stevenson's *The Master of Ballentrae* at the beginning of *The Midnight* illustrates, the boundaries between text and image, prose and poetry, and, perhaps especially, then and now, are always permeable, always being transgressed. The "poetic" sections of the text enact this transgression, letting words loose from punctuation and grammatical structure, allowing them to reverberate in the relational space between prose sections.

> Counterforce bring me wild hope
> non-connection is itself distinct
> connection numerous surviving
> fair trees wrought with a needle

> the merest decorative suggestion
> in what appears to be sheer white
> muslin a tree fair hunted Daphne
> Thinking is willing you are wild
> to the weave not to material itself (*Midnight*, 17)

Here, separation ("non-connection") and connection, "real" and represented objects, willing and wildness, the weaving and the woven, become parts of a single stream, each element capable, like "fair hunted Daphne," of transformation as means of escape. To engage with such writing is to be hunting meaning continually. Like Dickinson's, Howe's work is notable for its elusiveness, the way the words, just at the moment they are captured by an interpreting intelligence, cease to be what they were, or to mean what they meant.

Dramatizing in the slippery suggestiveness of her language thought's habit of "starting free and being captured and breaking free again and being captured again," Howe evokes the process at the heart of pragmatist thinking. In *Pierce-Arrow*, she alludes to this process, the germ of one of Peirce's important essays, as "[Alexander] Bain's belief-doubt theory" (74).[4] In "The Fixation of Belief," Peirce defines "inquiry" as the process in which "the irritation of doubt causes a struggle to attain a state of belief," suggesting that inquiry is motivated not by an impartial desire for truth, but rather by the need for "a firm belief . . . whether that belief be true of false" (114–15). Further, Peirce's description of the alternation between doubt and belief implies that the struggle is continuous, that the settlement of belief is always temporary. (This implication is made explicit elsewhere, for example in Peirce's description of science: "Science is . . . not standing upon the bedrock of fact. It is walking upon a bog, and can only say, this ground seems to hold for the present. Here I stay until it begins to give way" (*Collected*, 5:589). Both elements of the "belief-doubt theory" — the role of feeling in the pursuit of knowledge and the temporary nature of all truths — were to become essential for James's pragmatism.

James articulates his version of the "belief-doubt theory" in the lecture "What Pragmatism Means."

> The process here is always the same. The individual has a stock of old opinions already, but he meets a new experience that puts them to a strain. Somebody contradicts them; or in a reflective moment he discovers that they contradict each other; or he hears of facts with which they are incompatible; or desires arise in him which they cease to satisfy. The result is an inward trouble to which his mind till then had been a stranger, and from which he seeks to escape by modifying his previous mass of opinions. (*Writings*, 512)

In James's description, new knowledge — which is at first wild, existing outside the bounds of already-domesticated thought — is captured, assimilated, and brought into the previous store of knowledge.

In its meditations on, and movements between, prose and poetry, sanctioned and unsanctioned language, the authority and the wilderness of the archive, Howe's work enacts the process of "starting free and being captured and breaking free again and being captured again" that is at the heart of the pragmatist understanding of our acquisition of knowledge.

Conclusion: Trespassing

Implicit in my approach to this chapter is the belief that words matter: that language is not a conveyance for thought, but the material of which it is made. The kind of thinking described by James and enacted by Howe's poetics threatens the stability of the inherited form of literary scholarship, a form which, as Charles Bernstein demonstrates in his remarkable essay "Frame Lock," assumes a fundamental divide between thought and language. The accepted prose style for literary scholars, Bernstein writes, is characterized by "an insistence on a univocal surface, minimal shifts in mood either within paragraphs or between paragraphs, exclusion of extraneous or contradictory material, and tone restricted to the narrow affective envelope of sobriety, neutrality, objectivity, authoritativeness, or reanimated abstraction." Bernstein concludes that this rigidity of form, which he calls "frame lock," is derived from "what might be called the rule of the necessity of paraphrase[:] the argument must be separable from its expression so that a defined message can be extracted from the text" (92).

The rejection of the "rule of the necessity of paraphrase" is a hallmark of both modern and postmodern American poetics and pragmatist thought as embodied by Emerson and James, in particular. In her radical restatement of pragmatism as the application of evolutionary theory to thought and language, Joan Richardson highlights the pragmatist insight that "language [is] an organic form . . . as natural and necessary to the survival of human beings as the honeycomb to bees, the structure by which transformations essential to the life of the community are made" (6). The absorption of this lesson entails trespass: over the boundaries between thought and language, philosophy and poetry, "creative" and scholarly prose, subject and object. Bernstein: "Next to us is not the work that we study, which we love so well to explain, but the work we are. I unclothe myself in addressing a poem, and the poem returns to show me my bearings, my comportment, and the way to read the next poem or painting, person or situation" (98).

If we believe in it, the picture of confused, colliding, intimately connected subject and object that is at the heart of James's concept of relation and Howe's relational poetics demands a rethinking of the boundaries of literary studies. This rethinking has already begun: poets like Howe and Anne Carson have built their bodies of work on acts of useful trespass; the interdisciplinary work of scholars like Joan Richardson, Daniel Peck, Steven Meyer, and Laura Dassow Walls challenges the traditional boundaries between literature, philosophy, and science. While these writers and scholars contest the borders of literary studies, the emerging field of ecocriticism upends some of its foundational assumptions. As Lawrence Buell has observed, the recognition of the self as inseparable from environment "implies the dissolution of plot and calls into question the authority of the superintending consciousness. . . . But what sort of literature remains possible if we relinquish the myth of human apartness?" (*Environmental*, 145). We might ask a corollary question: what sort of writing becomes possible if we relinquish the myth of scholarly apartness?

Notes

[1] As Harold Bloom noted in a recent essay in the *New York Times*, "The oddity of Emerson in the public sphere is that he has the power to foster fresh versions of the two camps he termed the Party of Memory and the Party of Hope. The political right appropriates his values of remembering private interests as part of the public good, while the left follows his exaltation of the American Adam, a New Man in a New World of hope" (Bloom).

[2] Though James asserted that "there is no logical connexion between pragmatism, as I understand it, and a doctrine which I have recently set forth as 'radical empiricism,'" an important link may be observed between the epistemological underpinnings of pragmatism — the inseparability of the knower from the known — and the radical empiricist claim that subject and object are merely two aspects of the same substance (*Essays*, iv). As Ralph Perry writes in the introduction to James's posthumously published *Essays in Radical Empiricism*, the doctrine is "a theory of knowledge comprising pragmatism as a special chapter" (xii).

[3] Matthiessen famously excluded Emily Dickinson, among others, from his most important book. Howe notes, "in 1941 women were banished from Matthiessen's *American Renaissance: Art and Expression in the age of Emerson and Whitman*. At one time he intended to include Margaret Fuller but thought better of it" (*Birth-mark*, 18).

[4] In his account of the origins of pragmatism, Peirce notes the importance of Alexander Bain's definition of belief, which Peirce summarizes as "that upon which a man is prepared to act" (*Essential*, 2:399). Indeed, Peirce seems to have taken from Bain the idea of the discomfort engendered by doubt and the continual alternation of the settled state of belief and the unsettled state of doubt brought about by new experiences (Fisch, 420–21).

Works Cited

Altieri, Charles. "The Objectivist Tradition." In *The Objectivist Nexus: Essays in Cultural Poetics*, edited by Rachel Blau DuPlessis and Peter Quartermain, 25–36. Tuscaloosa: U of Alabama P, 1999.
Anastas, Peter. "re Olson inquiry" and "addenda." Email to Kristen Case. January 15, 2009.
Anderson, David Ross. "The Woman in the Tricorn Hat: Political Theory and Biological Portraiture in Marianne Moore's Poetry." *Journal of Modern Literature* 22, no. 1 (Autumn 1998): 31–45.
Anderson, Douglas. "Peirce's Common Sense Marriage of Religion and Science." In *The Cambridge Companion to Peirce*, edited by Cherly Misak, 175–92. Cambridge: Cambridge UP, 2004.
Bazin, Victoria. "Marianne Moore, Kenneth Burke and the Poetics of Literary Labor." *Journal of American Studies* 35, no. 3 (2001): 433–52.
Beck, John, 1963. *Writing the Radical Center: William Carlos Williams, John Dewey, and American Cultural Politics*. Albany: State U of New York P, 2001.
Bercovitch, Sacvan. "Emerson, Individualism, and the Ambiguities of Dissent." In *Ralph Waldo Emerson: A Collection of Critical Essays*, edited by Lawrence Buell, 101–29. New York: Prentice Hall, 1992.
———. "The Problems of Ideology in American Literary History." *Critical Inquiry* 12, no. 4 (Summer 1986): 631–53.
———. *The Puritan Origins of the American Self*. New Haven, CT: Yale UP, 2011.
Bernstein, Charles. "Frame Lock." In *My Way: Speeches and Poems*, 90–99. Chicago: U of Chicago P. 1999.
Blau, Joseph. Review of *Emerson's Angle of Vision: Man and Nature in American Experience* by Sherman Paul (1952). *Journal of Philosophy* 50, no. 6 (March 12, 1953): 195–96.
Bloom, Harold. "Out of Panic, Self-Reliance." *New York Times*, October 11, 2008, http://www.nytimes.com/2008/10/12/opinion.
Brent, Joseph. *Charles Sanders Peirce: A Life*. Bloomington: Indiana UP, 1993.
Brooks, Cleanth. *The Well-Wrought Urn: Studies in the Structure of Poetry*. New York: Houghton Mifflin, 1975.
Buell, Lawrence. *Emerson*. Cambridge: Harvard UP, 2003.
———. *The Environmental Imagination: Thoreau, Nature Writing and the Formation of American Culture*. Cambridge: Harvard UP, 1995.

———. "Introduction." In *Ralph Waldo Emerson: A Collection of Critical Essays*, edited by Lawrence Buell, 1–12. New York: Prentice Hall, 1992.
Burke, Kenneth. "Motives and Motifs in the Poetry of Marianne Moore." *Accent* (Spring 1942): 157–69.
Burke, Thomas F., D. Micah Hester, and Robert B. Talisse. Introduction to *Dewey's Logical Theory*, edited by Thomas F. Burke, Micah Hester, and Robert B. Talisse, xi–xxvi. Nashville, TN: Vanderbilt UP, 2002.
Butterick, George. *A Guide to the Maximus Poems of Charles Olson*. Berkeley: U of California P, 1978.
Buxton, Rachel. "Marianne Moore and the Poetics of Pragmatism." *Review of English Studies* 58:236 (September 2007): 531–51.
Byrd, Don. *Charles Olson's "Maximus."* Chicago: U of Illinois P, 1980.
Cameron, Sharon. *Writing Nature: Henry Thoreau's Journal*. New York and Oxford, UK: Oxford UP.
Cavell, Stanley. *Emerson's Transcendental Etudes*. Edited by David Justin Hodge. Stanford: Stanford UP: 2003.
———. *The Senses of Walden*. Chicago: U of Chicago P, 1981.
Colapietro, Vincent. "Experimental Logic: Normative Theory or Natural History?" in *Dewey's Logical Theory*, edited by Thomas F. Burke, Micah Hester, and Robert B. Talisse, 43–71. Nashville, TN: Vanderbilt UP, 2002.
Collis, Stephen. "Drawing the Curtain on *The Midnight*." *Jacket* 25 (February 2004), http://jacketmagazine.com/25/collis-s-howe.html.
———. *Through Words of Others: Susan Howe and Anarcho-Scholasticism*. Victoria, BC: English Literary Studies Editions, 2006.
Costello, Bonnie. *Marianne Moore: Imaginary Possessions*. Cambridge, MA: Harvard UP.
Cunningham, John. "The Human Presence in Frost's Universe." In *The Cambridge Companion to Robert Frost*, edited by Robert Faggen, 261–72. Cambridge: Cambridge UP, 2001.
Dean, Bradley. Introduction to *Wild Fruits: Thoreau's Rediscovered Last Manuscript*, by Henry David Thoreau, ix–xvii. Edited by Bradley Dean. New York: Norton, 2000.
———. "Henry D. Thoreau and Horace Greeley Exchange Letters of the 'Spontaneous Generation of Plants.'" *New England Quarterly* 66, no. 4 (December 1993): 630–38.
Derrida, Jacques. "Différance." In *Critical Theory Since 1965*, edited by Hazard Adams and Leroy Searle, 120–37. Revised edition. Gainesville: UP of Florida, 1986.
Dewey, John. *John Dewey: The Later Works, 1925–1953*. Vol. 1, *1925, Experience and Nature*. Edited by Jo Ann Boydston and Sidney Hook. Carbondale: Southern Illinois UP, 1981.
———. *John Dewey: The Later Works, 1925–1953*. Vol. 10, *1934, Art As Experience*. Edited by Jo Ann Boydston. Carbondale: Southern Illinois UP, 2008.

———. *John Dewey: The Later Works, 1925–1953*. Vol. 12, *1938, Logic: The Theory of Inquiry*. Edited by Jo Ann Boydston. Carbondale: Southern Illinois UP, 2008.

———. *The Middle Works, 1899–1924*. Vol. 9, *1916, Democracy and Education*. Edited by Jo Ann Boydston. Carbondale: Southern Illinois UP, 1980.

———. *The Middle Works, 1899–1924*. Vol. 10, *1916–1917, Journal Articles, Essays, and Miscellany Published in the 1916–1917 Period*. Edited by Jo Ann Boydston. Carbondale: Southern Illinois UP, 1985.

———. *The Middle Works, 1899–1924*. Vol. 12, *1920, Reconstruction in Philosophy and Essays*. Edited by Jo Ann Boydston. Carbondale and Edwardsville: Southern Illinois UP, 1988.

Eastman, Max. "John Dewey." *Atlantic Monthly* (December 1941): 671–85.

Edwards, Jonathan. *A Jonathan Edwards Reader*. Edited by John E. Smith, Harry S. Stout, and Kenneth P. Minkema. New Haven: Yale UP. 1995.

———. *Images and Shadows of Divine Things*. Edited by Perry Miller. New Haven, CT: Yale UP. 1948.

———. *The Works of Jonathan Edwards*. Vol. 6, *Scientific and Philosophical Writings*. Edited by Wallace E. Anderson. New Haven: Yale UP, 1980.

Emerson, Ralph Waldo. *The Complete Sermons of Ralph Waldo Emerson*. Vol. 2. Edited by Albert J. Von Frank. Columbia: U of Missouri P, 1989.

———. *Essays and Lectures*. New York: Library of America, 1983.

———. *Journals and Miscellaneous Notebooks of Ralph Waldo Emerson*. Vol. 2, *1822–1826*. Edited by William H. Gilman, Alfred R. Ferguson, and Merrell R. Davis. Cambridge, MA: Belknap, 1961.

———. *Journals and Miscellaneous Notebooks of Ralph Waldo Emerson*. Vol. 16, *1866–1882*. Edited by Ronald A. Bosco and Glen M. Johnson. Cambridge, MA: Belknap, 1982.

Erdt, Terrence. *Jonathan Edwards: Art and the Sense of the Heart*. Amherst, MA: U of Massachusetts P, 1980.

Faggen, Robert. "Frost and the Questions of Pastoral." In *The Cambridge Companion to Robert Frost*, edited by Robert Faggen, 49–74. Cambridge: Cambridge UP, 2001.

———. *Robert Frost and the Challenge of Darwin*. Ann Arbor: U of Michigan P, 1991.

———, ed. *Notebooks of Robert Frost*. Cambridge, MA: Belknap/Harvard UP, 2006.

Fisch, Max. "Alexander Bain and the Genealogy of Pragmatism." *Journal of the History of Ideas* 15, no. 3 (June 1954): 413–44.

Fletcher, Angus. *A New Theory for American Poetry: Democracy, the Environment, and the Future of Imagination*. Cambridge, MA: Harvard UP, 2004.

Fredman, Stephen. *The Grounding of American Poetry: Charles Olson and the Emersonian Tradition*. Cambridge: Cambridge UP, 1993.

Frost, Robert. *Collected Poems, Prose and Plays*. New York: Library of America, 1995.

———. *Complete Poems of Robert Frost*. New York: Holt, Rinehart and Winston, 1964.
———. *Poetry and Prose*. New York: Henry Holt, 1972.
———. *The Notebooks of Robert Frost*. Edited by Robert Faggen. Cambridge, MA: Belknap/Harvard UP, 2006.
———. *Selected Letters of Robert Frost*. Edited by Lawrence Thompson. New York: Holt, Rinehart and Winston, 1964.
Goldsmith, Kenneth. *The Weather*. North Hollywood, CA: MakeNow Press, 2005.
Goodman, Russell. *American Philosophy and the Romantic Tradition*. Cambridge: Cambridge UP, 1990.
Hall, Donald. "The Art of Poetry: Marianne Moore" *Writers at Work: The Paris Review Interviews*. Second series. New York: Viking, 1963. Reprinted in *Marianne Moore: A Collection of Critical Essays*, edited by Charles Tomlinson, 20–45. Englewood Cliffs, NJ: Prentice Hall.
Havelock, Eric. *Preface to Plato*. Cambridge, MA: Harvard UP, 1963.
Hickman, Larry. "Dewey's Theory of Interpretation." In *Reading Dewey: Interpretations for a Postmodern Generation*, edited by Larry Hickman, 166–87. Bloomington: Indiana UP, 1998.
Hollander, John. Foreword to *Robert Frost: The Work of Knowing*, by Richard Poirier, xi–xx. Palo Alto: Stanford UP, 1990.
Holley, Margaret. "The Model Stanza: The Organic Origin of Moore's Syllabic Verse." *Twentieth Century Literature* 30, no. 2/3. Marianne Moore Issue (Summer-Autumn 1984): 181–91.
———. *The Poetry of Marianne Moore: A Study in Voice and Value*. Cambridge: Cambridge UP, 1987.
The Holy Bible: King James Version. New York: American Bible Society, 1999.
Howarth, William. *The Book of Concord: Thoreau's Life as a Writer*. New York: Viking: 1982.
Howe, Susan. *The Birth-mark: Unsettling the Wilderness in American Literary History*. Hanover, NH: Wesleyan UP/UP of New England, 1993.
———. "Encloser." In *The Politics of Poetic Form*, edited by Charles Bernstein, 175–96. New York: ROOF Books, 1990.
———. *The Europe of Trusts*. New York: New Directions, 1990.
———. *Frame Structures: Early Poems, 1974–1979*. New York: New Directions, 1996.
———. *The Midnight*. New York: New Directions, 2003.
———. *My Emily Dickinson*. New York: New Directions, 1985, 2007.
———. *Pierce-Arrow*. New York: New Directions, 1999.
———. *Souls of the Labidie Tract*. New York: New Directions, 2007.
Hume, David. *A Treatise of Human Nature*. New York: Oxford UP, 2000.
James, William. *Essays in Radical Empiricism*. Edited by Ralph Perry. New York: Longmans, Green, 1922.
———. *The Principles of Psychology*. Vol. 1. New York: Dover: 1950.
———. *Writings, 1902–1910*. Edited by Bruce Kuklick. New York: Library of America, 1987.

Johnson, Rochelle L. *Passions for Nature: Nineteenth-Century America's Aesthetics of Alienation*. Athens, GA: U of Georgia P, 2009.
Johnson, Thomas H. Introduction to *Emily Dickinson: Selected Letters*, by Emily Dickinson, ix–xvi. Edited by Thomas H. Johnson. Cambridge, MA: Belknap/Harvard UP, 1986.
Jonik, Michael. "A Natural History of the Mind: Edwards, Emerson, Thoreau, Melville." PhD diss., State University of New York at Albany, 2009.
Judovitz, Dalia. "Philosophy and Poetry: The Difference Between Them in Plato and Descartes." In *Literature and the Question of Philosophy*, edited by Anthony J. Cascardi, 24–51. Baltimore: Johns Hopkins UP, 1987.
Kandinsky, Wassily. *Concerning the Spiritual in Art*. Edited by Robert Motherwell. New York: Wittenboom, Schultz, 1947.
Ketner, Kenneth Laine. *His Glassy Essence: An Autobiography of Charles Sanders Peirce*. Nashville, TN: Vanderbilt UP, 1989.
Kuhn, Thomas. "Objectivity, Value Judgment and Theory Choice." In *Critical Theory Since 1965*, edited by Hazard Adams and Leroy Searle, 383–94. Revised edition. Gainesville: UP of Florida, 1986.
———. *The Structure of Scientific Revolutions*. Chicago: U of Chicago P, 1962.
Leader, Jennifer. "'Certain Axioms Rivaling Scriptures': Marianne Moore, Reinhold Niebuhr, and the Ethics of Engagement." *Twentieth Century Literature* 51, no. 3 (Autumn, 2005): 316–40.
Lentricchia, Frank. "The Return of William James." *Cultural Critique* 4 (Autumn 1986): 5–31.
———. *Robert Frost: Modern Poetics and the Landscapes of Self*. Durham, NC: Duke UP. 1975.
Levin, Jonathan. *The Poetics of Transition: Emerson, Pragmatism and American Literary Modernism*. Durham, NC: Duke UP, 1999.
Lowance, Mason A., Jr. *The Language of Caanan: Metaphor and Symbol in New England from the Puritans to the Transcendentalists*. Cambridge, MA: Harvard UP, 1980.
Mariani, Paul. *William Carlos Williams: A New World Naked*. New York: McGraw-Hill, 1981.
Marsden, George. *Jonathan Edwards: A Life*. New Haven: Yale UP, 2003.
Marsh, Alec. *Money and Modernity: Pound, Williams and the Spirit of Jefferson*. Tuscaloosa: U of Alabama P, 1998.
Maud, Ralph. *Charles Olson's Reading: A Biography*. Carbondale: Southern Illinois UP, 1996.
Maud, Ralph, and Sharon Thesen, eds. *Charles Olson and Frances Boldereff: A Modern Correspondence*. Middletown, CT: Wesleyan UP, 1999.
Menand, Louis. *The Metaphysical Club: A Story of Ideas in America*. New York: Farrar Straus Giroux, 2001.
Michael, John. *Emerson and Skepticism: The Cipher of the World*. Baltimore: Johns Hopkins UP, 1988.
Milder, Robert. "From Emerson to Edwards." *New England Quarterly* 80, no. 1 (March, 2007): 96–133.

Miller, J. Hillis. Introduction to *William Carlos Williams: A Collection of Critical Essays*, by William Carlos Williams, 1–14. Edited by J. Hillis Miller. Englewood Cliffs, NJ: Prentice Hall, 1966.
———, ed. *Poets of Reality: Six Twentieth-Century Writers*. Twentieth Century Views series. Cambridge, MA: Harvard UP, 1965.
Miller, Perry. *Errand Into the Wilderness*. Cambridge: Belknap, 1956.
———. *Jonathan Edwards*. New York: Meridian, 1959.
Misak, Cheryl. "Charles Sanders Peirce (1839–1914)." In *The Cambridge Companion to Peirce*, edited by Cherly Misak, 1–26. Cambridge: Cambridge UP, 2004.
Moore, Marianne. *The Poems of Marianne Moore*. Edited by Grace Schulman. New York: Viking, 2003.
———. "The Steeple-Jack." Manuscript. 1:04:23. Marianne Moore Collection, The Rosenbach Museum and Library, Philadelphia, PA.
Morris, Charles. *The Pragmatic Movement in American Philosophy*. New York: George Braziller, 1970.
Neufeldt, Leonard. *The House of Emerson*. Lincoln: U of Nebraska P, 1982.
Nicholls, Peter. "'The Pastness of Landscape': Susan Howe's 'Pierce-Arrow.'" *Contemporary Literature* 43, no. 3 (Autumn 2002): 441–60.
Olson, Charles. "Human Universe." In *Collected Prose*, edited by Donald Allen and Benjamin Friedlander, 155–66. Berkeley: U of California P, 1997.
———. *The Maximus Poems*. Edited by George Butterick. Berkeley: U of California P, 1983.
———. *The Maximus Poems*. Vol. 3. Edited by Charles Boer and George Butterick. New York: Penguin. 1975.
———. "Projective Verse." In *Collected Prose*, edited by Donald Allen and Benjamin Friedlander, 237–39. Berkeley: U of California P, 1997.
———. *The Special View of History*. Edited by Ann Charters. Berkeley: Oyez, 1970.
Orange, Tom. "William Carlos Williams Between Image and Object." *Sagetrieb* 18, no. 2/3 (2002): 127–56.
Parini, Jay. *Robert Frost: A Life*. New York: Henry Holt, 1999.
Paton, Priscilla. "Apologizing for Robert Frost." *South Atlantic Review* 63, no. 1 (Winter 1998): 72–89.
Paul, Sherman. *Olson's Push: Origin, Black Mountain and Recent American Poetry*. Baton Rouge: Louisiana State UP, 1978.
Pearce, Roy Harvey. "Marianne Moore." In *Marianne Moore: A Collection of Critical Essays*, edited by Charles Tomlinson, 150–58. Englewood Cliffs, NJ: Prentice Hall, 1969.
Peck, H. Daniel. "Thoreau's Lakes of Light: Modes of Representation and the Enactment of Philosophy in *Walden*." *Midwest Studies in Philosophy* 28, no. 1 (September 2004): 85–101.
———. *Thoreau's Morning Work*. New Haven: Yale UP, 1990.
Peirce, Charles Sanders. *Collected Papers of Charles Sanders Peirce*. 8 vols. Edited by C. Hartshorne and P. Weiss (vols. 1–6) and A. Burks (vols. 7–8). Cambridge, MA: Harvard UP.

———. *The Essential Peirce: Selected Philosophical Writings.* Vol. 1, *1867–1893*, edited by Nathan Houser and Christian Kloesel. Bloomington: Indiana UP, 1992.
———. *The Essential Peirce: Selected Philosophical Writings.* Vol. 2, *1893–1913*, edited by Peirce Edition Project. Bloomington: Indiana UP, 1998.
Perloff, Marjorie. *Wittgenstein's Ladder.* Chicago: U of Chicago P, 1996.
Pihlström, Sami. "Peirce's Place in the Pragmatist Tradition." In *The Cambridge Companion to Peirce*, edited by Cherly Misak, 27–57. Cambridge: Cambridge UP, 2004.
Poirier, Richard. *Poetry and Pragmatism.* Cambridge, MA: Harvard UP, 1992.
———. *Robert Frost: The Work of Knowing.* New York: Oxford UP, 1977.
Rees, Ralph. "The Reality of Imagination in the Poetry of Marianne Moore." *Twentieth Century Literature* 30, no. 2/3 (Summer/Fall 1984): 231–42.
Rescher, Nicholas, "Process Philosophy." *The Stanford Encyclopedia of Philosophy* (Fall 2008), edited by Edward N. Zalta. http://plato.stanford.edu/archives/fall2008/entries/process-philosophy/.
Retallack, Joan. *The Poethical Wager.* Berkley: U of California P, 2003.
Rich, Motoko. "Editing of Frost Notebooks in Dispute." *New York Times*, January 22, 2008. http://www.nytimes.com/2008/01/22/ books/22frost.html.
Richardson, Joan. *A Natural History of Pragmatism: The Fact of Feeling from Jonathan Edwards to Gertrude Stein.* Cambridge, UK and New York: Cambridge UP, 2007.
Richardson, Robert. *Emerson: The Mind on Fire.* Berkley: U of California P, 1995.
———. *William James: In the Maelstrom of American Modernism.* New York: Houghton Mifflin, 2006.
Rorty, Richard. *Contingency, Irony and Solidarity.* Cambridge, UK: Cambridge UP, 1989.
———. "Dewey's Metaphysics." In *New Studies in the Philosophy of John Dewey*, edited by Stephen M. Cahn, 45–75. Hanover, NH: UP of New England, 1977.
———. *Philosophy and the Mirror of Nature.* Princeton: Princeton UP, 1979.
Rotella, Guy. "Comparing Conceptions: Frost and Eddington, Heisenberg, and Bohr." *American Literature* 59, no. 2 (May 1987): 167–89.
Royce, Josiah, and Fergus Kernan. *Journal of Philosophy, Psychology and Scientific Methods* 13, no. 26 (December 1916): 701–9.
Scheffler, Israel. *Four Pragmatists: A Critical Introduction to Peirce, James, Mead and Dewey.* London: Routledge & Kegan Paul, 1986.
Sears, John F. "William James, Henri Bergson, and the Poetics of Robert Frost." *New England Quarterly* 48, no. 3 (September 1975): 341–61.
Shaw, W. David. "The Poetics of Pragmatism: Robert Frost and William James." *New England Quarterly* 59, no. 2 (June 1986): 159–88.
Sheehy, Donald. "The Poet as Neurotic: The Official Biography of Robert Frost." *American Literature* 58, no. 3 (October 1986): 393–410.

Shulze, Robin. *Becoming Marianne Moore: Early Poems, 1907–1924.* Berkeley: U of California P, 2002.
Simon, Linda. *Genuine Reality: A Life of William James.* New York: Harcourt, 1998.
Sleeper, Ralph. *The Necessity of Pragmatism: John Dewey's Conception of Philosophy.* New Haven: Yale UP, 1986.
Steinman, Lisa. "Modern America, Modernism, and Marianne Moore." Marianne Moore Issue, *Twentieth Century Literature* 30, no. 2/3 (Summer/Autumn 1984): 210–30.
Thompson, Lawrence Roger, and R. H. Winnick. *Robert Frost: A Biography.* Edited by Edward Connery Lathem. Single volume edition. New York: Holt, Rinehart and Winston, 1981.
Thoreau, Henry David. *Journal of Henry David Thoreau.* Edited by Bradford Torrey and Francis Allen. 14 vols. Boston: Houghton Mifflin, 1906.
———. "Nature Notes, Charts and Tables: Autograph Manuscript." MA 610. The Pierpont Morgan Library, New York.
———. "Walking." In *The Essays of Henry David Thoreau*, edited by Lewis Hyde, 147–87. New York: North Point Press, 2002.
———. *A Week on the Concord and Merrimack Rivers; Walden, or, Life in the Woods; The Maine Woods; Cape Cod.* New York: The Library of America, 1985.
Trilling, Lionel. "A Speech on Robert Frost: A Cultural Episode." 1959. Reprinted in *The Moral Obligation to Be Intelligent: Selected Essays*, edited by Leon Wieseltier, 372–80. New York: Farrar Straus Giroux, 2000.
Tweney, Ryan. "Jonathan Edwards and Determinism." *Journal of the History of the Behavioral Sciences* 33, no. 4 (Fall 1997): 365–80.
Von Hallberg, Robert. *Charles Olson: The Scholar's Art.* Cambridge: Harvard UP, 1978.
———. "Olson, Whitehead and the Objectivists." *boundary 2* 2, no. 1/2 (Autumn 1973–Winter 1974): 85–112.
Wafa, Abdul Waheed. "Afghans Say New U.S. Strike Killed Civilians." *New York Times*, July 7, 2008, http://www.nytimes.com/2008/07/07/world/asia.
Waldrop, Rosmarie. "Charles Olson: Process and Relationship." *Twentieth Century Literature* 23, no. 4 (December 1977): 467–86.
Walls, Laura Dassow. *Seeing New Worlds: Henry David Thoreau and Nineteenth-Century Science.* Madison: U of Wisconsin P, 1995.
Weaver, Mike. *William Carlos Williams: The American Background.* Cambridge, UK: Cambridge UP, 1971.
Whitehead, Alfred North. *Adventures of Ideas.* New York: Macmillan, 1933.
———. *Process and Reality.* New York: Macmillan, 1957.
Whittemore, Reed. *William Carlos Williams: Poet from Jersey.* New York: Houghton Mifflin, 1975.
Williams, William Carlos. *Autobiography.* New York: New Directions, 1967.

———. *The Collected Poems of William Carlos Williams.* Vol. 1, *1909–1939.* Edited by A. Waltom Litz and Christopher MacGowen. New York: New Directions, 1986.
———. *The Collected Poems of William Carlos Williams.* Vol. 2, *1939–1962.* Edited by Christopher MacGowen. New York: New Directions, 1988.
———. *The Embodiment of Knowledge.* Edited by Ron Loewinsohn. New York: New Directions, 1988.
———. *Imaginations.* Edited by Webster Schott. New York: New Directions, 1970.
———. *Selected Essays.* New York: New Directions, 1969.
———. *Selected Letters.* New York: New Directions, 1985.
Wittgenstein, Ludwig. *Philosophical Investigations: The German Text, with a Revised English Translation.* Edited by G. E. M. Anscombe and Elizabeth Anscombe. Oxford, UK: Wiley-Blackwell, 1991.
Zabel, Morton. "A Literalist of the Imagination." *Poetry* 47, no. 6 (March 1936): 326–36.

Index

action. *See* practice
aesthetics, 2, 9, 28, 29, 37, 114, 116, 118
Afghanistan, U.S. military action in, xv, 40, 124, 128, 132
Agassiz, Luis, 121n7
Altieri, Charles, 87, 89
America, xi, 1, 13, 21, 27, 28, 35, 36, 38, 39–41, 47, 91, 92, 96, 98, 119, 123–26, 127, 131, 132, 134–36, 138, 141n1
Anastas, Peter, 96–97, 120n3, 120n4
Anderson, David Ross, 30
Anderson, Douglas, 60
Antinomianism (in Howe), 125, 127, 133, 135–37
Aristotle, 9, 102, 114, 121n10, 126, 129

Bain, Alexander, 139, 141n4
Bazin, Victoria, 40
Beck, John, 75, 83, 87
Bercovitch, Sacvan, 19n1, 39–40, 123–25
Bernstein, Charles, 140
Blake, William, 34, 96
Blau, Joseph, 28
Bloom, Harold, 132, 141n1
Boer, Charles, 114–15
Bolderoff, Frances, 96
Brent, Joseph, 44–45, 49, 51–52, 57, 62, 64
Brontë, Charlotte, 126
Brontë, Emily, 126, 133
Brooks, Cleanth, 19
Browning, Robert, 126
Buell, Lawrence, 25, 39, 98, 101, 119, 141
Burke, Kenneth, 33–34, 84

Burke, Thomas F., 73–74, 83
Butterick, George, 114–16, 120n2, 121n9
Buxton, Rachel, 35–36
Byrd, Don, 115, 117

Calvinism: and Edwards, 2, 5 19n3; and grace, 3–5, 8, 19n3; and Marianne Moore, 33; and Unitarianism, 2, 7. *See also* Edwards, Jonathan
Cameron, Sharon, 98, 101, 112, 118–19
Carson, Anne, 141
Cavell, Stanley, xii, 20n4, 27–28, 41, 42n2, 82, 96, 98, 100, 121n8
Colapietro, Vincent, 94n1
Coleridge, Samuel Taylor, 22, 27
Collis, Stephen, 69n6, 70n8, 132, 138
Concord, Massachusetts, 8, 26, 27, 95–96, 118, 123
Costello, Bonnie, 38, 42n6
Cunningham, John, 17

Darwin, Charles, 30, 32, 64–67, 74–75, 79, 83, 89, 93, 99, 121n7, 128. *See also* evolution
Davis, Ian. *See* Firth, Ian
Dean, Bradley, 98, 117, 121n7
Derrida, Jacques, 82
Descartes, René, xiii, 5, 29, 102, 129
Dewey, John, xi, xii, and Darwin, 74, 75, 79, 89, 128; and language, 71–72, 75–76, 80–82; logical theory of, 75–76, 94n1; nature in, 76, 94; and Peirce, 94n1; and practice, 73, 76, 81–81; and pragmatism, 70n8, 81; and science, 73, 76, 78–80, 83; and Williams, 71–73, 75, 82–87, 89, 92–94; and Wittgenstein, 81

Dewey, John, works by: "Americanism and Localism," 92–93; *Art as Experience*, 70n8; *Democracy and Education*, 5, 36, 79, 84, 128; *Experience and Nature*, 76–77, 80–81, 94, 94n2; *Logic, The Theory of Inquiry*, 75–76; "The Need for a Recovery of Philosophy," 74; *The Quest for Certainty*, 74; *Reconstruction in Philosophy*, 20n5, 73, 78–79; *Studies in Logical Theory*, 94n1; "The Superstition of Necessity," 76

Dial, The (magazine), 21, 39, 92

Dickens, Charles, 126

Dickinson, Emily, 125–27, 131, 133–35, 137, 139, 141n3

Eastman, Max, 83

ecocriticism, 141

Edwards, Jonathan, 3; and Calvinism, 2, 5 19n3; and Emerson, 7–8, 19n1; and feeling (affection), 3; and grace, 3–5, 8, 19n3; and the Great Awakening, 3; language of, 4–6; Locke, 4; and Newton, 5; Perry Miller's view of, 4; and practice, 3–6

Edwards, Jonathan, works by: *A Divine and Supernatural Light*, 4; "A Faithful Narrative of the Surprising Work of God," 6; *Images and Shadows of Divine Things*, 13; "Of Atoms," 5; *A Treatise Concerning Religious Affections*, 3, 8, 11

Einstein, Albert, 36, 83. *See also* relativity, theory of

Eliot, T. S., 30, 35, 84, 91

Emerson, Ralph Waldo, xi; and American poetry, 28; and Edwards, 7–8, 19n1; and "emanationist" vs. "evolutionary" form (Jonik), 24, 37; epistemology of, 40; and feeling, 7, 28; idealism of, 22–28, 37, 40, 42n3; illnesses of, 10; and James, xii–xiii, 1, 6–9, 29; and Moore, 21–22, 29–31, 33–35, 37–41; and nature, 10, 22–25, 27, 31, 35, 37; and the ordinary, 8–9, 26; as philosopher, 28; popular view of, 38–39; and practice, 2, 6–9, 37; and pragmatism, 2, 6–9, 20n4, 24, 26, 29, 41n1; as solipsist, 27; son Waldo's death, 26; and spirit/matter, 22, 40; and Thoreau, 96, 101, 105, 117; and Unitarianism, 10, 24; and vision/sight, 10, 31; writing practices of, 9, 37–38

Emerson, Ralph Waldo, works by: "The American Scholar," 9, 26–27, 29–30, 35, 37, 42n6; "Experience," xiv, 8, 9, 16, 22, 24–28; *Journals & Notebooks*, 8, 10, 37–38; *Nature*, 10, 22–24, 28, 31, 33, 67, 124; "Self-Reliance," 41; *Sermons*, 6–9; "Swedenborg; Or, The Mystic," 22

environment, xiii, xv, 20, 32, 47; and Darwin, 32, 74, 99; and Dewey, 20, 74–75, 83; and the Kalendar (Thoreau), 109, 117; and literary criticism (Buell), 101, 119, 141; and *The Maximus Poems*, 97, 103, 105, 115, 117; and self/subject, xi, xiii, 35, 57, 67, 97, 115, 119–20; text as (Fisher/Cavell), 100, 105, 121n8; and *Walden*, 97, 99–101, 103; and Williams, 83, 93. *See also* nature

epistemology, xi, xiii, 2, 17, 38, 120, 137; of Dewey, 5; of Edwards, 4; of Emerson, 24, 26, 31, 37–38, 40; of Frost, 15–16, 62; of James, 2, 35, 129, 141n2; of Moore, 30–31, 33, 35–38, 40; of Olson, 97, 102; of Peirce, 2, 45, 51, 62; pragmatist, xii, 5, 15–16, 35; of Thoreau, 97–100, 111; of Williams, 89

Erdt, Terrence, 19n1

ethics, 2, 7, 30, 101, 132

Euripides, 131

evolution, xii–xiii, 24, 33, 37, 38, 47, 51, 53, 56–57, 61, 64–67, 75, 93, 121, 128, 140. *See also* Darwin, Charles

Faggen, Robert, 44–45, 59, 63, 65, 69n1

Firth, Ian, xvii
Fisch, Max, 141n4
Fletcher, Angus, 105, 121n8
Fredman, Stephen, 120n1
Frost, Robert, xi; and conflict, 45–46, 52–53, 59, 69n6; and "correspondence," 50–51; and Darwinian evolution, 64–68; Derry, New Hampshire farm of, 43; elusiveness of, 47–49; epistemology of, 62–63; as failed farmer, 43; and James, xiii, 45, 59, 69n2; and Peirce, 43–47, 49–58, 60–62, 64–69; and poetic form, 46, 54, 57–58, 61; and practice of writing, 2, 15–16; and pragmatism, 2, 15–16, 45–46, 59, 62–64, 68; as "terrifying poet," 53; theology of, 59–62; and Lawrence Thompson, 47–48, 50
Frost, Robert, works by: "After Apple Picking," 15–16; "The Constant Symbol," 15–16, 43; "Design," 60–61; "Directive," 43; "Education by Poetry," 63–64, 68; "The Figure a Poem Makes," 17, 24, 54, 58; "For Once, Then, Something," 55–56; "The Hill Wife," 45; "Hyla Brook," 48–49; "Into My Own," 57–58; "Introduction to E. A. Robinson's 'King Jasper,'" 50, 52; "A Late Walk," 45; *Letters*, 18, 47–48, 54; *A Masque of Mercy*, 59; *A Masque of Reason*, 59; "Mending Wall," 55; "The Most of It," 56, 59–60; "Mowing," 62–64; "The Need of Being Versed in Country Things," 43, 66–67; *North of Boston*, 15; *Notebooks*, 16, 20n6, 44–45, 52–55, 57, 61, 64, 66–67, 69n1; "Stopping by Woods on a Snowy Evening," 45; "Storm Fear," 45; "The Subverted Flower," 45; "The Tuft of Flowers," 51

Gloucester, Massachusetts, 95–99, 103–4, 114, 116, 118, 120n2
Goldsmith, Kenneth, 20n7
Goodman, Russell, 24–25, 27

Great Awakening, the, 3. *See also* Edwards, Jonathan
Greeley, Horace, 121n7
Gregory, Horace, 84

Hall, Donald, 38
Hartley, Marsden, 90
Harvard University, 13–15, 18, 121n7, 133
Havelock, Eric, 28
Hawthorne, Nathaniel, 96
Hegel, Georg Wilhelm Friedrich, 76–78
Heidegger, Martin, 129
Hickman, Larry, 75
Higginson, Thomas Wentworth, 131
Hollander, John, 48
Holley, Margaret, 32, 34–35
Homer, 119, 131
Houser, Nathan, 69n7
Howarth, William, 98
Howe, Susan, xi, xii; and Antinomianism, 125, 127, 133, 135–37; and Emily Dickinson, 125, 126–28, 131, 133–35, 137, 139; on "enclosure," 132–33; and Harvard/Houghton library, 133–34; and James, xi, 123, 125, 130, 135–41; and poetic form, 131, 137–38; and Peirce, 130–31, 135, 139, 141n4; and relation, 125–31, 133–34, 138, 140–41
Howe, Susan, works by: *The Birthmark*, 124, 126–27, 131–34, 137, 141n3; "The Captivity and Restoration of Mrs. Mary Rowlandson," 132; "Encloser," 126, 132, 136–37; *The Europe of Trusts*, 131, 136; *Frame Structures*, 135–36; *The Midnight*, 127, 133, 137–39; *My Emily Dickinson*, 123, 126, 128, 133–35, 137; *Pierce-Arrow*, 130–31, 137, 139; *Souls of the Labadie Tract*, 130, 135, 137; "These Flames and Generosities of the Heart," 126
Humboldt, Alexander von, 111, 122n13

Hume, David, xiii, 29
Hutchinson, Anne, 127, 133, 134

idealism (philosophical)/the ideal, xi, xiii, 87; and Dewey, 76–77; and Emerson, 22–28, 37, 40, 42n3; and James, 8; and Marianne Moore, 30–31, 33–35, 39; of Plato, 30, 37, 39; and pragmatism, 64; and Thoreau, 97, 101, 109; and Williams, 87
imagism, 34, 85–86
Iraq war, xv, 124

James, Henry, 82
James, William, xi, 13–15; as anti-imperialist, 124–25; and Emerson, xii–xiii, 1, 6–9, 29; epistemology of, xiv, 2, 35, 129, 141n2; and Frost, xiii, 45, 59, 69n2; and Howe, xi, 123, 125, 130, 135–41; and language, 130, 136–37; and Peirce, 10–14, 64, 68; pragmatism of, xiv, 2, 6–8, 10–14, 125, 129, 139–40; radical empiricism of, xiv, 123, 129, 141n2
James, William, works by: *Essays in Radical Empiricism*, 123; "Is Life Worth Living?" 15; *The Meaning of Truth*, xiv, 125, 129–30; *Pragmatism*, xiv, 6–9, 10–12, 29, 35–36, 45–47, 74, 81, 125, 129, 139–41n2; "Pragmatism's Conception of Truth," xiv, 8–9, 35–36, 129; *The Principles of Psychology*, 19, 41, 125, 128–29, 135–36; "The Thing and Its Relations," 130; *The Varieties of Religious Experience*, 3–4, 8, 11, 45; "What Pragmatism Means," 6–7, 10–12, 74, 129, 139–40
Johnson, Rochelle, 98, 101
Johnson, Thomas H., 126
Jonik, Michael, 24, 31, 37
Judovitz, Dalia, 21, 28

Kandinsky, Wassily, 90, 92
Kant, Immanuel, xiii, 22, 24, 76, 87
Keats, John, 70n8, 96

Ketner, Kenneth Laine, 14
Kinbote, C. *See* Davis, Ian
Kuhn, Thomas, 79–80

language: Dewey's use of, 71–72, 75–76, 80–82; Edwards' use of, 4–6; Emerson's use of, 23–28, 31, 38; improvisational use of (Williams), 72–72, 90–91, 94n3; James on, 130, 136–37; Moore's use of, 31, 33–34, 38, 40; as organic form (Richardson), 47, 91, 140; and thinking, 47, 72; thought enacted in, 24–28, 31–32, 36, 40, 55, 84, 86, 94n3, 103, 119, 121n6, 140; Wittgenstein on, 2, 81, 82
Leader, Jennifer, 30
Lentricchia, Frank, 17, 48, 125
Levin, Jonathan, xii
Locke, John, xiii, 4, 19n2, 78
Logan, William, 69n1
Lowance, Mason A., 19n1

Mariani, Paul, 90
Marsden, George, 5–6, 19n2
Marsh, Alec, 84
Marsh, James, 22
materialism, 25, 42
Mather, Cotton, 126
Mather, Increase, 126
Matthew 17:16–20, 1–2; and Dewey, 20n5; and Edwards, 3–6; and Emerson, 6–10; and Frost, 14–18, 20n6; and James and Peirce, 10–14
Matthiessen, F. O., 133–34, 141n3
Maud, Ralph, 96
Melville, Herman, 96, 125, 134
Menand, Louis, xii, 52
metaphor, 1; America as, 124; and Emerson, 23; and Frost, 54, 56, 63, 68; and Thoreau, 101, 105
Meyer, Steven, 141
Michael, John, 29, 42n3
Milder, Robert, 19n1
Miller, J. Hillis, 85–86
Miller, Perry, 1–2, 4–5, 19n1, 133–34
Misak, Cheryl, 54

modernism, xi, 35, 48, 50, 88, 93, 98, 140
Moore, Marianne, xi, xii, 21; and "the actual," 30, 35, 37; critical response to, 33–34, 38–39; and Dewey, 36; and Emerson, 29–31, 33–35, 37–41; and facts, 34–37; and idealism/the ideal, 30–31, 33–35, 39, 34; imagination in works by, 32, 34–38; and nature, 31, 33, 35; and poetic form, 32, 37, 38; and pragmatism, 29, 35–36; and revision, 31–33, 37; and vision/sight, 31; writing practices of, 32, 38
Moore, Marianne, works by: "Armour's Undermining Modesty," 34; "He 'Digesteth Harde Y'ron,'" 34; "The Hero," 30, 37;"Is the Real Actual?" 30; "Part of a Novel, Part of a Poem, Part of a Play," 29–37, 40, 42; "Poetry," 42n4; *Reading Diary*, 36; "The Steeple-Jack," 29–37, 40, 42n4; "The Student," 30–32, 34–37, 42n5
Morris, Charles, 18

nature, xi, 29; and Dewey, 76, 94; and Emerson, 10, 22–25, 27, 31, 35, 37 (for *Nature*, see Emerson, Ralph Waldo, works by); and Frost, 60–61, 67; and Howe, 123; and Moore, 31, 33, 35; and Olson, 92, 96, 102; and Peirce, 11, 57, 64–66; and Thoreau, xi, 97, 99–101, 107–14, 117, 119–20, 122n13; and Williams, 85–87. *See also* environment
Neufeldt, Leonard, 25
New York Times, The, 132, 136, 137, 141n1
Nicholls, Peter, 130–31

objectivism (literary), 34, 87, 91–92
objectivism (philosophical), 98, 102, 109, 114
Olson, Charles, xi, xii; "composition by field," 102–3; death of, 114, 117–18; epistemology of, 97, 102; on the eternal, 92, 96, 102; function of writing for, 117; and Gloucester, Massachusetts, 95–99, 103–4, 114, 116, 118, 120n2; on history, 95, 97, 102–3, 114, 119; and manuscripts of, 117–18; and mythology, 114, 116; and nature, 92, 96, 102; and objectivism (literary), 91–92; and objectivism (philosophical), 102, 114; and process, 97–98, 102–4, 109, 114, 119, 120n5; and Thoreau, 95–98, 100–101, 103, 105–6, 114–20; and Alfred North Whitehead, 97, 102–4, 109, 114, 116, 119, 122n14; and Williams, 17, 91–92
Olson, Charles, works by: "Human Universe," 17, 102–3, 105, 118, 119, 121n10; "I, Maximus of Gloucester, to You," 95–96; "A Later Note on Letter #15," 102; "Letter 3," 105–6; "Letter, May 2, 1959," 103–4; "Maximus, in Gloucester Sunday, LXV," 116; *The Maximus Poems*, 95–98, 100–106, 114–21n9; "Maximus, to Gloucester," 104; "Projective Verse," 91–92, 102; *The Special View of History*, 97, 103–4; "The winter the Gen. Starks was stuck," 115
Oppen, George, 87
Orange, Tom, 89
ordinariness, 8, 13, 26, 27, 28–29, 37, 81, 135

Parini, Jay, 43
Paton, Priscilla, 48
Paul, Sherman, 28, 120n1, 121n6
Pearce, Roy Harvey, 35
Peck, H. Daniel, 98, 101, 106–7, 109, 112, 114, 120n1, 120n4, 122n11, 141
Peirce, Charles Sanders, xi, xii; and Arisbe, 14, 43–44, 130–31; categories of, 56–57, 130–31; Christianity of, 12, 60–62; and community, 50–51, 53, 64; and conflict, 45–46, 53; cosmology of, 56, 65; and

Peirce, Charles Sanders—*(cont'd)*
Darwinian evolution, 64–68; and Dewey, 94n1; on doubt and belief, 56–57, 139, 141n4; elusiveness of, 47, 49; epistemology of, 2, 45, 51, 62; and Frost, 43–47, 49–58, 60–62, 64–69; and Howe, 130–31, 135, 139, 141n4; and James, 10–14, 64, 68; manuscripts of, 14, 50, 131; metaphysical system of, 56; pragmatic maxim of, 6, 10, 12, 64; pragmatism of, 2, 6, 10–24, 46, 62, 64, 69n4, 139, 141n4; and Josiah Royce, 14, 44, 49–50, 52–53, 64–65, 69n3; scholastic realism of, 11, 13, 64; and science, 13, 51–52, 54–55, 68, 139

Peirce, Charles Sanders, works by: "The Architecture of Theories," 44, 53; "Design and Chance," 57; "Evolutionary Love," 52, 61–62, 65–66; "The Fixation of Belief," 45, 56–57, 64, 139; "A Guess at the Riddle," 49, 57; "How to Make Our Ideas Clear," 10–12, 56, 64, 70n10; "The Law of Mind," 57; letters, 12–13, 45, 94n1; "A Neglected Argument for the Reality of God," 12; "Some Consequences of Four Incapacities," 51

Peirce, Juliette, 14, 52, 131
Perloff, Marjorie, 72
Perry, Ralph, 141n2
Pihlström, Sami, 11, 13, 64
Plato, 21, 22, 24, 28, 30, 37, 74
Poe, Edgar Allan, 96
poetry, xi–xii, 18–19, 21, 132; choice in writing of, 18–19, 20n7; "environmental" (Fisher), 105; forms of, 38, 58, 85, 88, 131, 137–38; and imagination (Moore), 34, 36, 40; and metaphor, 56, 63; and objects/things (Williams), 85–86; objectivist, 34, 87, 91–92; and philosophy, xi–xv, 1, 18, 19, 21–22, 27–28, 38–39, 46–47, 67, 72–73, 84, 140; and pragmatism, xi–xii, 1–2, 18–19, 69n2; and process, 91; and

relation (Howe), 128, 131, 138, 140; and science, 36, 54, 65, 68, 79, 84; and speech, 58, 68, 91; as "thirdness" (Peirce) in Frost, 57; work in American, 17

Poirier, Richard, xii, xiii, 14, 17, 20n4, 41n1, 48, 52, 57, 69n2, 81–82
Pope, Alexander, 131
Pound, Ezra, 17, 86, 91
practice, 1; and Dewey, 73, 76, 81–81; and Edwards, 2, 3–6; and Emerson, 2, 6–9, 37; and Frost, 2, 15–16, 46; and James, 2, 10–13; and methodology of this text, xv, 19; and Peirce, 2, 10–13, 46, 56; poetic, xii, 2, 15–19, 20n5, 38, 46–47; and pragmatism, 1–2, 16, 18, 46; vs. theory, 73. *See also* pragmatism

pragmatic maxim, the, 6, 10, 12, 64. *See also* Peirce, Charles Sanders

pragmatism, xi–xiii, xv, 1, 18–19, 129; of Dewey, 70n8, 81; and Edwards, 2, 3–6; and Emerson, 2, 6–9, 20n4, 24, 26, 29, 41n1, 139; and evolution, xii, 47, 93, 140; and Frost, 2, 15–16, 45–46, 59, 62–64, 68; and Howe, 125, 134–35, 139–40; of James, xiv, 2, 6–8, 10–14, 125, 129, 139–40; and methodology of this text, xv, 19, 126, 139–40; and Moore, 29, 35–36; of Peirce, 2, 6, 10–24, 46, 62, 64, 69n4, 139, 141n4; and poetry, xi–xii, 1–2, 18–19, 69n2; politics of, 124–25; and practice, 1–2, 16, 18, 46; and radical empiricism, 129, 141n2; and transcendentalism, xii, 2; and Williams, 85, 93. *See also* practice

process philosophy, 97–98, 102–4, 109, 114, 119, 120n5. *See also* objectivism; Whitehead, Alfred North

Puritanism, 2, 19n1. *See also* Calvinism

radical empiricism (James), xiv, 123, 129, 141n2
realism (philosophical), 11, 13, 41, 64, 77

Rees, Ralph, 34
relativity, theory of, 83, 116
romanticism, 49, 87
Rescher, Nicholas, 120n5, 121n5
Retallack, Joan, 94n3
Rich, Motoko, 69n1
Richardson, Joan, xii, 33, 42n2, 47, 81–82, 93, 140–41
Richardson, Robert, 9, 10, 13, 22, 38, 69n3
Rorty, Richard, 22, 62, 74, 77–78
Rotella, Guy, 64, 70n9
Rowlandson, Mary, 126–27
Royce, Josiah, 13–14, 44, 49–50, 52–53, 64–65, 69n3

Santayana, George, 77
Scheffler, Israel, 12
Schulman, Grace, 42n4
science, 141; and Dewey, 73, 76, 78–80, 83; and Frost, 63, 65, 68; and Moore, 30, 36; and Peirce, 13, 51–52, 54–55, 68, 139; and Thoreau, 111; and Williams, 83–84
Sears, John, 14–15
Shakespeare, William, 126
Shaw, W. David, xiii, 59, 69n2
Sheehy, Donald, 69n5
Shelley, Mary, 93
Shulze, Robin, 32
Simon, Linda, 13–14
Sitar, James, 69n1
Sleeper, Ralph, 76–77, 80–81
Stein, Gertrude, xii, 82, 86, 94, 137
Steinman, Lisa, 30, 34–36, 42n5
Stevens, Wallace, xii, 82
Stevenson, Robert Louis, 138
Sydney, Philip, 63

Thompson, Lawrence Roger, 43, 47, 50, 62, 69n5
Thoreau, Henry David, xi, xii; and Darwin, 99; and Emerson, 96, 101, 105, 117; epistemology of, 97–100; function of writing for, 112–13, 117–18; and Alexander von Humbolt, 111, 122n13; idealism of, 97, 101, 109; manuscripts of, 97, 98, 101, 106–13, 117–20, 122n11, 122n12, 122n13; and metaphor, 101, 105; and nature, xi, 97, 99–101, 107–14, 117, 119–20, 122n13; and objectivism (philosophical), 98, 109; and Olson, 95–98, 100–101, 103, 105–6, 114–20, 120n1; and place/environment, xi, 97, 99–101, 103, 119–20; and science, 111
Thoreau, Henry David, works by: Journal, 98–99, 101, 106, 109, 111–13, 118–19; Kalendar, 97, 98, 101, 106–13, 117–20, 122n11, 122n12, 122n13; *Walden*, 41, 95–101, 105, 112, 119–20, 121n6, 121n8; "Walking," xi; *A Week*, 96–98, 112, 117; *Wild Fruits*, 117
transcendentalism, xii, 2, 19n1
Trilling, Lionel, 52–53
truth, pragmatist conception of, xiv, 1–20, 20n5, 35–36, 52, 54–57, 62–64, 81, 129, 135, 139
Tweney, Ryan, 19n3

Unitarianism, 7, 22, 24

Von Hallberg, Robert, 114, 116, 122n14

Wafa, Abdul Waheed, 132, 136
Waldrop, Rosmarie, 102, 118
Walls, Laura Dassow, 98, 111, 122n13, 141
Weaver, Mike, 91–92
Whitehead, Alfred North, 97, 102–4, 109, 114, 116, 119, 122n14, 126
Whitman, Walt, 96
Whittemore, Reed, 85, 90
Williams, William Carlos, xi; and Dewey, 71–73, 75, 82–87, 89, 92–94; epistemology of, 89; and idealism, 87; imagism of, 85–86; and improvisation, 72–72, 90–91, 94n3; and Wassily Kandinsky, 90, 92; and nature, 85–87; objectivism (literary) of; and objects/things, 85–89; and Olson, 91–92;

Williams, William Carlos—*(cont'd)*
  and place/environment, 83–93;
  poetics of, 92; and pragmatism, 85,
  93; and romanticism, 87; and science, 83–84
Williams, William Carlos, works by:
  Autobiography, 72, 93; "By the
  Road to the Contagious Hospital,"
  85–86; *The Embodiment of Knowledge*, 72–73, 83–84, 90; *Imaginations*, 87; *Kora in Hell*, 90; *Letters*, 82–84, 91; "The Red Wheelbarrow," 85–86, 91; *Spring and All*, xiii, 82, 84–92; "Young Sycamore," 86
Wittgenstein, Ludwig, 2, 72, 81, 94n3
Wordsworth, William, 27, 63

Yeats, William Butler, 34

Zabel, Morton, 34
Zukofsky, Louis, 87

www.ingramcontent.com/pod-product-compliance
Lightning Source LLC
Chambersburg PA
CBHW070807230426
43665CB00017B/2518